# IMPERFECT COMPETITION, DIFFERENTIAL INFORMATION, AND MICROFOUNDATIONS OF MACROECONOMICS

# IMPERFECT COMPETITION, DIFFERENTIAL INFORMATION, AND MICROFOUNDATIONS OF MACROECONOMICS

KIYOHIKO G. NISHIMURA

CLARENDON PRESS · OXFORD
1992

*Oxford University Press, Walton Street, Oxford* OX2 6DP
*Oxford New York Toronto*
*Delhi Bombay Calcutta Madras Karachi*
*Petaling Jaya Singapore Hong Kong Tokyo*
*Nairobi Dar es Salaam Cape Town*
*Melbourne Auckland*
*and associated companies in*
*Berlin Ibadan*

*Oxford is a trade mark of Oxford University Press*

*Published in the United States*
*by Oxford University Press, New York*



*British Library Cataloguing in Publication Data*
*Data available*

*Library of Congress Cataloging in Publication Data*
*Nishimura, Kiyohiko. 1953–*
*Imperfect competition, differential information, and microfoundations of macroeconomics/Kiyohiko G. Nishimura*
*p. cm.*
*Includes bibliographical references and index.*
*1. Competition, Imperfect. 2. Macroeconomics. I. Title*
*HB238.N 57 1992 339-dc20 91-35239*
*ISBN 0–19–828617–1*

*Typeset by Taj Services Ltd., Noida, U.P., India*
*Printed and bound in*
*Great Britain by Bookcraft (Bath) Ltd.*
*Midsomer Norton, Avon*

*To*
*Yukiko, Keiko, and Eiko*

# Preface

The past two decades witnessed a substantial change in the field of macroeconomics. The fall of the Keynesian approach after the inflationary episode of the 1970s was followed by the rise of the New Classical approach, but the New Classical approach was overtaken in the 1980s by the Real Business Cycle and New Keynesian approaches. The driving force behind the change is a desire for sound microeconomic foundation of macroeconomic theory.

This book seeks to link a microeconomic model of imperfectly informed firms and unions in monopolistic competition to a general theory of wage and price-setting in a macroeconomic model. The analysis is based on profit maximization and rational behaviour. It is thus broadly in line with the newly emerged New Keynesian approach which emphasizes the importance of imperfect competition in explaining macroeconomic phenomena. However, this book differs from the existing literature of the New Keynesian economics in its emphasis on the 'synergism' of imperfect competition and imperfect and differential information. It is shown in various chapters that these two forms of market imperfection are capable of producing such macroeconomic phenomena as nominal price rigidity, relative price rigidity, and cost-oriented prices, although neither can produce the phenomena in any significant way if it acts independently. In this sense, this book integrates the New Keynesian Approach emphasizing imperfect competition and the new Classical Approach emphasizing imperfect and differential information.

Some of the material appearing in this book has been adapted from articles that appeared originally in journals. In particular, I am grateful to the editors and publishers of *Review of Economic Studies* (Ch. 5), *International Economic Review* (Ch. 6), *Economica* (Ch. 8), *European Economic Review* (Ch. 4), *Journal of Economic Behavior and Organization* (Ch. 9), and *Economic Studies Quarterly* (Ch. 7) for their permission to include material that was originally published in their journals. I am also pleased to acknowledge the financial assistance of the Mishima Kaiun Foundation, the Seimeikai Foundation, and the Nihon Keizai Kenkyu Shorei Zaidan.

In undertaking a project of this size one necessarily incurs many debts. Jean-Pascal Benassy and Nils Gottfries read an earlier version of Chapter 1 and made suggestions that lead me to rewrite it entirely. The anonymous reader of the Oxford University Press also gave me helpful suggestions about the structure of the book. In addition, I have benefited from discussions with Thomas Russell and Kee Nam Cheung. The opinions and ideas expressed here have resulted from conversations over many years with my colleagues. I cannot possibly give adequate attribution to all, but I would be very remiss not to cite the important contributions of Takashi Negishi and Katsuhito Iwai, my teachers and colleagues. I am also indebted to numerous students in my graduate courses, especially Susumu Imai and Yuji Genda, who read earlier manuscripts and gave me valuable comments.

Andrew Schuller at the Oxford University Press was always helpful whenever I needed assistance in preparing this book. I am also grateful to Machelle Buchman, Yuriko Hiratuka, and Sachiko Otuki for their editorial assistance. Finally, I am indebted to my wife, Yukiko, and my daughters, Keiko and Eiko, for their encouragement towards the completion of this book.

K. G. N.

Tokyo, Japan,
July, 1991.

# Contents

# 1
# Introduction

## 1. MOTIVATION OF THIS BOOK: THREE 'STYLIZED FACTS' AND THE NEW KEYNESIAN APPROACH

One of the most salient features of macroeconomic time series in the United States and other industrialized countries is that large movements in quantities are often associated with little or no significant movement in relative prices, including real wages (relative price rigidity). Moreover, shifts in aggregate demand induced, for example, by changes in the money supply are largely accommodated by changes in quantities rather than by changes in nominal prices (nominal price rigidity). By contrast, prices are sensitive to changes in cost (cost-based prices).[1]

The Keynesian approach of the 1960s and early 1970s attempted to explain these facts by assuming that wages and prices are sticky.[2] Individual wages respond to changes in demand only gradually, and thus in the short run can be treated as constant. Prices are determined by mark-ups over wages, and mark-ups are insensitive to short-run changes in demand. Consequently, the general price level is also sticky, so that output is affected by changes in aggregate demand. Because of sticky mark-ups, there is no systematic relationship between relative prices (real wages) and output.

The assumption of price rigidity was considered a convenient short-cut, which facilitated short-run macroeconomic analysis.[3] In medium- and/or long-run analyses, the short-run rigidity of prices and wages was augmented by the Phillips curve, that is, the empirical relationship between wage movements and the unemployment rate. In most cases, rigidity and the Phillips curve relationship were simply assumed; they were not explained from the rational behaviour of economic agents.[4]

The inflationary experiences of many industrialized economies in the 1970s at first seemed contradictory to the above three 'stylized facts', i.e. relative price rigidity, nominal price rigidity, and cost-based prices; however, counter-inflationary policies of the early 1980s that reduced aggregate demand caused a sharp decline in output with only small changes in nominal and relative prices, which was consistent with the stylized facts. Moreover, a seemingly unstable Phillips curve in the 1970s was shown to be stable when augmented, for example, by material costs. Thus, the three stylized facts can still be considered a relatively accurate description of the United States and other industrialized economies (see Blanchard 1990).

Nevertheless, the experiences of the 1970s and 1980s raised serious doubts about the soundness of the Keynesian approach of the 1960s and early 1970s as a theory of prices and wages, because it assumed, rather than derived, the three stylized facts. Prices increased rapidly in the face of excess demand in the 1970s, while they were 'sticky' when aggregate demand was reduced in the 1980s. Thus, an explicit theory of price and wage determination was needed, which would explain the conditions under which changes in aggregate demand induced large changes in output.

The direction of research in the Keynesian tradition was thus changed in the late 1970s and the 1980s in order to account explicitly for price movements, and the so-called 'New Keynesian' approach emerged.[5] The general method in this approach is to start from explicitly specified market imperfections and to attempt to explain the degree of price and wage stickiness and other macroeconomic phenomena by examining the optimal behaviour of economic agents under such imperfections. The interdependence of the agents' actions is the central theme of these studies. In this sense, the New Keynesian approach stresses the importance of the microeconomic foundations of macroeconomic models. The approach goes beyond the microfoundation approach of the 1960s and 1970s and insists on providing complete general equilibrium macroeconomic models.

This book has two objectives. The first is to explain the three stylized facts presented at the outset within a coherent New Keynesian framework. From among various New Keynesian features, I have chosen imperfect competition and imperfect and differential information as the building blocks of macroeconomics. The starting-point is the absence of a Walrasian auctioneer, not only for setting prices, but also for transmitting price information to all market participants. The book assumes (1) that markets are imperfectly competitive and firms set their prices (imperfect competition), and (2) that market information is transmitted to consumers only gradually, and that any attempts to expedite the process are costly (imperfect and costly information). A major feature of this book is 'predetermined prices', in which firms announce their prices before they have perfect knowledge of either their markets or the economy.

The second objective of this book is to explore the relationship between competitiveness and the short-run movements of economic variables in imperfectly competitive economies under imperfect and differential information. Although many empirical studies have reported a wide diversity in nominal as well as relative price rigidity in industrialized economies,[6] few theoretical attempts have been made to explain this diversity within the framework of the New Keynesian approach. The differences may be traced back to the diversity in competitiveness among countries. I shall investigate this issue.

This book is divided into four parts: this introductory chapter and Parts I, II, and III. The rest of this chapter presents a general introduction and overview of the book. Part I takes up the second stylized fact, nominal price rigidity under nominal disturbances. Part II concerns the third stylized fact, cost-based prices, as well as the effect of competition on short-run movements in prices and investments. Part III investigates the first stylized fact, the relative price rigidity.

Throughout the book, the emphasis is placed on product markets rather than labour markets, except in Chapter 4, which analyses imperfectly competitive unions. This is by no means meant to argue that product-market imperfect competition and imperfect information are more important than labour-market imperfect competition and imperfect information. I have chosen product markets partly because the Keynesian approach of the 1960s and early 1970s left product-market analysis rather underdeveloped compared with its sophisticated labour-market analysis, and partly because the effects of imperfect competition and imperfect information emphasized in this book are more easily understood using a product-market analysis. Labour markets are subject to various market imperfections, of which imperfect competition and imperfect information constitute only a part.

## 2. OUTLINE OF THE CHAPTER

The remainder of Chapter 1 briefly surveys the New Keynesian approach and other related macroeconomic approaches, and presents a detailed outline of the book.

Among market imperfections, imperfect competition, or monopolistic competition as its stand-in, has attracted much attention in the New Keynesian approach.[7] Section 3 deals with this literature. In Section 3.1 imperfect competition is compared with perfect competition as a model of markets. Several 'anomalies' are pointed out which are inconsistent with the perfect-competition paradigm. These suggest that imperfect competition—or, more precisely, monopolistic competition—is more appropriate for use in macroeconomic analysis.

Section 3.2 examines the properties of monopolistically competitive models by using a simple illustrative model. It is shown that monopolistically competitive models have such Keynesian characteristics as demand-determined quantities and underemployment; however, they still have classical properties. In particular, there is no nominal price rigidity, and we have monetary neutrality, even in the short run.

Section 3.3 surveys attemps to explain nominal rigidity and the non-neutrality of money by adding extra elements to the basic monopolistically competitive framework: less than full rationality (near-rationality) and/or the existence of physical costs of changing nominal prices (menu costs). However, it is shown that the near-rationality/menu-cost argument has several theoretical and empirical problems as a theory of nominal price rigidity. In particular, only a small part of output fluctuations can be accounted for by this type of argument.

Section 4 takes up the other ingredient of this book, imperfect and differential information. In Section 4.1, perfectly competitive models of nominal price rigidity based on imperfect and differential information are examined as a frame of reference. These models are based on imperfect information on the side of perfectly competitive suppliers and are capable of producing nominal price rigidity. However, they have often been criticized on the grounds that they make unrealistic informational assumptions and have insufficient explanatory power. Based on the results presented in Section 3.1, it is argued in Section 4.2 that prices are likely to be predetermined, and that imperfect and differential information is a natural assumption in monopolistically competitive models. I also consider the three implications of imperfect information under monopolistic competition which form a basis for the results obtained in this book. Lastly, Section 5 outlines the subsequent chapters in non-technical terms.

## 3. IMPERFECT COMPETITION

### 3.1. *Imperfect Competition as a Model of Markets*[8]

The paradigm of perfect competition has been a central part of economics for more than a century, as well as a building block of macroeconomics. In many macroeconomic textbooks perfect competition is assumed, at least for product markets (see e.g. Sargent 1987: Chs. 1, 2). This is sometimes the case even in the Keynesian tradition.

In textbook perfect competition, there is a Walrasian auctioneer who determines prices to equate demand to supply and allocates consumers to firms. Taking these prices as given, consumers determine their demand, and firms determine their supply.

However, several facts about the product markets of industrialized economies are inconsistent at least with the textbook model of perfect competition. Among them, three observations have attracted much attention in recent years: (1) the existence of price distribution in the market of seemingly homogeneous products; (2) the non-convergence of experimental economies to perfect competition; and (3) the prevalence of non-competitive behaviour among various industries. Together they suggest that imperfect competition may be more appropriate for describing many product markets in industrialized economies.

#### *The existence of price distribution*

The first observation that is inconsistent with perfect competition is the existence of price distribution in the market of seemingly homogeneous products. Under perfect competition, the Law of Single Price prevails. However, casual observation of consumer-goods markets immediately reveals that in many markets this is not the case. Various sellers often offer the same product with different price tags.[9]

It should be noted here that the existence of price distribution is also found in intermediate-goods markets in which professional buyers purchase the products, as well as in consumer-goods markets. This is emphasized by Carlton (1986; 1989), who examined in detail the individual price data of intermediate products reported in Stigler and Kindahl (1970).

The theory of imperfect competition provides us with two possible explanations of the existence of price distribution.

The first explanation is based on product differentiation.[10] Unlike the hypothetical competitive market in which many firms produce homogeneous goods and trade them in the same location, firms in the real market produce differentiated goods and sell them to consumers in different locations. This is clearly the case in consumer-goods markets. Moreover, seemingly homogeneous intermediate goods, such as steel bars, may in fact be differentiated by accompanying services (for example trade credit). From the viewpoint of product differentiation, the existence of price distribution simply reflects the inadequacy of the definition of products, and the Law of Single Price still holds. However, producers are no longer price-takers. They now have a partial monopoly on their customers. The market is now imperfectly competitive, with producers determining their price taking into account the power of their partial monopoly.

The second interpretation is based on the buyers' imperfect information about prices and the location of sellers.[11] If information about sellers is instantaneously transmitted to buyers at no cost, competition among sellers will ensure one price for one product. However, if for some reason information about sellers is costly and search costs differ among buyers, competition does not ensure one price for one product. One seller sells his products to consumers having high search costs, and makes profits with a high price and small sales volume; another seller sets his price low enough to induce a large sales volume, and also makes profits. Like product differentiation, buyers' imperfect information also results in imperfect competition. Depending on the distribution of search costs among consumers, sellers have partial monopoly power over their customers. Thus, although the two imperfectly competitive markets have different origins, their market structure is quite similar. In fact, these two models of imperfect competition should be considered as complements, rather than substitutes. For example, the model based on buyers' imperfect information often assumes the homogeneity of goods. This assumption is sometimes criticized on the grounds that search costs are almost negligible if goods are homogeneous, because consumers can easily get price information at an almost negligible cost by simply telephoning sellers and asking their prices. Consequently, in order for search costs to be non-negligible, goods must be differentiated, and quality information must not be so easily obtained. This in turn suggests that, if there are many differentiated products in the market, it is generally very costly for consumers to have perfect information about the market all the time. Thus, in an economy with many differentiated products, consumers are likely to be only imperfectly informed.

Moreover, in a market of imperfectly informed consumers, firms have an incentive to differentiate their products from those of other firms and to make them particularly suited to their current buyers, in order to keep them as their customers. When buyers' information is not perfect, firms cannot expect a large increase in sales volume even if they cut their prices substantially. Consequently, firms are inclined to make profits by producing goods that have a large value added, instead of pursuing a larger sales volume by offering low prices.

*Results in experimental economics*

The results of experimental economics constitute the second observation that is inconsistent with perfectly competitive models.[12] Although markets having Walrasian auctioneers or the like are rather rare, even in industrialized economies, this does not necessarily imply the inadequacy of perfectly competitive models of markets. Suppose that firms set their prices by trial and error. Nevertheless, if their prices converge to perfectly competitive prices as they learn about the market, perfectly competitive models are appropriate for analysing the market, at least in the long run. This issue is examined in experimental economics, and the general conclusion is that prices do not converge to perfectly competitive prices in settings corresponding to existing consumer-goods markets.

The results of experimental economics can be summarized as follows. First, in the case of the double auction, in which both buyers and sellers can negotiate prices with each other, there is a general tendency for the market outcome to converge to the Walrasian outcome as market participants[13] accumulate experience in the experimental setting. By contrast, in the case of the posted offer, in which sellers determine their prices and buyers are allowed only to decide whether or not to buy from them, there is no clear tendency to convergence in most cases. Prices are higher than competitive prices. Even in cases in which there seems to be such a tendency, the convergence takes a very long time, so that prices are significantly higher than competitive prices for most of the experimental period.

In many markets in industrialized economies, especially in consumer-goods markets, prices are determined by sellers on a take-it-or-leave-it basis. Thus, trade is organized mostly by the posted offer, not by the double auction. Consequently, the results of experimental economics described above suggest that imperfectly competitive models make more appropriate building blocks for macroeconomics.

Experimental economics also provides information about the appropriate selection from among imperfectly competitive models. Except for cases in which the number of sellers is very small, the market outcome does not significantly depend on the number of sellers in the experiment. This result, together with the importance of product differentiation in many industrialized economies, suggests that monopolistically competitive markets consisting of many firms producing differentiated products provide the most appropriate market model for the microeconomic foundation of macroeconomics.[14]

*Recent studies in industrial organization*

The third observation supporting imperfectly competitive models is found in studies of industrial organization. Imperfect competition is one of the core concepts in the literature of industrial organization, and a number of empirical studies have been undertaken on this subject. In general, these empirical studies have found that many industries in industrialized economies are far from perfectly competitive. The behaviour of prices is inconsistent with perfect competition.[15] If many industries are imperfectly competitive, it is likely that macroeconomic variables are also influenced by this non-competitive behaviour. In fact, recent macroeconomic studies suggest that the behaviour of productivity in business cycles can be neatly explained in the imperfectly competitive framework (see e.g. Hall 1986).

### 3.2. *Monopolistically Competitive Macroeconomic Models*

In the previous section, it was argued that imperfect competition (and monopolistic competition as its stand-in) is the appropriate model of markets in macroeconomic analysis. In this section I examine the behaviour of the monopolistically competitive economy.

To model a monopolistically competitive economy, careful analysis of the market constraints faced by each economic agent is needed (see Benassy 1988). Because this usually involves a complicated general equilibrium argument, let us take a short-cut and illustrate the basic characteristics of monopolistically competitive macroeconomic models in a simple reduced-form monopolistically competitive macroeconomic model.[16] Although it is admittedly too simplistic, this type of monopolistically competitive model is widely used in investigating the macroeconomic consequences of monopolistic competition (see e.g. Blanchard and Fischer 1989: Ch.8). Another reason for using this specific model is to facilitate a comparison in the next section between this perfect-information monopolistically competitive model and imperfect-information perfectly competitive macroeconomic models, which are usually formulated in similar reduced forms. However, the characteristics of monopolistically competitive models described below are not dependent on this particular simple model, but are in fact quite general.[17]

A monopolistically competitive economy has four fundamental characteristics: strategic interdependence among economic agents, demand-determined quantities, underemployment and insufficient aggregate demand, and lack of both nominal and real price rigidity. In the following, these characteristics are discussed in non-technical terms in a general setting, and then their particular importance in the simple illustrative model is illustrated.

### *A simple illustrative reduced-form macroeconomic model*

In the model that follows, all variables are in log, if not otherwise stated. On the demand side, the aggregate demand of this economy is determined by the money supply. Let $\bar{y}$ be the real aggregate demand, $m$ the money supply, and $\bar{p}$ the price level. We have

$$\bar{y} = m - \bar{p}. \tag{1}$$

On the supply side, the economy consists of numerous price-setting agents who have a partial monopoly on customers for their products. I assume that the agents are 'symmetric,' in the sense that they face the same form of both the demand and the cost functions. Let us consider a representative agent. To make the analysis as simple as possible, I assume that the price-setting agent faces the following downward-sloping demand curve, which depends on the average price and the real aggregate demand, as well as on the agent's own price:

$$q = -k\,(p - \bar{p}) + \bar{y}, \tag{2}$$

where $q$ and $p$ are the demand for and price of this agent's products, respectively. Note that $p - \bar{p}$ is the relative price of the agent's products. Thus, the parameter $k$ is the relative price elasticity of the demand, which satisfies $k > 1$.

The parameter $k$ indicates the degree of competition in the economy.[18] If $k$ is large, then the agent cannot set his price higher than the price level without losing most of his customers. By contrast, if $k$ is small, the agent has a significant monopoly power and can put a substantially higher price tag on his products than the price level and still make profits.

The technology of the agent is such that the log of the real cost of producing output $q^s$ is $(1 + c_1)q^s$, where $c_1 > 0$. Thus, the agent's real profits $\Pi$ are giving by

$$\Pi = \exp\,(p - \bar{p})\,\exp\,(q^s) - \exp\,[(1 + c_1)q^s]. \tag{3}$$

The agent maximizes $\Pi$ with respect to $p$ subject to

$$q^s \leqslant q, \tag{4}$$

taking the demand function and other firms' prices as given.

The real aggregate demand (1), the demand function (2), and the agent's profit function (3) completely characterize this simple monopolistically competitive economy.

*Strategic interdependence*

The fundamental characteristic of monopolistically competitive macroeconomic models in the New Keynesian tradition is a strategic interdependence among agents. In monopolistically competitive models, one agent's utility depends not only on his own actions, but also on the actions of other agents. In the simple macroeconomic model described above, one agent's real profits are influenced by other agents' prices through the average price, as well as by the agent's own price. The agent has to take other agent's prices (the average price) into account in determining his own price. This is because the agent has only a partial monopoly on his customers. Thus, strategic interdependence causes an externality.

In the simple illustrative model described earlier, this externality has a special form when we add the following assumption. Suppose that there are a number of small agents, so that an agent ignores the effect of his own price change on the average price. Hereafter I shall call this the *monopolistically competitive assumption in the strong form.* Under this assumption, the agent takes $\bar{p}$ as given in determining his own price. Then, a reduction in one agent's price reduces the average price a bit, which induces an increase in the real aggregate demand. However, because the effect of such an increase on the real aggregate demand is spread over all kinds of products, the effect on the demand for this agent's products is negligible, and thus the agent ignores the effect in determining his own price. This is often called the aggregate demand externality, which, in fact, is one particular form of externality arising from strategic interdependence in monopolistically competitive models. The strategic interdependence and its induced externality play a crucial role in monopolistically competitive macroeconomic models.

*Demand-determined quantities*

In monopolistically competitive models, price-setting agents are constrained by demand. Because markets are imperfectly competitive, prices are always higher than marginal cost. Thus, if additional demand appears at these prices, price-setting agents are willing to serve it. Consequently, decisions about quantity are demand-constrained in monopolistically competitive models.[19] This, of course, is a familiar property of imperfect competition, but it plays a crucial role in monopolistically competitive models by bringing out an equilibrium characterized by underemployment and insufficient aggregate demand.

The property of demand-determined quantities in the simple illustrative model is expressed as $q^s = q$. The agent always supplies the quantity demanded. Then, under the strong monopolistically competitive assumption, it is easy to show that the agent's price $p$ is determined by

$$p = \frac{1}{1+c_1k}\left[\log\,(1+c_1) + \log\frac{k}{k\,-\,1}\right] + \frac{c_1}{1+c_1k}\,m + \left(1 - \frac{c_1}{1+c_1k}\right)\bar{p}. \quad (5)$$

In the symmetric macroeconomic equilibrium, the representative agent's price is equal to the average price:

$$\bar{p} = p. \quad (6)$$

Thus, the price level and the output of the monopolistically competitive macroeconomic equilibrium are, from (5) and (1),

$$\bar{p} = \frac{1}{c_1}\left[\log\,(1+c_1) + \log\frac{k}{k-1}\right] + m \quad (7)$$

and

$$\bar{y} = -\frac{1}{c_1}\left[\log\,(1+c_1) + \log\frac{k}{k-1}\right]. \quad (8)$$

*Underemployment and insufficient aggregate demand*

As explained earlier, the monopolistically competitive economy is characterized by strategic interdependence and induced externality. One agent's utility depends on the actions of other agents. This externality generally causes inefficiency, which takes the form of underproduction and underemployment in the monopolistically competitive economy, because prices are higher than marginal costs.[20]

In our illustrative model, a relevant yardstick of social welfare is the output level when competition is perfect (i.e. when $k$ goes to infinity).[21] If $\bar{y}$ is less than this level, the economy is underemployed; if greater, the economy is overemployed.

The monopolistically competitive equilibrium, (7) and (8), shows that the monopolistically competitive economy is underemployed. The output level (8), and ultimately the employment level, is lower than in the perfectly competitive case ($k = \infty$) if the degree of competition ($k$) is finite. This, of course, is due to the inefficiency of monopoly, as mentioned above. However, in this particular model it can also be considered the consequence of the so-called aggregate demand externality described in the previous section.

In this model, a decrease in the price level implies an increase in real balances, which is translated into an increase in real aggregate demand. Thus, if all agents concertedly reduced their prices from the equilibrium price (7), real aggregate demand would increase. It is well known that in a monopolistically competitive economy price is always higher than marginal cost. So, if real aggregate demand increased, monopolistically competitive agents would be willing to satisfy the increase. Thus, the monopolistically competitive economy is characterized by insufficient aggregate demand.

The reason for insufficient aggregate demand lies in the externality arising from strategic interdependence in monopolistic competition. The agent takes the average price as given and does not take into account the macroeconomic effect of his price decision on aggregate demand. Moreover, he does not assume that a concerted price cut takes place. This is because such a price cut induces a free-rider problem. Suppose that other agents cut their price slightly by the same amount, say, $x$ per cent. Then, the agent can obtain more profits by reducing his price by less than $x$ per cent than by reducing it by $x$ per cent. Because the agent knows that other agents have the same incentive, the agent expects that the concerted price cut will never materialize. This expectation is realized in the equilibrium.[22]

*Lack of price rigidity and short-run monetary neutrality*

Although the monopolistically competitive economy has such Keynesian features as demand-determined quantities, underemployment, and insufficient aggregate demand, as described in the previous section, it still retains a few classical characteristics. There is neither nominal nor relative price rigidity. In the monopolistically competitive economy, as in the perfectly competitive economy, money (or, more precisely, a once-and-for-all change in the money supply) is neutral, even in the short run. This is because rational economic agents are concerned only with real terms, regardless of whether competition is monopolistic or perfect. The change in the money supply simply induces a proportional increase in the price level and leaves the real variables unchanged. Thus, monopolistically competitive models are capable of producing steady-state Keynesian properties (such as underemployment) but fail to explain Keynesian features during adjustment (such as business cycles).[23]

In our illustrative model, the equilibrium price level and output, (7) and (8), show that the change in the money supply is completely absorbed by the change in $\bar{p}$, and that $\bar{y}$ is independent of the money supply. The reason can be easily understood when the price competition model is restructured as the quantity competition model. From (2), the reverse demand function is

$$p - \bar{p} = -\,(1/k)\,(q - \bar{y}). \qquad (9)$$

Substituting this into (3), we get

$$\Pi = \exp\,[-\,(1/k)\,(q - \bar{y})]\,\exp\,(q) - \exp\,[(1 + c_1)q]. \qquad (10)$$

The agent maximizes (10) with respect to $q$. In the macroeconomic equilibrium, we have

$$q = \bar{y}. \qquad (11)$$

Consequently, the economy is completely characterized only by real variables. This equilibrium should be the same as (7) and (8). Thus, monetary factors cannot influence the real sector in the monopolistically competitive economy.

### 3.3. *Adding New Elements: Near-Rationality and Menu Costs*

The reason we get monetary neutrality in monopolistically competitive macroeconomic models is that economic agents are concerned only with relative price, not nominal prices. An increase in nominal demand simply induces a proportional increase in all prices, leaving relative prices and real variables unchanged.

In order to get monetary non-neutrality, it is then necessary to make the decision of economic agents depend on nominal variables, as well as on relative prices. The simplest way to introduce such dependence is to assume that it is costly to change nominal prices.[24] However, such costs are in general quite small, except possibly for mail-order businesses, which depend heavily on catalogues.[25] It costs little to change menus in restaurants. Thus, we need an additional ingredient to make nominal prices rigid.

The argument of near-rationality may fill the gap between small price adjustment costs and nominal price rigidity (see Akerlof and Yellen 1985). The economic agent is called near-rational if, although his action deviates from complete rationality, the cost of the deviation is very small. The argument claims that if economic agents are near-rational they do not change their prices, and that output is increased when the money supply is altered, as long as the change is small.

Here the aggregate demand externality described in Section 3 plays an important role. Let us first consider the decision of each economic agent. Suppose that the economy is initially in equilibrium. The first-order condition of the optimal price implies that the first-order change in real profits must be zero at that price. Suppose then that the money supply increases by a small amount. Because the change is small and the price is initially optimal, the loss in real profits arising from not adjusting the price is of second-order smallness. Thus, non-adjustment is near-rational for economic agents. However, this failure to adjust prices to changes in the money supply causes a first-order change in the economy because of the aggregate demand externality caused by real balances. Because real balances increase, output increases.

The near-rationality argument can also be interpreted in a completely rational framework. It implies that a very small cost of changing prices, called a 'menu cost', is sufficient completely to prevent rational economic agents from adjusting their prices to a small change in the money supply. This is often described as the menu-cost argument (see Mankiw 1985, and Blanchard and Kiyotaki 1987).

*Problems*

Although the near-rationality/menu-cost argument seems promising at first sight, it still has several problems.

On the empirical side, the argument seems only partially capable of explaining the three stylized facts presented in Section 1. There are two major empirical problems: the magnitude of fluctuations, and the inconsistency with cost-based prices. Let us examine each of these in turn.

The first empirical problem is the magnitude of nominal price rigidity that can be explained by the argument. The argument is based on the assumption of a small change in the money supply. However, what we want to know is the effect of a large change in the money supply. In order for a large change in the money supply not to induce agents to change their prices and thus increase their output, the cost of non-adjustment must be smaller than the menu cost, even in the case of a large change in nominal demand. This is the case only if marginal cost is almost flat and the optimal price is itself constant, because the menu cost is by definition very small and almost negligible. However, empirical studies suggest that marginal cost is at least moderately increasing (see e.g. Bils 1987). It is easy to show that a moderately increasing marginal cost requires the menu cost to be non-negligible and significantly larger than zero in order to prevent firms from changing their prices.[26]

The second empirical problem is that this argument cannot explain why prices respond differently to demand and cost changes. The argument is based on price-adjustment costs, and these costs are the same, regardless of whether adjustment is induced by changes in demand or in cost.

As for the first problem, there is one approach that overcomes the difficulty by adding a new element, namely, the real price rigidity. (See Ball and Romer 1990 for this kind of treatment.) Suppose, for example, that there is a change in the money supply, but other firms do not adjust their prices to this change. Then, if a firm adjusts its *nominal* price, a change in the *relative* price is implied. Assume that a firm does not gain much by changing its relative price. (This is the cause of relative price rigidity.) Then, a small price-adjustment cost may be sufficient to prevent a firm from adjusting its nominal price to a change in the money supply. If the price-adjustment cost is larger than the benefit, then firms do not adjust their prices in an equilibrium, and money becomes non-neutral. The larger the degree of relative price rigidity, the smaller the price-adjustment cost that causes monetary non-neutrality.

The combination of the menu cost and relative price rigidity, however, finds cost-based prices (the second problem) still difficult to explain. This is because the argument depends on the cost of nominal price adjustment, which should be the same for both demand and cost changes.

Besides problems with the empirical explanatory power of the argument, there are also two theoretical problems. The first is that of price-adjustment cost versus quantity-adjustment cost. To begin with, it is not clear why we should consider the near-rational behaviour of price determination, rather than that of quantity determination. The fundamental assumption in the near-rationality/menu-cost argument is that 'doing nothing' implies no price adjustment. However, in the perfect-information framework, price determination is equivalent to quantity determination. Thus, there is no a priori reason to choose the near-rational behaviour of price determination instead of that of quantity determination. If we assume the near-rational behaviour of quantity determination, economic agents do not change their supply when the money supply is changed, and we get monetary neutrality.

Another theoretical problem of the near-rationality/menu-cost argument which has attracted much attention in recent years is that, although it explains a lack of price adjustment, it does not give us a theory of price adjustment. It is impossible to keep all prices unchanged in a changing economy, and prices should eventually be adjusted to changes in economic conditions. However, it is generally very difficult to formalize a complete general equilibrium dynamic model of the economy in the face of the cost of changing prices, with the possible exception of the steady-state model.

There are two approaches to circumventing the last problem. In the first approach, instead of pursuing general equilibrium dynamics, attention is concentrated on the analysis of individual agents in a partial equilibrium setting.[27] The second approach starts by assuming plausible rules of changing prices and wages, instead of deriving them from rational behaviour, and then analyses general equilibrium dynamics based on these rules. This approach includes the literature of long-term and staggered contracts (see Fischer 1977*a*; Taylor 1979, 1980; Blanchard 1986), as well as the *S–s* policy approach (see Caplin 1985; Caplin and Spulber 1987).

The contract approach assumes fixed timing and intervals of contract negotiation, which determine prices (or, more precisely, price paths) during the contract period. This introduces imperfect information into the model, because agents have to determine future prices without knowing future economic conditions. This imperfect information results in monetary non-neutrality in a way similar to the imperfect-information perfectly competitive model, which will be discussed in the next section.

The *S–s* policy approach assumes that the agent changes his price if the deviation from the optimum exceeds certain thresholds. (The upper bound is called *S*, and the lower bound, *s*.) Thus, the *S–s* policy is a state-dependent rule of changing prices, in contrast to long-term and staggered contracts, which lead to time-dependent rules. While the contract approach always produces monetary non-neutrality owing to imperfect information, the *S-s* approach does not necessarily induce monetary non-neutrality. In fact, Caplin and Spulber (1987) give a completely worked out example which shows that, even though individual prices are rigid because of menu costs, the aggregate price level is completely flexible and money is neutral.[28]

## 4. IMPERFECT AND DIFFERENTIAL INFORMATION

The fundamental assumption behind the near-rationality/menu-cost argument—that 'doing nothing implies no price adjustment rather than no quantity adjustment—implicitly assumes that economic agents find it more convenient and profitable to post prices and keep them for some time than to adjust prices to every change in economic condition. However, there is no explicit structure justifying this behaviour in the monopolistically competitive models of Section 3.2, in which both consumers and firms are informed as to the conditions of the economy at no cost.

As indicated in Section 3.1, however, monopolistic competition is likely to be accompanied by imperfect information, costly search, and sluggish information diffusion on the side of consumers. The imperfect-information argument for monopolistic competition clearly implies that this is the case in many markets. The product differentiation argument for monopolistic competition also suggests that consumers are imperfectly informed, because to collect information about prices and the quality of various differentiated products (including services accompanying them) is costly and time-consuming. The monopolistically competitive market is different from the well organized perfectly competitive markets in which information is transmitted instantaneously and costlessly among market participants.

Before analysing imperfect information under monopolistic competition, however, it is worthwhile to examine perfectly competitive macroeconomic theories of imperfect information as a frame of reference.[29] This is partly because this theory was the chief vehicle of macroeconomic discussions in the 1970s, and partly because it was perhaps the first significant attempt to introduce imperfect information into macroeconomic general equilibrium analysis.

### 4.1 *Imperfect-Information Perfectly Competitive Models*

A stripped version of imperfect-information perfectly competitive macroeconomic models can be described as follows. The model is quite similar to the monopolistically competitive economy discussed in the previous section, except that (1) goods are homogeneous; (2) markets are perfectly competitive; and (3) there are demand disturbances.

The economy is composed of a large number of separate, perfectly competitive markets. Markets are homogeneous except for idiosyncratic demand disturbances. The demand function in one market is

$$q^d_u = m + u - p_u, \tag{12}$$

where $m$ is the money supply, which is common to all markets, $u$ is the idiosyncratic demand disturbance, $q^d_u$ is the quantity demanded, and $p_u$ is the price. As in the monopolistically competitive model of the previous section, all variables are in log, if not otherwise stated. Both $m$ and $u$ are independent random variables, whose distributions are normal with $Em = Eu = Emu = 0$, $Em^2 = \sigma^2_m$, and $Eu^2 = \sigma^2_u$.

In each market there are homogeneous suppliers. The representative supplier's real profits are given by

$$\Pi = \exp(p_u - \bar{p}_u)\exp(q_u) - \exp[(1 + c_1)q_u], \tag{13}$$

where $\bar{p}_u$ is the average price in the economy. The supplier maximizes $\Pi$ with respect to $q_u$.

The fundamental assumption is that perfectly competitive markets in this economy are informationally separated. The supplier cannot observe the economy-wide variables $\bar{p}_u$, $m$, and $u$ in determining his supply (imperfect information). Instead, he can observe the local price $p_u$ and form rational expectations about the global price level $\bar{p}_u$ (differential information). Let the supplier assume that $\bar{p}_u$ is distributed normally with mean $e(\bar{p}_u|p_u)$, where $e(\bar{p}_u|p_u)$ is the linear least-squares regression of $\bar{p}_u$ on $p_u$. (It can easily be shown that this is equal to the mathematical expectation of $\bar{p}_u$ conditional on information $p_u$ in our models.) Then, the supplier maximizes the expected profits $\hat{E}\Pi$ with respect to $q_u$, where $\hat{E}$ is the expectation operator with respect to the supplier's subjective distribution of the $\bar{p}_u$ just described. To make analysis simple, in this section (and only in this section) I employ the approximation that $e[\exp(-\bar{p}_u)|p_u] = \exp[e(-\bar{p}_u|p_u)]$.[30] Using this approximation, we then have $\hat{E}\Pi \approx \exp[p_u - e(\bar{p}_u|p_u)]\exp(q_u) - \exp[(1 + c_1)q_u]$. Consequently, the supply of the representative supplier is given by

$$q^s_u = \frac{1}{c_1}[-\log(1+c_1) + p_u - e(\bar{p}_u|p_u)]. \tag{14}$$

This is the Lucas supply function, except for a constant term.

In equilibrium, from $q^d_u = q^s_u$ we have

$$p_u = \frac{1}{1+c_1}[\log(1+c_1) + c_1(m+u) + e(\bar{p}_u|p_u)]. \tag{15}$$

Because $\bar{p}_u$ is the average of $p_u$, it can be shown from the above expression that

$$e(\bar{p}_u|p_u) = (1 - \theta)\bar{p}_L + \theta p_u, \tag{16}$$

where $\bar{p}_L = [\log(1 + c_1)]/c_1$, and $\theta = \sigma_m^2/(\sigma_m^2 + \sigma_u^2) < 1$;[31] $\bar{p}_L$ is the long-run price level, which is the price level where $m = 0$.

Rational expectations about $\bar{p}_u$ show that the expectations are sticky with respect to $\bar{p}_u$. In the framework of informationally separated local markets, suppliers have to form expectations based on information about local equilibrium prices. However, local equilibrium prices are nothing more than noisy information about the global prices level, because of local demand shocks. Since suppliers are aware of the possibility that they may confuse local demand shocks with global ones, their expectations become conservative and sticky with respect to local equilibrium prices.

This stickiness of expectations causes the monetary non-neutrality in this imperfect-information perfectly competitive macroeconomic model. The Lucas supply function implies that if $p_u = e(\bar{p}_u|p_u)$, then the money supply $m$ becomes neutral. However, because of sticky rational expectations, $e(\bar{p}_u|p_u)$ reflects only a part of the change in $p_u$. Consequently, an increase in $m$ results in an increase in output. In equilibrium, from (15) and (16) we obtain

$$\bar{p}_u = \bar{p}_L + \frac{c_1}{1-\theta+c_1} m \text{ and } \bar{q}_u = -\bar{p}_L + \frac{1-\theta}{1-\theta+c_1} m. \tag{17}$$

*Problems*

There are several problems with imperfect-information perfectly competitive macroeconomic models which caused a decline in their popularity as a theory of business cycles.[32] I shall consider three of the criticisms that have often been made against the model. Some of them are quite similar to the criticisms of the near-rationality/menu-cost arguments explained in the previous section.

The first criticism is empirical and regards the magnitude of output fluctuations that this model can explain. The equilibrium value of $\bar{q}_u$ (17) shows that $c_1$ should be very small (marginal cost is almost flat) in order to obtain large output fluctuations. For example, if $c_1 = 3$ and $\theta = ½$, then the fluctuation in the log of the output is only one-seventh of that in the log of the money supply. However, empirical studies of labour supply show that the labour-supply elasticity is likely to be small, suggesting that $c_1$ is large (see e.g. Killingthworth 1983). This substantially reduces the plausibility of the imperfect-information perfectly competitive model as a model of nominal price rigidity. Thus, the imperfect-information perfectly competitive model runs into the same problem as the near-rationality/menu-cost argument described in the previous section. Both require an almost flat marginal cost curve in order to explain the observed magnitude of output fluctuations.

The second criticism is theoretical and regards 'unrealistic' informational assumptions. The model is criticized on the grounds that the setting of informationally separated, perfectly competitive markets is unrealistic in industrialized economies that have sophisticated information technology.[33] Although in each local market there are Walrasian auctioneers who have quite sophisticated mechanisms for transmitting information within their own markets (they can costlessly transmit price information to all market participants), they cannot communicate with one another (they do not have aggregate information). Moreover, whereas the unobservability of the economy-wide price level $\bar{p}_u$ and the money supply $m$ plays a crucial role in this model, information about the price level and the money supply is available publicly within weeks and could be made available faster at a small cost in many industrialized countries. In addition, there are economy-wide securities markets in industrialized economies. Security prices may aggregate and reveal information about economy-wide shocks. Information about these securities markets is available at little cost.

The third problem of this approach concerns the types of shocks that affect output. This model predicts that only unanticipated monetary shocks affect output, and that their effects are not persistent. However, empirical studies on this subject show that output appears to be affected by current perceptions of monetary stocks,[34] and that their effects persist for several periods.

There are, however, attempts to resolve the last problem by adding additional elements to the basic framework. First, if some economic agents have to make their decisions well in advance for institutional reasons, then currently perceived monetary shocks have persistent effects on output. This is the case if there are long-term contracts.[35] Second, if nominal shocks mingle with velocity shocks, then the misperception needed to generate persistent effects of monetary shocks on output can arise, even though economic agents continuously observe the money supply. In this case, the money supply is at best noisy information about the true demand condition. Finally, a similar argument may be applied to the case in which, first, permanent shocks and transitory shocks have different effects on economic agents' behaviour and, second, the agents are unable to distinguish between the two.[36]

### 4.2. *Predetermined Prices: Imperfect Information and Monopolistic Competition*

Let us now return to the monopolistically competitive models of Section 3. In the following, based on the discussion of buyers' imperfect information in Section 3.1, I argue that prices are likely to be predetermined in monopolistically competitive economies. I relate this observation to the theoretical difficulties of the near-rationality/menu-cost argument in Section 3.3. Predetermined prices induce imperfect and differential information on the side of firms, which resembles the imperfect and differential information of perfectly competitive suppliers in the imperfect-information perfectly competitive macroeconomic models of Section 4.1. Thus, imperfect information on both sides of the market is a natural assumption in the monopolistically competitive models. I go on to consider the interaction between imperfect competition and imperfect information, which is a driving force behind the analysis in this book.[37]

*Predetermined prices*

My starting-point is Arthur Okun's observation about pricing behaviour in industrialized economies. Okun (1981) argues that many firms in various markets, industries, and economies seem to follow a 'predetermined price' strategy, in which firms announce their prices well before they have complete knowledge about the economy, including the reaction of other firms (imperfect information).[38] Firms determine their prices using all local information available at the time of decision (differential information), but they do not adjust their prices afterwards, even if new information arrives about global demand. Thus, prices are predetermined.[39]

This behaviour is clearly irrational in the framework of complete information. However, as indicated in Section 2.1, consumers are likely to be only imperfectly informed about the market, as they suffer from non-negligible search costs. The diffusion of information among consumers is at best sluggish in many markets. Monopolistically competitive markets are not like well organized commodity markets and are likely to be characterized by buyers' imperfect information, sluggish information diffusion, and costly search. In such markets, firms must incur costs (such as advertising costs) to inform their customers of the location, price, and quality of their products.

If the market is not well organized, and if, in addition, monopolistic competition is coupled with both buyers' imperfect information and sluggish information diffusion, frequent changes in prices (and quality) may cause a serious information transmission problem for firms. Information diffuses among consumers only gradually, and any attempts to expedite the process are costly. If firms frequently change their prices, they must inform their customers of the changes through costly methods such as newspaper adverts and direct mailings. Moreover, if firms fail to inform customers of the changes, customers may be confused and become antagonized. This may lead to a depletion of customers. In such a setting, the *imputed* cost of changing prices is no longer trivial, although the *physical* cost of rewriting menus is likely to remain negligible. Moreover, the imputed cost of changing prices may be substantially larger than the cost of changing quantities. Thus, the two problems of the near-rationality/menu-cost argument is Section 3.3.[40] are not likely to be major problems in the framework of the imputed cost of changing prices. In fact, this seems to provide a basis for the arguments of Okun (1981), Rotemberg (1982), and others, who based their analyses on the non-negligible cost of changing prices.

The fact that frequent price changes involve substantial cost implies two things. First, prices are likely to be determined before firms have perfect knowledge of exogenous conditions in their markets and the economy, and tend to be kept constant for a prolonged period of time. Second, firms must determine their prices under imperfect and incomplete information about their rivals. If firms do not exchange information about prices, they cannot know the price decisions made by their competitors when setting their own prices. Informational exchange among firms is not likely to take place because of anti-trust law considerations. Anti-trust law authorities may be suspicious of such activity because it may lead to tacit collusion.[41]

The imperfect and incomplete information suffered by firms in monopolistically competitive economies resembles the imperfect competition of suppliers in the perfectly competitive macroeconomic models of Section 4.1. The perfectly competitive supplier has local demand information, which is the equilibrium price in the local market. He estimates global demand conditions, such as the average price, from this local information. The firm in the monopolistically competitive setting corresponds to the local market in the perfectly competitive setting. The monopolistically competitive firm has imperfect local demand information, which is also imperfect information about global demand conditions. Based on this local information, the firm estimates global exogenous demand conditions and the reaction of other firms.

*Interaction between imperfect information and monopolistic competition*

Imperfect information introduces three informational elements into New Keynesian models, in addition to the strategic interdependence of economic agents. I argue in this book that these three elements together explain the three stylized facts (relative price rigidity, nominal price rigidity, and cost-based prices) in a coherent way, and at the same time clarify the relationship between the competitiveness of markets and the short-run movements of aggregate economic variables.

The first ingredient of imperfect-information monopolistically competitive models is an externality in the acquisition of information. The argument is quite similar to that involving the externality of price changes in the near-rationality/menu-cost argument.

In the near-rationality/menu-cost argument, if a firm adjusts its price when global demand conditions are altered, it may stabilize output. However, the possible benefits of this firm's price adjustment spread over to consumers and other firms, and the direct effect on this particular firm's profits, may be quite small. This is the externality in price changes. Facing the cost of price adjustment, the firm may ignore the benefits and choose no adjustment. Similarly, if a firm acquires costly information about global conditions, this may help stabilize output through price adjustment. However, the private benefits from this stabilization may be small, although it may be socially beneficial because of the externality. So the firm may choose not to acquire information because of its cost. The argument suggests that imperfect information may be voluntarily chosen by firms. Thus, imperfect information may be self-sustained in the monopolistically competitive economy.

The second ingredient of this model is that competitiveness determines the degree of price rigidity and output volatility. Under monopolistic competition, the firm's optimal choice depends on the average level of other firm's choices as well as on its individual demand and cost conditions. If information is imperfect, the firm's optimal choice is dependent on its expectations about average choice, rather than on the actual average choice. Competitiveness determines the relative importance of expectations about both average and individual conditions in determining the firm's optimal price. The more competitive the market is, the larger the weight that is given to expectations about the average. As explained in Section 4.1, imperfect information makes *expectations* about the average be rigid compared with the actual average because of the possibility of confusing local and global changes. Since competitiveness influences the relative importance of rigid expectations in firms' optimal decisions, it also affects price rigidity and output volatility.

The third characteristic of imperfect-information monopolistically competitive models is the interdependence of consumer behaviour and the optimal decisions of firms. In the imperfect-information framework, search is costly, and information about firms is transmitted to consumers only gradually. Consumers decide on their supplier using partial, imperfect information about the economy. This implies that a consumer's choice in the imperfect-information economy depends not only on relative prices but also on other characteristics of firms' offers, including information provision, such as advertising. In fact, the relevant criterion for consumers when choosing a supplier is not the relative price, but the total utility gain provided by the offer. This characteristic of the monopolistically competitive economy is in sharp contrast to the perfectly competitive economy, where the relative price is the only variable that determines a consumer's decision. In the monopolistically competitive economy, firms may gain customers by methods other than price cuts.

## 5. OUTLINE OF THE BOOK

### *Part I*

Part I investigates nominal price rigidity under nominal demand disturbances. Here we are concerned with the stylized fact where shifts in nominal aggregate demand are accommodated largely by changes in quantities, rather than by changes in nominal prices.

Chapters 2 and 3 are directly related to the theoretical and empirical problems of the near-rationality/menu-cost models of Section 3.1 and the imperfect-information perfectly competitive models of Section 4.1 as theories of nominal price rigidity.

Chapter 2 examines monopolistically competitive economies with predetermined prices, assuming that information about the money supply is not available when firms determine their prices. This chapter has four objectives. First, it examines the plausibility of predetermined prices. By analysing a stylized information transmission process, it derives conditions ensuring that predetermined prices are in fact an equilibrium strategy for firms. The result suggests that predetermined prices and the resulting imperfect information are an equilibrium strategy for a wide range of parameters in markets of differentiated products and sluggish information diffusion. The argument in this chapter is based on the externality in information acquisition described in Section 4.2.

Second, the chapter investigates the degree of price rigidity arising from predetermined prices. It shows that prices are still rigid even if supply elasticity is small (i.e. if marginal cost is rapidly increasing). Thus, it suggests that imperfect information, together with monopolistic competition, may provide an explanation of the phenomenon that both perfect-information menu-cost models and imperfect-information perfectly competitive models fail to explain: namely, large fluctuations in output with little change in nominal prices despite small supply elasticity.

The third objective of this chapter is to clarify the relationship between competitiveness and price rigidity in economies with predetermined prices. The firm's optimal price depends on expectations about the average price, as well as on its own individual conditions. Increased competition causes the firm's price to depend more on rigid expectations about the average price (owing to imperfect information) than on its own conditions. In this case, increased competition decreases the sensitivity of prices and thus enhances their rigidity. Consequently, a 'highly competitive' monopolistically competitive economy has more rigid prices than a 'non-competitive' monopolistically competitive economy.

Finally, this chapter provides a welfare analysis of the monopolistically competitive economy. It presents a simple characterization of social welfare in this economy and reveals that the deviation from the social optimum can be decomposed into a deviation that is due to non-competitive pricing and one that is due to imperfect information. Competitiveness influences social welfare not only directly, through non-competitive pricing, but also indirectly, through its interaction with imperfect information. In particular, because increased competition decreases price sensitivity and increases output variability, an increase in competitiveness may increase, rather than decrease, the social cost of fluctuations in nominal demand.

In the simplistic model of the predetermined price economy discussed in Chapter 2, the optimal policy is trivial, taking the form either of announcing necessary monetary information to the public, or of controlling the money supply and removing monetary uncertainty. The first policy (information provision) has the same effect as the second (aggregate demand management). Thus, there are no a priori grounds for preferring aggregate demand management to simple information provision. Although the model in Chapter 2 has the Keynesian characteristic of nominal price rigidity, it does not given strong support to the Keynesian notion of the desirability of aggregate demand management. In fact, because the government actually provides such monetary information to the public in most industrialized economies, one may argue that the scope of active demand management policies are rather limited. Chapter 3 takes up this issue.

A common criticism of monetary non-neutrality models based on imperfect information about monetary disturbances, including the one in Chapter 2 and the perfectly competitive models surveyed in Section 4.1, is that information about the money supply is available at small cost and with a short lag. If gains from acquiring and using such information were large, then firms would obtain the information, and they would be perfectly informed about monetary disturbances.

Chapter 3 shows that this need not be the case: private gains from information acquisition may be small, whereas social gains for the economy as a whole are large. If firms fail to acquire and use information about the money supply, prices will not be adjusted to changes in it. Thus, given that other firms fail to acquire and use money supply information in forming their expectations, monopolistically competitive firms may find that failure to incorporate information about the money supply into their expectations may cost them very little. This is because of the externality in information acquisition discussed in Section 4.2. The monetary information usually contains substantial noise. In order to utilize this information, firms have some workers who analyse it. Because this is costly, firms may choose not to acquire the information and remain imperfectly informed about the money supply. However, the macroeconomic equilibrium results in rigid nominal prices and large fluctuations in output, and this may reduce the welfare of consumers and workers (and possibly of the firms themselves).

This argument suggests that information provision may not work in monopolistically competitive economies. In fact, in the simple model of Chapter 3, private gains from acquiring monetary information are zero, so that even a very small cost of acquiring monetary information is sufficient to prevent firms from doing so. In this case, aggregate demand management is clearly preferable in order to overcome problems that arise in the private sector owing to lack of information.

Although Chapters 2 and 3 analyse monopolistic competition in product markets, similar arguments may be applied to monopolistically competitive labour markets and may provide us with one possible explanation of the predetermined nominal wage. In Chapter 4, we investigate an issue that has been discussed extensively in the last decade, namely, the implications of wage indexation in the monopolistically competitive framework. Under predetermined nominal wage contracts incorporating cost-of-living adjustments, the conventional wisdom is that full indexation always insulates the economy from nominal shocks. This chapter, however, shows that this is no longer true under monopolistic or, more generally, imperfect competition in labour markets. This is because monopolistically competitive unions are concerned not only with the level of real wages, but also with the level of employment. Although full indexation enables unions to determine real wages, it does not resolve uncertainty about employment. The union must estimate the location of labour demand from available local information in order to forecast the level of employment. Because the determination of real wages by the union depends on its estimated location of labour demand, imperfect information about labour demand affects real wage determination, and thus causes imperfect insulation under full indexation.

*Part II*

Part II explores a possible explanation of the third stylized fact (cost-based prices) described in the introductory section in the predetermined price framework. At the same time, it clarifies the effect of competition on pricing and investment in a more general framework than that of Part I, allowing both (and possibly correlated) demand and cost disturbances. However, in order to make the analysis tractable, the approach taken in Part II is a partial equilibrium approach, that is, an analysis of a monopolistically competitive industry, rather than a general equilibrium approach, as in Part I.

Chapter 5 considers the behaviour of prices. This chapter gives an explanation of cost-based pricing, which is widely observed in industrialized economies, but which previous New Keynesian models have found difficult to explain. I analyse the general case of correlated demand and cost shocks. It is shown that in a realistic setting, where cost disturbances are more uniform than demand disturbances, prices are more sensitive to changes in cost than to changes in demand.

Under imperfect information, uniform cost disturbances and dispersed demand disturbances imply that local cost information is more valuable than local demand information in estimating macroeconomic, global disturbances in demand and cost. Consequently, a firm's price is more dependent on local cost information, so that the price becomes more sensitive to cost changes. Thus, the behaviour of prices under monopolistic competition and imperfect information can be characterized as cost-based prices. In addition, in this chapter's correlated shock framework I examine the robustness of Chapter 2's conclusion that increased competition enhances price rigidity.

Chapter 6 investigates the effect of competition on the volatility of investment, under the assumption of imperfect information about other firms' investments. Investment is an important determinant of aggregate demand and one of the main sources of its volatility, although investment is excluded in the analysis of Part I to provide analytical tractability. In this chapter I analyse the effect of imperfect information and increased competition on the sensitivity of investment to demand and supply shocks. The main conclusion is that increased competition among firms unambiguously increases the sensitivity of investment to both demand and supply shocks, and thus makes investment more volatile.

The rigidity of expectations about industry-wide variables plays a crucial role here. Under this chapter's simple structure, a firm's optimal investment depends negatively on its expectations about average investment within the industry. Suppose there is an unexpected increase in productivity. Because expectations are rigid, the firm's expectations about average investment do not increase as much as the actual average investment. This implies that a firm will increase its investment more under imperfect information than under perfect information. Increased competition implies that a firm's investment becomes more dependent on rigid expectations. Thus, increased competition enhances the investment-increasing effect and increases the volatility of investment.

Chapter 7 is a temporary detour from the analysis of rigid prices and volatile output. It explores the characteristics of a monopolistically competitive industry under imperfect information in more detail. Specifically, it examines the possibility of a stochastic expectational equilibrium in such an industry. In the imperfect-information models of the preceding chapters, it was assumed that it is impossible or costly for firms to obtain information about other firms' prices before they determine their own prices. In this chapter, firms are allowed to get partial information about other firms' prices at no cost. The resulting equilibrium is a stochastic one, in which firms keep changing their prices to meet competition, but the distribution of prices does not change. I investigate the possibility of multiple expectational equilibria in this framework and its relationship to the degree of competition.

## *Part III*

The subject of Part III is relative price rigidity in product markets. In Parts I and II attention is concentrated primarily on the effect of firms' imperfect information about the economy and the decisions of other firms on their own decisions about nominal prices. In Part III it is seen that consumers' imperfect information and its effect on firms' strategies lead to relative price rigidity. Unlike in Parts I and II, firms in Part III are assumed to have perfect information about the market, so the results obtained in Part III are due solely to imperfect information on the side of consumers.

Chapter 8 deals with price behaviour in customer markets under uncertainty. A customer market is defined in this chapter as a non-Walrasian market in which price-setting, quantity-taking firms compete for imperfectly informed, repetitive consumers, called 'customers'. Price information diffuses only gradually among customers. Customers are virtually immobile in the short run and are 'attached' to particular firms (suppliers), although they can freely choose their suppliers in the long run as the offers of other firms become known to them. There is uncertainty about market conditions, which customers cannot observe. Prices may be adjusted to these changes.

The temporary immobility of customers arising from imperfect information implies that firms and customers are, in the short run, involved in a bilateral monopoly. Efficient allocation requires that firms take into account their customers' preferences under uncertainty in determining their prices. Thus, firms' prices are influenced by customers' imperfect information. If customers are price-risk-averse, then customer market prices are rigid, and increased competition among firms makes them even more so. In this chapter it is argued that the scope of rigid customer market prices is quite wide, if near-rational behaviour and adjustment cost in the consumption process are taken into consideration.

Chapter 9 considers a market in which consumers actively search, although the cost of search is substantial. This is the case, for example, if products are expensive and their quality-adjusted prices vary. The chapter investigates the plausibility of the rigid-price argument in this market. This argument states that, by advertising its price and location well in advance and thus reducing the search costs of consumers, a firm may gain customers and increase profits, even though it must abandon the fine-tuning of its price to market conditions. Using a simple search framework, this chapter shows that such a rigid price strategy is likely to be an equilibrium strategy.

Unlike Parts I and II, in which price rigidity is *nominal* price rigidity, rigidity in Part III is *real* (or *relative*) price rigidity. This is because the primary sources of rigidity are consumer preference (price risk aversion) and technology (search costs), and these are based on real terms. Relative price rigidity, however, may cause nominal price rigidity if it is supplemented by a (physical and/or imputed) cost of changing nominal prices, as explained in Section 3.3. Thus, relative price rigidity as explained in Part III may also cause monetary non-neutrality and other Keynesian phenomena.

# Notes

1. Blanchard (1990) presented a concise assessment of empirical results on which the above three stylized facts are based. Tobin (1972) summarized the results of empirical studies about the behaviour of prices and wages in the US economy in the 1960s and early 1970s, based on these stylized facts. Coutts *et al.* (1978) obtained the same results for the UK in the 1960s and 1970s. See also Gordon (1981), Rotemberg (1987), and Blanchard and Fischer (1989: Ch. 1) for a survey of the empirical studies in the USA after the Second World War. 'Rigidity' of nominal and relative prices seems to be present even before the war (see Sachs 1980; Schultze 1981, 1986). Rigidity is also found in other industrialized economies (see Gordon (1983; 1990), Sachs (1979), and Geary and Kennan (1982)).

   There are, however, other interpretations of the time series that minimize the importance of demand shocks but emphasize supply shocks (especially technological shocks) in economic fluctuations: see Blanchard and Fischer (1989: Ch. 1) for a survey of this literature.
2. This statement may be misleading, because there are many economists who do not agree with this characterization of the Keynesian approach. To be more precise, the Keynesian approach should here be read as the *American* Keynesian approach, or as the textbook treatment of Keynesian theory found in most popular textbooks on macroeconomics.
3. So-called 'fixprice' macroeconomics exemplifies this trend: see Barro and Grossman (1976).
4. There were attempts to explain the Phillips curve relationship in the microeconomic framework: see e.g. Phelps *et al.* (1970). Their attempts paved the way for research on the microfoundations of Keynesian economics. However, these early attempts were generally partial rather than general equilibrium (see below).
5. An alternative, the competitive equilibrium business-cycle approach, also appeared in the late 1970s: see e.g. Barro (1989) for a survey of this literature. I do not discuss the relative weakness and strength of the two approaches in detail in this book. See Blanchard and Fischer (1989) for an assessment of the two approaches from a New Keynesian viewpoint, and Lucas (1987) for the view of an economist sympathetic to the competitive equilibrium business-cycle theory.

   Here I use the term 'New Keynesian' in a broader sense than in the surveys of Rotemberg (1987) and Blanchard and Fischer (1989: Ch. 8). These authors refer mainly to the imperfectly competitive approaches that appeared in the 1980s in the USA; however, similar approaches were also found in Europe and Japan in the late 1970s and the 1980s. Negishi (1978) and Benassy (1976) are seminal works in this field. For a survey of this literature, see Benassy (1990a; 1992).
6. See the references cited in n. 1, especially Gordon (1990).

7. There is a rich array of market imperfections in the real economy: the models in the New Keynesian approach differ from one another, depending on which of the market imperfections is taken as the main building block of the model. Market imperfections other than imperfect competition include a bilateral monopoly in labour and goods markets, asymmetric information in labour and financial markets, increasing returns, and multiple equilibria. See Blanchard and Fischer (1989: Ch.9); Greenwald and Stiglitz (1987a, b); and Azariadis and Cooper (1985) for the New Keynesian approach based on market imperfections other than imperfect competition.
8. This section is not intended to be a survey of the literature and is rather superficial in its treatment of the subject. The aim is simply to point out various empirical and theoretical microeconomic results supporting imperfect competition as a model of markets for macroeconomic research. For more on this subject, readers are referred to the references cited in the subsequent footnotes.
9. Pratt *et al.* (1979) report interesting data on price distribution in consumer goods markets.
10. See Spence (1976) and Dixit and Stiglitz (1977). Eaton and Lipsey (1989) surveys the literature. For a compact survey of the literature from a New Keynesian viewpoint, see Benassy (1992). The following argument may underlie the current popularity of product differentiation as the source of imperfect competition.
11. See e.g. Salop (1976); Salop and Stiglitz (1977); Butters (1977); Wolinsky (1986). Stiglitz (1989) surveys this literature.
12. See Plott (1982) for a survey of results in experimental economics. The results reported here are obtained in Ketcham *et al.* (1984).
13. They are usually students paid for their participation in the experiment.
14. However, this conclusion may be premature, because hypothetical markets in experimental economics may fail to incorporate some important characteristics of real-world competition. Some researchers base their macroeconomic analysis of prices and quantities on oligopolistic competition, rather than monopolistic competition: see e.g. Sweezy (1939); Green and Porter (1984); Rotemberg and Saloner (1986); Maskin and Tirole (1988).
15. See e.g. Domberger (1979); Qualls (1979); Domowitz *et al.* (1986).
16. This model is a simplified version of the microfoundation model developed in Chapter 2.
17. See Benassy (1992) for a survey of monopolistically competitive macroeconomic models which are explicitly based on the general equilibrium argument. Ses also Dixon (1987) for a model similar to the one described below.
18. Sattinger (1984) presents a model of product differentiation in which $k$ is the number of products (and, consequently, the number of agents).
19. This is forcefully emphasized by Weitzman (1984).
20. For a more complete discussion of underemployment in general monopolistically competitive models, see Benassy (1992). Negishi (1978) and Benassy (1978) study the underemployment equilibrium in the monopolistically competitive economy under the subjective-demand assumption. Akerlof and Yellen (1985), Dixon (1987), Benassy (1987), and Blanchard and Kiyotaki (1987) obtained underemployment under the objective-demand framework.

(See Benassy 1990*a* for the subjective-demand approach, as well as the objective-demand approach, the latter of which I adopt in the following analysis.) The treatment here follows Blanchard and Kiyotaki (1987).

D'Aspremont *et al.* (1989), Silvestre (1988), and Dehez (1985) go further beyond the underemployment property, and show that, under a certain configuration of preferences, technology, and expectations, the monopolistically competitive economy entails unemployment, in the sense that, for all levels of nominal wage, including zero wage, labour demand is always short of labour supply, even if labour supply is exogenously fixed. The reason is as follows. In the monopolistically competitive economy, firms set the prices at which marginal revenue is equal to marginal cost. Thus, even if marginal cost (the nominal wage) is zero, the firm's demand for labour may be bounded, and the price will not necessarily go to zero. Thus, if the initial wealth of consumers is small (so that the Pigou effect is small), equilibrium labour demand may be smaller than labour supply even if the wage goes to zero. See also Schultz (1989) for the robustness of their results.

21. This procedure is justified as long as the number of firms is the same. If the number varies, then we have to take preference for diversity into account.
22. Other macroeconomic issues have also been investigated in this imperfectly competitive framework, including crowding-out (Snower 1983; Dixon 1987), optimal fiscal policies (Benassy 1991); interaction between product markets and asset markets (Svensson 1986); investment in macroeconomic rationing models (Sneessens 1987); the effect of wage rigidity on economic stability (Iwai 1981); the effect of kinked demand curves in a macroeconomic setting (Negishi 1979 and Woglom 1982); increasing returns to scale (Weitzman 1982); and finally, profit-sharing (Weitzman 1985).
23. See Benassy (1992) for an exposition of this monetary neutrality in imperfectly competitive models in a general setting. Blanchard and Kiyotaki (1987) and Dixon (1987) explain this property in a simple framework similar to the illustrative model of this section.
24. There are many studies about the implications of the cost of changing prices in a monopolistically competitive economy. For earlier studies, see Barro (1972); Iwai (1974); Sheshinski and Weiss (1977, 1983); Rotemberg (1982); and Parkin (1986). Recent studies concentrate primarily on the dynamic effects of price adjustment costs. The issues include staggering and time-dependent *v.* state-dependent rules. See Blanchard and Fischer (1989: Ch. 8) for a survey of the literature.
25. Okun (1981) provides another explanation of large price adjustment costs. He argues that, in a market in which consumers keep long-term customer–supplier relationships with firms, customers buy from the present supplier and do not shop around, as long as the current price is the same as the past price. He calls this behaviour 'intertemporal comparison shopping'. Nishimura (1982) provides a microeconomic foundation for this behaviour; however, the scope of this type of market seems rather limited.
26. See Ch. 2. However, in order to analyse the issue more satisfactorily, we should distinguish variations in work-hours from variations in employment. The former are related to microeconomic labour-supply elasticity, as indicated in the text, whereas the latter depend on institutional factors in labour markets.

Because I do not analyse institutional factors in labour markets in detail, I shall not pursue this issue any further in this book.

27. This approach is taken, for example, by Sheshinski and Weiss (1977, 1983).
28. However, Caplin and Leahy (1989) presents an example in which money is not neutral in this framework.
29. I analyse Lucas's model in the following discussion (see Lucas 1973). See also Cukierman (1984) for a survey of the literature.
30. This approximation is often used in the literature. However, it may result in misleading conclusions, especially in a long-run analysis (see Ch. 4). For this reason, I avoid this approximation in the following chapters as much as possible.
31. Rational expectations are obtained by the method of undetermined coefficients. Let $e(\bar{p}_u|p_u) = J + Lp_u$. On the one hand, substitute this into the equilibrium condition, and get $\Lambda = m + u$, here $\Lambda = (1/c_1)[(1 + c_1 - L)p_u - \log(1 + c_1) - J]$. By definition, $\Lambda$ is observable. Then, we have $e(m|p_u) = \theta\Lambda$. (This is an application of the optimal forecast theory; see e.g. Sargent (1987: Ch. 10.) On the other hand, from the equilibrium condition, we obtain $(1 + c_1 - L)\, e(\bar{p}_u|p_u) = \log(1 + c_1) + c_1 e(m|p_u) + J$. Substituting $e(m|p_u) = \theta\Lambda$ into this expression, and collecting the terms, we obtain the rational expectations in the text.
32. Many critical surveys of imperfect-information perfectly competitive macroeconomic models are available; see especially McCallum (1986); Blanchard and Fischer (1989: Ch. 7); and Grossman (1989).
33. Of course, most assumptions made in economics are 'unrealistic', in the sense that they are not literally true. The issue is whether or not the results of the analysis hang on such unrealistic assumptions.
34. The long list of empirical studies inconsistent with imperfect-information perfectly competitive models includes Bean (1984); Boschen (1985); Boschen and Grossman (1982); Barro and Hercowitz (1980); and Frydman and Rappoport (1987).
35. This has been emphasized in the context of long-term labour contracts common in the USA and, in turn, connects the imperfect-information perfectly competitive models with the contract approach described in the near-rationality/menu-cost argument in Section 3.2; e.g. Fischer (1977*a*) and Taylor (1979, 1980). This approach, however, has been criticized because it assumes, rather than explains, the nominal price rigidity inherent in such long-term contracts (Barro 1977). In fact, the near-rationality/menu-cost argument has been presented to overcome such criticisms.
36. See e.g. Brunner *et al.* (1980, 1983). Also, see Froyen and Waud (1987, 1988) for recent developments in the imperfect-information perfectly competitive approach.
37. To my knowledge, Andersen (1985) and Nishimura (1986*a*) are the first two attempts to explain nominal price rigidity based both on imperfect competition and on differential (imperfect) information. They independently reached a similar conclusion.
38. See Okun's discussion of fixed-time scheduling, pre-notification, and meeting competition as the standards of price changes in customer markets.

39. The predetermined nature of prices in industrialized economies is also emphasized by Gordon (1981). See also Bosworth and Lawrence (1982).
40. That is, the problems of the magnitude of menu costs necessary for large output fluctuations and of why we consider the cost of changing prices rather than that of changing quantities.
41. Moreover, non-co-operative firms may not find it profitable to exchange information. (See the literature of information sharing in oligopolistic markets, such as Clarke (1983); Vives (1985); Gal-Or (1986).) Although collusion coupled with information exchange always yields the maximum profit (monopoly profit), a binding information exchange agreement under non-co-operative behaviour does not always increase profits.

# PART I
# NOMINAL PRICE RIGIDITY

# 2
# The Predetermined-Price Economy

## 1. INTRODUCTION

In this chapter I construct a choice-theoretic microfoundation model of the monopolistically competitive economy with predetermined prices. The model is based on rational behaviour of consumers and firms, takes account of general equilibrium relations, and explicitly considers the transmission of information that leads to imperfect information on the side of firms. The mode is laid out in Section 2. Throughout this chapter, it is assumed that information about the money supply is not available. The issue of monetary information acquisition is postponed to Chapter 3.

The information diffusion process analysed in this chapter is quite stylized and is not intended to be realistic. Rather, it is constructed to capture the essence of the observation made by Okun (1981), Gordon (1981), and others that information transmission is costly and time-consuming. In this economy, only the firms themselves provide information about their offers (location, price, and quality). Consumers choose their supplier from among firms about which they already have information, instead of searching actively for the best offer among unknown firms.[1] It takes time for firms to inform consumers of their offers, and any attempt to speed up the information diffusion process is costly.

In Section 2, the firm is required to announce its price in advance (predetermined prices). In this case, the firm's price information is assumed to reach consumers at no cost, but the firm has to predetermine its price before having perfect knowledge about its market and the economy. In this section I first construct a model of the predetermined-price economy in a game-theoretic framework. The predetermined-price economy is formulated as an incomplete-information game of price-making firms, and its Bayesian Nash equilibrium is derived. However, although the game-theoretic framework has the advantage of making underlying assumptions clear, it has the disadvantage of being complicated. Thus, I also present an alternative reduced-form rational expectations model of the predetermined-price economy, whose rational expectations equilibrium is identical to the Bayesian Nash equilibrium of the incomplete-information game. This reduced-form model is easily analysed and related to other macroeconomic models surveyed in Chapter 1. I characterize the equilibrium using this reduced-form model.

In Section 3 I examine the plausibility of predetermined prices, introducing the possibility of waiting until uncertainty is resolved and being perfectly informed at the time of price decision. The firm then has two alternatives. First, as in Section 2, the firm can announce its price well in advance. I shall call this the 'imperfect-information (predetermined-price) strategy'. Second, the firm can wait until it has sufficient knowledge about the current state of the economy, and then determine its price. However, because at this stage little time is left for the firm to reach consumers before they visit other firms, the firm must use costly methods of advertisement, such as direct mailings. I shall call the second strategy the 'perfect-information strategy'. If the extra advertising cost is larger than the informational gain from the perfect-information strategy, the firm chooses the imperfect-information (predetermined-price) strategy. I show that the minimum extra advertising cost supporting a predetermined-price equilibrium is relatively small. This is the case even if supply is not elastic, in the sense that the slope of the marginal cost curve is steep. This suggests a wide scope of predetermined-price behaviour, as Okun and Gordon emphasized.

In Section 4 I analyse the effects of inelastic supply on prices and quantities in the predetermined-price economy. They are shown to be different from those in other models of nominal price rigidity. It is well known that, in order to obtain large fluctuations in output, the supply elasticity must be very large, both in the imperfect-information perfectly competitive model of Lucas (1973) and in the menu-cost monopolistically competitive model of Blanchard and Kiyotaki (1987). This characteristic is considered a weakness of these models as regards their ability to explain nominal price rigidity, because empirical analysis suggests that supply is rather inelastic. By contrast, in the predetermined-price framework, monetary disturbances still have a significant effect on the real sector, even if supply is not elastic.

The relationship between competitiveness in the economy and the short-run behaviour of prices and quantities is also investigated in Section 4. Contrary to the commonly held view, increased competition among firms in the predetermined-price economy reduces price flexibility, and thus increases the volatility of output, whereas a change in competitiveness has little effect on price flexibility under perfect information. Thus, the behaviour of a monopolistically competitive economy is heavily dependent on whether it is subject to perfect or imperfect information.

Section 5 presents a welfare analysis of the predetermined-price economy. In this section I show that it is possible to decompose the deviation of the predetermined-price economy from the social optimum into the deviation due to non-competitive pricing behaviour and the deviation due to imperfect information. Using this property, I show that increased competition is not necessarily associated with an increase in social welfare (or, more precisely, a decrease in the deviation from the social optimum) for a given magnitude of nominal disturbances. This is mainly because increased competition increases output volatility by decreasing price flexibility. If consumer's utility is sufficiently concave in consumption and leisure, there is even a case where, for a given magnitude of nominal disturbances, an increase in competition actually decreases social welfare (or increases the deviation from the social optimum). In this case, increased competition increases, rather than decreases, the social cost of nominal disturbances.

Section 6 concludes this chapter with remarks on the possible extensions and the robustness of the results obtained in the chapter.

## 2. A SIMPLE MACROECONOMIC MODEL OF MONOPOLISTIC COMPETITION WITH PREDETERMINED PRICES

In developing a macroeconomic model of monopolistic competition under imperfect information, I make five basic choices. I first choose a representative household. Here I use one representative household, which sells labour to firms and receives firms' profits as dividends. This aggregation of households enables us to analyse social welfare explicitly.

Second, in order to link real variables with nominal ones in the simplest way, I assume real balances in the utility function. As sources of uncertainty, I assume disturbances in the money supply and in the representative household's preferences. The confusion between the former macroeconomic nominal disturbances and the latter microeconomic real ones provides the source of monetary non-neutrality in this model.

Third, in order to make the economy monopolistically competitive, I assume that products are differentiated, each being produced by one firm. As in the recent literature of monopolistic competition (Weitzman 1985 and Blanchard and Kiyotaki 1987), I adopt the constant elasticity of substitution (CES) specification of the utility function of the representative household.

Fourth, I assume that labour inputs are differentiated and that one firm uses only one labour input, which is specific to it. Thus, a particular firm and the supplier of the firm-specific labour input (the household) form a bilateral monopoly in the labour market. Following Hall and Lilien (1979), we assume individual efficient bargains between firms and the household. A given firm and the household determine wages and employment efficiently, taking as given the results of negotiation between the other firms and the household.

Fifth, I assume that firms know the structure of the economy. They know the household's utility function and the other firms' production functions. They do not, however, have information about monetary and preference disturbances. About these they have only imperfect information.

The fourth assumption of efficient bargains is made in order to concentrate our attention on the effect of product-market monopolistic competition on the behaviour of the monopolistically competitive economy. Because wage and employment bargains between firms and the household are assumed to be efficient, there is no nominal rigidity in the labour markets. Thus, any nominal rigidity found in this monopolistically competitive economy stems from product-market monopolistic competition.[2]

One may object to the fifth assumption of perfect knowledge, because this requires too much information that firms in the real economy are not likely to possess. Later in this section I give an alternative assumption that requires less information for firms but produces the same results as the main model; however, the alternative assumption still requires substantial knowledge about the economy on the part of firms. The reason I make the perfect knowledge assumption, or something like it, is that I am concerned with the behaviour of the economy under an expectational equilibrium, where the formation of expectations by firms is consistent with the endogenous mechanisms generating the forecasted variables, contingent on the information available to firms. The possibility of firms using rules-of-thumb in their expectations and possible changes in the analysis will be discussed in section 6.

### *The model*

The economy consists of one representative consumer and $n$ firms. Each firm produces a specific good that is an imperfect substitute for the other goods, employing labour specific to the firm. The household derives utility from the consumption of goods, liquidity services of real money balances, and leisure. It gets initial money balances through transfer payments from the government and receives wages and dividends from firms. It maximizes its utility by choosing consumption of goods and money balances, taking prices as given.

Note that one representative household supplies labour to firms and receives wages and dividends from them. Thus, under the assumption of bilateral monopoly and efficient bargains, employment (work-hours and thus leisure) is determined by firms in such a way as to maximize the household's utility with respect to their price, by taking the prices of other firms as given. Because of the construction of a single representative household, it does not matter how revenues are divided into wages and profits (dividends). This greatly reduces the complexity of the model.

### *The sequence of events*

Before presenting the details of the model, it is worthwhile to specify its sequence of events. There are two stages: the price-decision stage, and the consumption-decision stage.

At the beginning of the first stage, nature chooses a particular realization of monetary and preference disturbances. The government then allocates money to the household through transfer payments. Firms are allowed to conduct market research and get imperfect information about monetary and preference disturbances. Firms simultaneously choose their prices based on this imperfect information.

In the second stage, after all prices have been determined, the household decides how much to buy from each firm and places its orders. The household observes all disturbances and prices. It determines consumption and real money holdings, taking prices, wages, dividends, and initial money holdings as given. All firms are obliged to satisfy the demand that their price offers create, and thus there are no rations.[3] Firms employ labour and produce the demanded quantities. Then, the household actually purchases the goods from the firms and consumes them, and firms pay wages and dividends to the household.

*Symmetry*

Firms are assumed to be symmetric in that they have the same demand and production functions. The assumption of symmetry allows us to simplify our welfare analysis. However, demand disturbances differ from firm to firm. These disturbances are determined by monetary and preference disturbances.

## 2.1. *The Second Stage: Consumption Decision and Monetary Equilibrium*

It is convenient to analyse the economy backwards, from the second stage to the first. In the second stage, there is no uncertainty for the household.

*The representative household*

The representative household derives utility from consumption, real money balances, and leisure. Its utility function $\Psi$ is the composite of the CES and Cobb-Douglas functions, such that

$$\Psi \equiv \left[ D(n\bar{Y})^{\zeta} \left( \frac{\tilde{M}}{\bar{P}} \right)^{1-\zeta} \right] - \sum_{i=1}^{n} L_i^{\mu}, \tag{1}$$

where $D$ is a normalization factor such that $D = \zeta^{-\zeta}(1-\zeta)^{-(1-\zeta)}$; $n$ is the number of goods (and the number of firms); $\bar{Y}$ is the average consumption index defined below; $\tilde{M}$ represents the end-of-period nominal money holdings; $\bar{P}$ is the price index associated with $\bar{Y}$, which is defined below; and $\zeta$ is a parameter which satisfies $0 < \zeta < 1$. Real balances $\tilde{M}/\bar{P}$ are included in the utility function, because real balances yield liquidity services. $L_i$ is the labour input specific to the $i$th firm, and $L_i^{\mu}$ represents the disutility that comes from the labour input specific to the $i$th firm.

Thus, $\Sigma_{i=1}^{n} L_i^{\mu}$ is the total disutility of labour. We assume that $1 < \mu$, which implies increasing marginal disutility of labour.

The average consumption index $\bar{Y}$ is defined as follows:

$$\bar{Y} = \bar{Y}(\{Q_i\}: i=1, \ldots, n) \equiv \left[ \left( \sum_{i=1}^{n} U_i^{1/k} \, Q_i^{(k-1)/k} \right) / n \right]^{k/(k-1)}, \tag{2}$$

where $Q_i$ is the consumption of the $i$th product. The parameter $k$ satisfies $1 < k$. The assumption is necessary for profit maximization, which will be specified later in this section.

$U_i$ represents the *product-specific* preference disturbance. I assume that $U_i$ is a draw from a log-normal distribution; that is, $\log U_i$ is a draw from a normal distribution with mean zero and variance $\sigma_u^2$.

$\bar{P}$ is the price index associated with the average consumption index $\bar{Y}$:

$$\bar{P} = \bar{P}(\{P_i\}: i=1, \ldots, n) \equiv \left[ \left( \sum_{i=1}^{n} U_i \, P_i^{1-k} \right) / n \right]^{1/(1-k)}, \tag{3}$$

where $P_i$ is the price of the $i$th product.

The household's demand for each product and the demand for real balances are both derived from the maximization of $\Psi$ with respect to $Q_i$ and $\tilde{M}/\bar{P}$, subject to the following budget constraint:

$$\sum_{i=1}^{n} P_i \, Q_i + \tilde{M} = B, \tag{4}$$

where $B$ is the beginning-of-period asset of the household.

Let us now consider $B$. The household obtains money from the government in the form of transfer payments, and wage payments and dividends from firms. Then,

$$B = \sum_{i=1}^{n} (\bar{P}\Lambda_i + \bar{P}\Pi_i) + M,$$

where $\Lambda_i$ is the real wage payment, and $\Pi_i$ the real dividend from the $i$th firm. The beginning-of-period money holdings are equal to the money supply, $M$.

The money supply is a random variable. I assume that $M$ is a draw from a log-normal distribution; that is, $\log M$ is a draw from a normal distribution with mean zero and variance $\sigma_m^2$. $\log M$ and $\log U_i$ are independent.

### *Demand functions and monetary equilibrium*

Using the properties of the CES and Cobb–Douglas functions, we can derive the demand $Q_i$ for the $i$th product and the demand for real balances

$\tilde{M}/\bar{P}$. They are

$$Q_i = \left(\frac{P_i}{P}\right)^{-k} \bar{Y}U_i, \tag{5}$$

where

$$n\bar{Y} = \zeta \frac{B}{\bar{P}}, \text{ and } \frac{\tilde{M}}{\bar{P}} = (1-\zeta)\frac{B}{\bar{P}}.$$

In order for the economy to be in monetary equilibrium at the second stage, the money demand should be equal to the money supply. Thus, the end-of-period money holdings should equal the beginning-of-period money holdings. That is,

$$\tilde{M} = M \tag{6}$$

should be satisfied. Because of (5) and (6), we obtain from the monetary equilibrium condition

$$\bar{Y} = H_1 \frac{M}{\bar{P}}, \tag{7}$$

where

$$H_1 = [\zeta/(1-\zeta)]/(1/n).$$

Thus, in equilibrium, the average demand is proportional to the initial real money holdings.

*The household's utility in equilibrium*

Substituting demand functions (5) and (7) into (1), we obtain the household's utility in equilibrium, such that

$$\Psi = \frac{B}{\bar{P}} - \Sigma_i L_i^{\mu} = \left(\frac{n}{\zeta}\bar{Y}\right) - (\Sigma_i L_i^{\mu}), \tag{8}$$

where $L_i$ is determined by firms in the first stage.

## 2.2. *The First Stage: Price Decision and the Incomplete-Information Game*

Because firms have perfect knowledge about the economy except for the particular realization of monetary and preference disturbances, firms know the household's consumption functions (5) and its indirect utility function (8).

*Firms' payoff function*

Firms are indexed by $i$, $i$=1, . . . , $n$. The demand for the $i$th firm's product, $Q_i$, is, from (5) and (7),

$$Q_i = \left(\frac{P_i}{\bar{P}}\right)^{-k} \bar{Y}U_i = H_1 \left(\frac{P_i}{\bar{P}}\right)^{-k} \frac{A_i}{\bar{P}}, \tag{9}$$

where

$$A_i = MU_i.$$

In order to produce output $Q_i$, the $i$th firm needs labour inputs. I assume

$$Q_i = L_i^{\phi}, \tag{10}$$

where $L_i$ is labour input, and $\phi$ satisfies $0 < \phi < \mu$. Thus, I allow increasing returns to scale, as long as this is dominated by an increasing marginal disutility of labour.

The $i$th firm's nominal profit $\bar{P}\Pi_i$ is given by

$$\bar{P}\Pi_i = P_i\, Q_i - \bar{P}_i\, \Lambda_i \tag{11}$$

where $\Lambda_i$ is the real-wage payment.

The $i$th firm maximizes the joint benefit of its stockholders and its workers. Because the representative household is the stockholder of the firm and at the same time its worker, the firm maximizes the representative household's utility (8) with respect to its price.

From (8) and the above relations, we have

$$\Psi \equiv \frac{B}{\bar{P}} - \Sigma_i L_i^{\mu} = \Lambda_i + \Pi_i - L_i^{\mu} + \Psi_{-i} = \frac{1}{\bar{P}} P_i Q_i - Q_i^{1+c_1} + \Psi_{-i},$$

where $c_1$ is a parameter depending on the degree of increasing marginal disutility of labour, $\mu$, and the degree of returns to scale, $\phi$, such that

$$c_1 = (\mu/\phi) - 1 > 0;$$

and where

$$\Psi_{-i} = \sum_{j \neq i} (\Lambda_j + \Pi_j) - \sum_{j \neq i} L_j^{\mu} + \frac{M}{\bar{P}} = \sum_{j \neq i} \left(\frac{1}{\bar{P}} P_j Q_j\right) - \sum_{j \neq i} Q_j^{1+c_1} + \frac{M}{\bar{P}}.$$

Consequently, from (9) we obtain

$$\Psi = \Upsilon\,(P_i,\ \bar{P},\ A_i) + \Psi_{-i}, \tag{12}$$

where

$$\Upsilon\,(P_i,\ \bar{P},\ A_i) \equiv H_1\left(\frac{P_i}{\bar{P}}\right)^{1-k} \frac{A_i}{\bar{P}} - \left[H_1\left(\frac{P_i}{\bar{P}}\right)^{-k} \frac{A_i}{\bar{P}}\right]^{1+c_1} \tag{13}$$

and

$$\Psi_{-i} = \sum_{j \neq i} \Upsilon\,(P_j,\ \bar{P},\ A_j) + \frac{M}{\bar{P}}. \tag{14}$$

*The monopolistically competitive assumption in the strong form and the firm's payoff function*

Throughout this chapter (and throughout this book), I make the following strong form of the monopolistically competitive assumption. I assume that the number of firms (and the number of goods), $n$, is so large that the dependence of the price index $\bar{P}(\{P_i\})$ on a particular $P_i$ is negligible. This implies that the firm ignores the dependence of $\bar{P}$ on its own price $P_i$ when determining its price. Thus, the firm takes $\bar{P}$ as given under this strong form of the monopolistically competitive assumption.

Under this monopolistically competitive assumption in the strong form, the firm's objective is reduced to maximizing $\Upsilon(P_i, \bar{P}, A_i)$, because $\Psi_{-i}$ in (12) does not depend on the $i$th firm's $P_i$ (see (14)).

*Imperfect information about demand and the incomplete-information game*

At the beginning of the first period, the firm gets information about $M$ and $U_i$. Let $\Omega_i$ be the information that the firm receives. Let us consider the case in which $\Omega_i = \{A_i\}$.[4] It should be noted here that the firm can observe $A_i = MU_i$, but $M$ and $U_i$ themselves are not independently observed.

The firm's strategy is its price, which depends on the information $\Omega_i$. The first stage can be described as the incomplete-information game in the sense used by Harsanyi (1967–8). Under the monopolistically competitive assumption in the strong form, where the dependence of $\bar{P}$ on $P_i$ is negligible, the Bayesian Nash equilibrium of the incomplete-information game[5] is defined as the set of policy functions $\{\phi_i(\Omega_i)\}_{i=1, \ldots, n}$ such that, for all $i = 1, \ldots, n$, $M \in [0, \infty)$, and $U_i \in [0, \infty)$,

$$E\left[\Upsilon\Big(\phi_i(\Omega_i), \bar{P}\{[\phi_s(\Omega_s)]\}, A_i\Big) \,\Big|\, \Omega_i\right] \geqq E\left[\Upsilon\Big(P_i, \bar{P}\{[\phi_s(\Omega_s)]\}, A_i\Big) \,\Big|\, \Omega_i\right]$$

is satisfied for all $P_i \in [0, \infty)$. Note that the price index $\bar{P}(\{P_s\}:_{s=1, \ldots, n})$ is defined in (3).

*Two simplifying assumptions and the price index*

To simplify the analysis, we make two additional assumptions. First, we consider the symmetric equilibrium; that is, assume that, if $\Omega_i = \Omega_j = \Omega$, then $\phi_i(\Omega) = \phi_j(\Omega) = \phi(\Omega)$. Second, we restrict our attention to the case of log-linear policy functions. Thus, we assume $\phi(\Omega_i) = \Phi A_i^{\rho}$ for some real numbers $\Phi$ and $\rho$.

The monopolistically competitive assumption in the strong form, together with the symmetric and log-linear policy assumptions, simplifies the expression of the price index. Let us define the following price index function:

$$\bar{P}^* (x_1, x_2, x_3, x_4) \equiv x_2 x_1^{x_3} \exp\left[-z(x_4)\,\sigma_u^2\right], \tag{15}$$

where

$$z(x_4) = \frac{[1 - (k-1)\, x_4]^2}{2\,(k-1)}\,. \tag{16}$$

Then, the price index is[6]

$$\bar{P}\ \{[\phi\ (A_s)]:\ _{s\ =1,\ \ldots\ldots,\ n}\} = \bar{P}^*\ (M, \Phi,\ \rho,\ \rho). \tag{17}$$

*The symmetric, log-linear-policy, monopolistically competitive Bayesian Nash Equilibrium*

Under the above assumptions, the symmetric Bayesian Nash equilibrium of the incomplete-information game is defined as a policy function $\phi(\Omega_i) = \phi(\{A_i\}) = \Phi A_i^\rho$, such that

$$E\left\{Y\left[\phi\ (A_i),\ \bar{P}^*(M,\ \Phi,\ \rho,\ \rho),\ A_i\right] \middle| \Omega_i\right\} =$$

$$\max_{P_i \in [0,\ \infty)}\ E\left\{Y\left[P_i,\ \bar{P}^*(M,\ \Phi,\ \rho,\ \rho),\ A_i\right] \middle| \Omega_i\right\} \tag{18}$$

is satisfied for all $M \in [0, \infty)$, and $U_i \in [0, \infty)$, where $\Omega_i = \{A_i\} = \{MU_i\}$.

The Bayesian Nash equilibrium of the incomplete-information game (18) completely characterizes the economy. Although computing the Bayesian Nash equilibrium is generally difficult, the game (18) has a log-linear log-normal framework which is simple enough to make the computation fairly easy. Appendix A at the end of this chapter shows that the Bayesian Nash equilibrium pair $(\Phi,\ \rho)$ is such that

$$\Phi = \Phi_\theta \equiv \left[\frac{(1+c_1)k}{k-1}\right]^{1/c_1} H_1 \exp\left[\frac{1}{c_1}\ \omega\rho_\theta^2\ \theta\sigma_u^2 - \frac{1+c_1(k-1)}{c_1}\ z(\rho_\theta)\sigma_u^2\right], \tag{19}$$

and

$$\rho = \rho_\theta \equiv \frac{c_1}{1+c_1k - [1+c_1\ (k-1)]\theta}, \tag{20}$$

where

$$\theta = \frac{\sigma_m^2}{\sigma_m^2 + \sigma_u^2} \quad \text{and}\ \omega = \frac{1}{2}\left[(1+c_1)^2\ (k-1)^2 - (k-2)^2\right]. \tag{21}$$

## 2.3. *The Equivalent Reduced-Form Rational Expectations Model*

One may object to the assumption underlying the Bayesian Nash equilibrium, that is, the assumption of perfect knowledge about the economy except for the short-run disturbances $M$ and $U_i$. There is, however, an alternative assumption often made in macroeconomics which requires less information on the part of firms but produces the same equilibrium. We gain additional insight into the Bayesian Nash equilibrium by considering this alternative model.

In the alternative assumption, firms have perfect knowledge about the reduced-form model of the economy, and form subjective expectations about unknown disturbances. Instead of knowing the true mathematical expectation conditional on available information, as in the Bayesian Nash equilibrium described above, firms in this alternative model are assumed to form subjective expectations based on their own information. However, these expectations are constructed so as to be rational, in the sense that they coincide with the true mathematical expectation conditional on available information. As will be clear later in this section, the resulting equilibrium is identical to the Bayesian Nash equilibrium of the incomplete-information game described above. This alternative model can be called the reduced-form rational expectations model, because it depends on perfect knowledge about the reduced-form model of the economy and on the assumption of rational expectations.

The reason for considering this equivalent rational expectations model is that it is easier to analyse and interpret the properties of the equilibrium in this framework than in the original incomplete-information-game framework. The procedure for obtaining rational expectations equilibrium just described is frequently used in the macroeconomic literature, and we can thus compare the results obtained in our monopolistically competitive economy with those of other macroeconomic models that incorporate rational expectations. I use this framework in this and the following two sections to investigate the properties of the Bayesian Nash equilibrium and to compare it with other macroeconomic models of nominal price rigidity.

In the remainder of this section, I first reformulate (18) in a linear framework by taking the log of all variables and by using the log of the geometric average price instead of the log of the price index (17). The latter procedure facilitates the following equilibrium analysis, because the log of the geometric average price is simply the average of the log of the individual prices. I then examine the monopolistically competitive model by using firm's subjective expectations about the log of the geometric average price, instead of the mathematical expectation conditional on the information $\Omega_i$, as in (18). These subjective expectations are chosen so as to be rational in the sense that they are equal to the true mathematical expectation conditional on information $\Omega_i$. Thus, the resulting equilibrium is the same as the Bayesian Nash equilibrium in (18). Finally, I give an intuitive explanation of the equilibrium pricing rule in this model and compare inperfect-information equilibrium with its perfect-information counterpart.

In the following, the lower-case letter variable is the log of the upper-case letter variable, if not otherwise stated; that is, $z = \log Z$. I also suppress the subscript $i$ in $\Omega_i$ and let $p_u$ and $q_u$ be the price and the quantity of the products of the firm whose $U_i$ is equal to $U$. Because we are concerned with a symmetric equilibrium, these notations should not be confusing.

*The log-linear representation of the Bayesian Nash Equilibrium*

Under our assumptions, the log of the price index, $\bar{p}$, and the log of the geometric average price, $\bar{p}_u$, satisfy the following relations:[7]

$$\bar{p} = \bar{p}_u - z(\rho)\sigma_u^2, \tag{22}$$

where

$$\bar{p}_u = \int_u p_u f(u)\,du \tag{23}$$

and

$$p_u - \bar{p}_u = \rho u. \tag{24}$$

Here $f(u)$ is the density function of $u = \log U$, whose distribution is normal with mean zero and variance $\sigma_u^2$. Consequently, the demand for a particular firm's products is, from (9),

$$q_u = -k(p_u - \bar{p}_u) + x - \bar{p}_u, \tag{25}$$

where $x$ is the individual nominal-demand condition of this firm, consisting of the monetary disturbance $m$ and the idiosyncratic disturbance $u$:

$$x = r + m + u, \tag{26}$$

where

$$r = r(\rho) \equiv h_1 + (1 - k)z(\rho)\sigma_u^2. \tag{27}$$

From (13), the firm's payoff function can now be rewritten as

$$\Upsilon = \exp(v)\ \exp(p_u - \bar{p}_u)\exp(q_u) - \exp[(1+c_1)q_u], \tag{28}$$

where

$$v = v(\rho) \equiv z(\rho)\sigma_u^2. \tag{29}$$

Thus, taking into account that $\log A = x - r$, the Bayesian Nash equilibrium of this economy is a pair $(\Phi, \rho)$ such that $\bar{p}_u = \int_u p_u f(u)du$, and such that $p_u = \log\Phi + \rho(x - r)$ maximizes the expected payoff,

$$E\{\exp(v)\exp(p_u - \bar{p}_u)\exp(q_u) - \exp[(1 + c_1)q_u] \mid \Omega\},$$

conditional on information $\Omega = \{x - r\}$ and subject to (25).

*The reduced-form rational expectations model*

Instead of assuming that the firm knows the true mathematical expectations of its payoff, conditional on $\Omega$, suppose that the firm forms subjective expectations about the average price $\bar{p}_u$ relying on available information. This information includes the reduced-form model of the economy. The firm knows the functional forms and parameters of the demand functions. In addition, it is known that all firms are identical except for the firm-specific disturbances $u$. Firms form their expectations about the average price using available information, namely, the demand information $A_i$.

The Bayesian expectation formation of these firms differs from that of one independent decision-maker, because it necessarily involves acquiring information about endogenous variables. Because the model is monopolistically competitive, the demand at one firm is dependent on the average price, which is contingent on the prices of other firms. The average price is determined by the interplay of these ignorant firms' price decisions. In general, this leads to the well-known infinite regress problem,[8] even if all firms know all the structural parameters of the reduced-form model.

In order to avoid this infinite regress problem, we make the rational expectations assumption. Specifically, the firm assumes that $\bar{p}_u$ is normally distributed with mean $e(\bar{p}_u|\Omega)$ and variance $V(\bar{p}_u|\Omega)$, where $e(\bar{p}_u|\Omega)$ is the linear least-squares regression of $\bar{p}_u$ on $\Omega$ including $x$, and $V(\bar{p}_u|\Omega)$ is its error variance. It can be shown that these expectations in fact turn out to be rational, in the sense that they coincide with the true mathematical expectation and variance of the distribution of $\bar{p}_u$ conditional on $\Omega$.

The firm's problem in this subjective-expectation framework is, from (23), (25), (26), and (28), to maximize

$$\hat{E}Y=\hat{E}\left(\exp[v+(1-k)(p_u-\bar{p}_u)+x-\bar{p}_u]-\exp\{(1+c_1)[-k(p_u-\bar{p}_u)+x-\bar{p}_u]\}\right),$$

with respect to $p_u$, where $\hat{E}$ is the expectation operator with respect to the firm's subjective distribution of $\bar{p}_u$. It can be shown that the optimal price formula is[9]

$$p_u=\frac{1}{1+c_1k}\,b+\frac{c_1}{1+c_1k}\,x+\left(1-\frac{c_1}{1+c_1k}\right)e\,(\bar{p}_u|\Omega), \tag{30}$$

where $b$ is a constant term determined by $\rho$ and $V(\bar{p}_u|\Omega)$, such that

$$b=b[\rho,V(\bar{p}_u|\Omega)]\equiv-v(\rho)+\log\,(1+c_1)+\log\left(\frac{k}{k-1}\right)+\omega V(\bar{p}_u|\Omega), \tag{31}$$

where $\omega$ is defined as in (21). The optimal price formula (30) shows that the individual price is the weighted average of the individual nominal demand condition $x$ and the expected average price $e(\bar{p}_u\mid\Omega)$.

From (30) we can get the rational expectations equilibrium by using the undetermined coefficient method.[10] The equilibrium individual price $p_u$ and the equilibrium average price $\bar{p}_u$ are given by

$$p_u=\log\Phi_\theta+\rho_\theta(x-r),\qquad\text{and}\qquad\bar{p}_u=\log\Phi_\theta+\rho_\theta m, \tag{32}$$

where

$$\log\,\Phi_\theta=\frac{1}{c_1}b\left(\rho_\theta,\rho_\theta^2\theta\sigma_u^2\right)+r(\rho_\theta)$$

and $\rho_\theta$ is defined in (20). Thus, we arrive at an equilibrium that is the same as the Bayesian Nash equilibrium of the incomplete-information game.

*Characteristics of the individual optimal price formula*

This individual optimal price formula (30) has an intuitive meaning. Let $d = x - \bar{p}_u$ be the individual real demand condition, and let its unconditional mean be $\bar{\bar{d}} = \int_m \int_u d\, g(m)\, f(u)\, dm du$, where $g(m)$ and $f(u)$ are the density functions of $m$ and $u$, respectively. From (26) and (32), we get

$$\bar{\bar{d}} = \bar{\bar{d}}_\theta \equiv -[b(\rho_\theta, \rho_\theta^2 \theta \sigma_u^2)/c_1]. \tag{33}$$

Using this relation, and taking $e(d|\Omega) = x - e(\bar{p}_u|\Omega)$ into account, we can transform the optimal price formula (30) into

$$p_u - e(\bar{p}_u|\Omega) = \frac{c_1}{1+c_1 k}\left[e(d|\Omega) - \bar{\bar{d}}\right]. \tag{34}$$

Note that $d$ is the firm's current real demand condition, and that $\bar{\bar{d}}$ can be considered its 'normal' average real demand condition. Thus, $d - \bar{\bar{d}}$ represents the relative strength of demand, and $e(d \mid \Omega) - \bar{\bar{d}}$ is its (subjective) expected value. Because $p_u - e(\bar{p}_u \mid \Omega)$ is the (subjective) expected relative price, the individual optimal price formula (34) indicates that, when (subjective) expected demand is strong relative to normal demand, a firm will increase its price in order to increase its (subjective) expected relative price.

The responsiveness of the individual price to the expected relative strength of demand depends on $c_1$ and $k$.

First, let us show that competition reduces individual price responsiveness. On the one hand, suppose that $k$, the degree of competition, increases. Because markets become more competitive, the firm cannot increase its relative price without inducing depletion of its customers. The firm shuns price increases, so competition decreases individual price responsiveness.

On the other hand, an increasing degree of increasing marginal cost (which is the composite of the degree of increasing marginal disutility of labour and that of decreasing returns to scale) raises individual price responsiveness. If $c_1$ (which is the degree of increasing marginal cost) increases, then the individual price becomes more responsive to the expected relative strength of demand.

*The imperfect-information equilibrium and the perfect-information equilibrium*

Next, consider the equilibrium average price in (32). It is worthwhile to compare it with its perfect-information counterpart as a frame of reference. If all firms know all relevant information, then there is no uncertainty about $\bar{p}_u$. Thus, $e(\bar{p}_u \mid \Omega) = \bar{p}_u$, and $V(\bar{p}_u \mid \Omega) = 0$. We substitute them into the individual optimal price formula (30), average over all firms, and rearrange the terms to obtain[11]

$$p_u = \log \Phi^* + m + \rho^* u, \qquad \text{and} \qquad \bar{p}_u = \log \Phi^* + m, \qquad (35)$$

where

$$\log \Phi^* = \frac{1}{c_1} b(\rho^*, 0) + r(\rho^*)$$

and

$$\rho^* = \frac{c_1}{1 + c_1 k}.$$

Comparing (32) and (35), we arrive at two 'short-run' characteristics of equilibrium prices in the imperfect-information monopolistically competitive models, which are closely related to those of the imperfect-information perfectly competitive models of Lucas (1972, 1973) and others. First, because $\rho_\theta < 1$, the average price $\bar{p}_u$ is insensitive to the money supply disturbance $m$. Thus, money is not neutral. Second, the relative price $p_u - \bar{p}_u$ is too sensitive to the idiosyncratic disturbance $u$, because $\rho_\theta > \rho^*$. Consequently, relative prices are volatile.

In this economy, the firm has to infer macroeconomic variables (the average price) from individual demand conditions. Because individual conditions consist of both macroeconomic and microeconomic variables, and because the firm cannot observe two variables independently, there exists the possibility of local–global confusion. Because an increase in the individual condition may stem solely from an increase in the microeconomic, firm-specific variable, the firm does not increase its expectation about the macroeconomic variable as much as the observed increase in the individual condition. Thus, the firm's expectation is insensitive to the macroeconomic variable, and excessively sensitive to the microeconomic variable. Because the firm's price depends on its expectation, it is also insensitive to macroeconomic shocks and excessively sensitive to microeconomic shocks. This argument is similar to that of the imperfect-information perfectly competitive models, in which confusion about local and global market conditions makes expectations about global macroeconomic variables, and ultimately the average price, rigid with respect to macroeconomic shocks.

The similarity between the monopolistically competitive model and the perfectly competitive model, however, ends here. The monopolistically competitive economy's price responsiveness to changes in supply elasticity and competitiveness is different from that of the imperfect-information perfectly competitive economy. This will be examined in Section 4.

## 3. PREDETERMINED PRICES AS AN EQUILIBRIUM STRATEGY

In the previous section, I presented a model of the monopolistically competitive economy with predetermined prices. In this section I examine the robustness of predetermined prices, explicitly considering the possibility of waiting until uncertainty is resolved. I also compare the predetermined price argument with a simple (and single-minded) version of the menu-cost argument[12] in order to clarify the properties of the predetermined-price argument as a theory of nominal price rigidity.[13]

### 3.1. *Predetermined-Price (Imperfect-Information) Strategy versus Perfect-Information Strategy*

In order to introduce the possibility of being perfectly informed before price decisions are made, let us further specify the stylized process of information transmission in Section 2. In this revised process, events occur in the following sequence, as illustrated in Fig. 2.1. In the first stage, firms choose between the predetermined-price (imperfect-information) strategy and the perfect-information strategy.[14] In the second stage, the monetary disturbance $m$ and the idiosyncratic product-demand disturbance $u$ are realized. In the third stage, although information about $m$ and $u$ is not available, firms are allowed to conduct market research about consumers. At this stage, consumers know their nominal demand for each product (or, more accurately, the level of the individual nominal demand condition, if the firm's price is equal to the average price), which is equal to $x = r + m + u$. They do not know, however, the individual real demand condition, because the average price $\bar{p}_u$ is not determined. (Price offers have not yet been made.) Thus, firms have perfect information only about the nominal individual demand condition $x$.

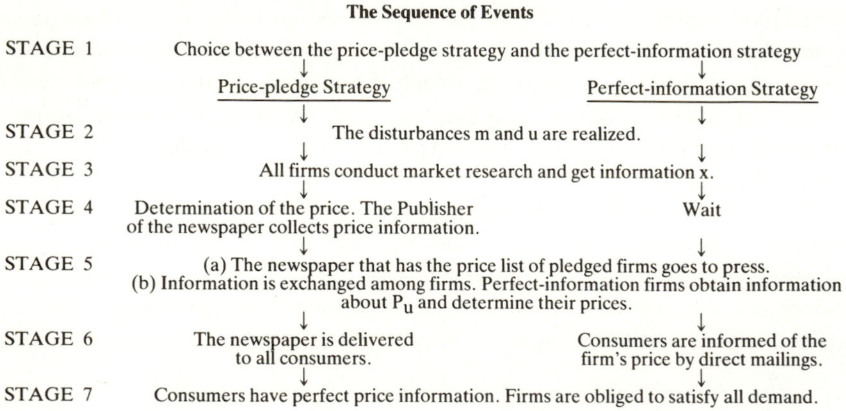
The Sequence of Events
STAGE 1
Choice between the price-pledge strategy and the perfect-information strategy
Price-pledge Strategy
Perfect-information Strategy
STAGE 2
The disturbances m and u are realized.
STAGE 3
All firms conduct market research and get information x.
STAGE 4
Determination of the price. The Publisher of the newspaper collects price information.
Wait
STAGE 5
(a) The newspaper that has the price list of pledged firms goes to press.
(b) Information is exchanged among firms. Perfect-information firms obtain information about Pu and determine their prices.
STAGE 6
The newspaper is delivered to all consumers.
Consumers are informed of the firm's price by direct mailings.
STAGE 7
Consumers have perfect price information. Firms are obliged to satisfy all demand.

FIG. 2.1. An information transmission process

In the fourth stage, firms that have chosen the predetermined-price strategy pledge their prices through a newspaper which all consumers read. For simplicity, we assume that this newspaper publishes their prices at no charge.[15] The newspaper is printed in the fifth stage and distributed among consumers at the end of the sixth stage. Thus, all consumers are perfectly informed of the pledged firms' prices at the end of the sixth stage.

Although price information about the predetermined-price firms reaches all consumers at no cost, these firms have to determine their prices in the fourth stage without knowing the average price $\bar{p}_u$.[16] They form rational expectations about $\bar{p}_u$ using available information and determine their prices based on these expectations. On the other hand, firms that have chosen the perfect-information strategy wait until the fifth stage, in which firms exchange information about their prices. Suppose that a trade association collects all price information and informs all firms of the average price $\bar{p}_u$.[17] Firms using the perfect-information strategy then determine their prices based on this information.

In the sixth stage, the perfect-information firms advertise their prices. However, these firms must reach consumers by using a costly advertising method, such as direct mailings, because the newspaper has already gone to press in the fifth stage. It is assumed that the perfect-information firms must pay a positive fixed extra advertising cost $F$.[18] By incurring $F$, the perfect-information firms can inform all consumers of their prices at the end of the sixth stage.

In the final stage, consumers actually visit firms and buy products. At this stage, consumers have perfect knowledge about price offers in the economy, received through the newspaper and direct mailings.

### 3.2. *The Minimum Extra Advertising Cost Supporting the Predetermined-Price (Imperfect-Information) Equilibrium*

Let us consider the choice of a given firm between the predetermined-price strategy and the perfect-information strategy in the first stage, when all other firms adopt the predetermined-price strategy. The choice is based on the unconditional expected value of the objective function Y: $R = \int_m \int_u Y g(m) f(u) dm du$, where

$$Y = \exp[v + (1-k)(p_u - \bar{p}_u) + x - \bar{p}_u] - \exp\{(1+c_1)[-k(p_u - \bar{p}_u) + x - \bar{p}_u]\}.$$

Because all other firms adopt the predetermined-price strategy, the average price $\bar{p}_u$ is determined in (32).

On the one hand, under the predetermined-price strategy, the $p_u$ equation in (32) determines the firm's optimal price. Thus, the relative price is $p_u - \bar{p}_u = \rho_\theta u$. Similarly, we have

$$x - \bar{p}_u = r_\theta + m + u - [(b_\theta/c_1) + r_\theta + \rho_\theta m] = \bar{\bar{d}}_\theta + (1 - \rho_\theta) m + u,$$

where $\bar{\bar{d}}_\theta = -b_\theta/c_1$, $b_\theta = b(\rho_\theta, \rho_\theta^2\theta\sigma_u^2)$, and $r_\theta = r(\rho_\theta)$, because of (26), (32), and (33). Thus, the expected value of the objective function under the predetermined-price strategy, $R^I$, is[19]

$$R^I = \exp\left\{\bar{\bar{d}}_\theta + v_\theta + \frac{1}{2}\,[(1-k)\,\rho_\theta + 1]^2\sigma_u^2 + \frac{1}{2}\,(1-\rho_\theta)^2\,\sigma_m^2\right\}$$

$$-\exp\left\{(1+c_1)\,\bar{\bar{d}}_\theta + \frac{1}{2}\,(1+c_1)^2\left[(-k\rho_\theta+1)^2\,\sigma_u^2 + (1-\rho_\theta)^2\,\sigma_m^2\right]\right\}, \qquad (36)$$

where $v_\theta = v(\rho_\theta)$.

On the other hand, if the firm adopts the perfect-information strategy, it can observe $\bar{p}_u$ in the sixth stage. We have $e(\bar{p}_u \mid \Omega) = \bar{p}_u$ and $V(\bar{p}_u \mid \Omega) = 0$. Because the other firms have adopted the predetermined-price strategy, the equilibrium average price, $\bar{p}_u$, still satisfies (32). Thus, the optimal perfect-information strategy price denoted by $p_u'$ is, from (30),

$$p_u' = \frac{1}{1+c_1k}\,b_\theta' + \frac{c_1}{1+c_1k}\,x + \left(1 - \frac{c_1}{1+c_1k}\right)\bar{p}_u. \qquad (37)$$

where

$$b_\theta' = -\,v(\rho_\theta) + \log(1+c_1) + \log\left(\frac{k}{k-1}\right).$$

Consequently, because $\bar{p}_u = (b_\theta/c_1) + r_\theta + \rho_\theta m$, the relative price under the perfect-information strategy is

$$p_u' - \bar{p}_u = \frac{1}{1+c_1k}\,(b_\theta' - b_\theta) + \frac{c_1}{1+c_1k}\,u + \frac{c_1}{1+c_1k}\,(1-\rho_\theta)m. \qquad (38)$$

Consequently, by substituting (38) into Υ, rearranging the terms, and integrating with respect to $u$ and $m$, we obtain the unconditional mean of the objective function of the firm under the perfect-information strategy, $R^P$, such that

$$R^P = \exp\left\{\bar{\bar{d}}_\theta + \frac{1-k}{1+c_1k}\,(b_\theta' - b_\theta) + v_\theta + \frac{1}{2}\left(\frac{1+c_1}{1+c_1k}\right)^2[\,\sigma_u^2 + (1-\rho_\theta)^2\sigma_m^2]\right\}$$

$$-\exp\left\{(1+c_1)\,\bar{\bar{d}}_\theta - \frac{(1+c_1)k}{1+c_1k}\,(b_\theta' - b_\theta)\right.$$

$$\left. + \frac{1}{2}\left(\frac{1+c_1}{1+c_1k}\right)^2 [\sigma_u^2 + (1-\rho_\theta)^2\sigma_m^2]\right\} - F. \qquad (39)$$

where $F$ is the extra advertising cost.

Let $F^*$ be such that $R^I = R^P$. $F^*$ is equal to benefit of perfect information. Although there is no simple representation of $F^*$, the benefit of perfect information can be decomposed into two parts.

First, since disturbances are multiplicative, the effect of forecast errors is large when demand is large. Consequently, the optimal price under imperfect information is set at a higher level than that under perfect information, in order to reduce demand and the cost of forecast errors. If, however, there is no forecast error, the firm can reduce its price ($b'_\theta - b_\theta < 0$) in (38) inducing more demand, and thus it can increase the value of its objective function.

Second, imperfect information makes the firm's price insensitive to the general demand condition, $m$, and excessively sensitive to the idiosyncratic disturbance, $u$. Both reduce the firm's real payoff.[20] By eliminating both, the perfect-information strategy raises production efficiency and increases the value of its objective function.

These benefits of the perfect-information strategy, however, should be compared with the associated extra advertising cost $F$. If $F$ is larger than $F^*$, we have $R^I > R^P$, so that the firm chooses the predetermined-price strategy. Thus, $F^*$ is the minimum extra advertising cost that supports a predetermined-price (imperfect-information) equilibrium.

The plausibility of a predetermined-price (imperfect-information) equilibrium is thus dependent on the magnitude of $F^*$. $F^*$ is a complicated function of $c_1$, $k$, $\sigma_u$, and $\sigma_m$. It is straightforward to show that, if at least one of $\sigma_u$ and $\sigma_m$ approaches zero, then $F^*$ becomes negligible.[21] This is because in both cases imperfect information about $\bar{p}_u$ does not matter. If $\sigma_u$ is close to zero, then the firm can correctly infer $m$, and ultimately, $\bar{p}_u$, from information $x$. If $\sigma_m$ is close to zero, $\bar{p}_u$ does not fluctuate, so there is little uncertainty about $\bar{p}_u$. Because the firm can gain little in both cases, a very small $F$ is sufficient to prevent the firm from using the perfect-information strategy.

Next consider the effects of $c_1$ and $k$ on $F^*$. In general, $F^*$ is small when $c_1$ is small but becomes larger as $k$ increases.[22] If $c_1$ is small (that is, if supply is elastic), then the individual optimal price is insensitive to demand conditions (the weight on $x$ in (30) is small); consequently, the average price is also insensitive to the demand change $m$. Thus, uncertainty about $\bar{p}_u$ decreases, implying a smaller forecast error. The incentive for the firm to obtain accurate information about $\bar{p}_u$ also decreases. A small $F$ becomes sufficient to prevent a firm from adopting the perfect-information strategy.

By contrast, if $k$ increases (that is, if competition among firms increases), a forecast error implies a larger unexpected change in demand. As long as marginal costs increase with output, this implies a larger reduction in the expected real payoff. Consequently, the incentive to obtain accurate information about $\bar{p}_u$ increases, and thus $F^*$ increases.

Table 2.1 illustrates the effects of $c_1$ and $k$ on the magnitude of $F^*$. In this table, $F^*$ is shown as the percentage of the expected real payoff of the firm adopting the perfect-information strategy. We consider three cases as illustrative examples. In case A we have $\sigma_m = 0.02$. This is the case in

TABLE 2.1. The Minimum Extra Advertising Cost that Supports a Predetermined-Price Equilibrium

Case A ($\sigma_m = 0.02$)

| $k$ | $c_1$ (%) | | | |
|---|---|---|---|---|
| | 0.24 | 3 | 6.7 | 30 |
| 2.67 | 0.002 | 0.019 | 0.038 | 0.157 |
| 6.7 | 0.008 | 0.053 | 0.106 | 0.439 |
| 15 | 0.016 | 0.076 | 0.149 | 0.605 |

Case B ($\sigma_m = 0.05$)

| $k$ | $c_1$ (%) | | | |
|---|---|---|---|---|
| | 0.24 | 3 | 6.7 | 30 |
| 2.67 | 0.013 | 0.117 | 0.237 | 0.978 |
| 6.7 | 0.049 | 0.331 | 0.663 | 2.713 |
| 15 | 0.097 | 0.471 | 0.925 | 3.724 |

Case C ($\sigma_m = 0.2$)

| $k$ | $c_1$ (%) | | | |
|---|---|---|---|---|
| | 0.24 | 3 | 6.7 | 30 |
| 2.67 | 0.200 | 1.857 | 3.723 | 14.554 |
| 6.7 | 0.787 | 5.160 | 10.092 | 35.598 |
| 15 | 1.539 | 7.278 | 13.818 | 45.510 |

*Note*: The minimum extra advertising cost is measured as a percentage of the expected real payoff of the firm adopting the perfect-information strategy.

*Source*: This table is based on equations (36) and (39) in the text.

which most of the change in the money supply is less than 2 per cent. Similarly, we have $\sigma_m = 0.05$ in case B, and $\sigma_m = 0.2$ in case C. In all cases, we arbitrarily set $\sigma_u = 2\sigma_m$.[23] It is evident from this table that $F^*$ is almost negligible if $c_1$ and $k$ are small. Moreover, except for the case in which $\sigma_m$, $k$, and $c_1$ are all very large, $F^*$ remains relatively small. For example, in case B, where $\sigma_m = 0.05$, we still have the moderate result of 3.7 per cent, even if $c_1 = 30$ and $k = 15$.

The case where $c_1 = 6.7$ and $k$=2.67 is of some interest. Empirical studies of labour supply which assume wage-taking workers often find inelastic labour supply. If their result is reinterpreted in the bilateral-monopoly labour-market relationship, their estimate implies that $c_1 = 6.7$ if the production function exhibits constant returns. Hall (1986) investigates the mark-up in many industries; his estimate of the mark-up in durables and non-durables in manufacturing implies that $k=2.67$. If their estimates regarding manufacturing can be generalized on to the whole economy, then, as shown by our table, $F^*$ is still small even if the change in nominal demand is substantial (see case C).

## 3.3. *The Predetermined-Price Approach and the Menu-Cost Approach*

Let us compare our predetermined-price approach with the menu-cost approach, which has attracted much attention in recent years. The menu-cost approach assumes imperfectly competitive firms which have perfect knowledge of the economy when they decide whether to adjust their prices to changes in economic conditions. There is, however, a small fixed (physical) cost of changing nominal prices. Suppose that the money supply increases. If the change is small, the gain from adjusting the prices is very small (by the envelope theorem), and thus a small cost of changing nominal prices is sufficient to prevent a firm from adjusting its price. It is sometimes further suggested that the gain from the adjustment is small even if the change in the money supply is not small, and that a small menu cost is capable of generating the observed magnitude of monetary non-neutrality.

There are two important differences between the predetermined-price approach and the menu-cost approach, if we take a literal and simple-minded view of the above menu-cost argument.

First, in our framework, where the firm has noisy information about uncertain demand conditions, the menu-cost approach (in the simple-minded form just described) implies that the firm does not adjust its price to such information before the demand uncertainty is resolved (*ex ante* price rigidity): rather, it chooses between adjustment and no adjustment after it has perfect demand information (*ex post* price flexibility).[24] By contrast, in the predetermined-price approach, the firm adjusts its price to noisy demand information (*ex ante* price flexibility), but does not adjust its price after the demand uncertainty is resolved (*ex post* price rigidity). Thus, in the menu-cost approach prices either fully reflect changes in demand or do not respond to them at all (adjustment or no adjustment), while in the predetermined-price approach prices only partially reflect changes in demand (partial adjustment).

Because of *ex ante* price rigidity in the menu-cost approach, the minimum menu cost that prevents the firm from adjusting its price is much larger than the minimum extra advertising cost in the predetermined-price approach, which allows *ex ante* price flexibility. Table 2.2 shows the minimum menu cost preventing the firm from adjusting its price.[25] The model is the same as in the foregoing analysis, except that we assume $u=0$. Since there is no firm-specific shock, this is the most favourable case

TABLE 2.2. The Minimum Menu Cost that Supports a No-Adjustment Equilibrium When there is No Firm-Specific Shock.

Case A ($\Delta = 0.02$)

| $k$ | $c_1$ (%) | | | |
|---|---|---|---|---|
| | 0.24 | 3 | 6.7 | 30 |
| 2.67 | 0.002 | 0.041 | 0.091 | 0.471 |
| 6.7 | 0.008 | 0.064 | 0.133 | 0.652 |
| 15 | 0.014 | 0.074 | 0.149 | 0.720 |

Case B ($\Delta = 0.05$)

| $k$ | $c_1$ (%) | | | |
|---|---|---|---|---|
| | 0.24 | 3 | 6.7 | 30 |
| 2.67 | 0.015 | 0.265 | 0.618 | 4.257 |
| 6.7 | 0.051 | 0.417 | 0.904 | 5.926 |
| 15 | 0.091 | 0.484 | 1.019 | 6.557 |

Case C ($\Delta = 0.2$)

| $k$ | $c_1$ (%) | | | |
|---|---|---|---|---|
| | 0.24 | 3 | 6.7 | 30 |
| 2.67 | 0.248 | 5.267 | 15.481 | 100.000 |
| 6.7 | 0.874 | 8.521 | 23.247 | 100.000 |
| 15 | 1.589 | 9.999 | 26.476 | 100.000 |

*Note*: The minimum menu cost is measured as a percentage of the expected real payoff of the firm adjusting its price.

*Source*: This table is based on equations in Appendix B.

for the menu-cost model. Initially all prices are optimal; then, the money supply is changed from $m$ to $m' = m + \Delta$. Table 2.2 shows the minimum menu cost in the cases of $\Delta = 0.02$, 0.05, and 0.2, which correspond to the cases in Table 2.1. As in Table 2.1, the minimum menu cost is measured as a percentage of the real payoff of the adjusting firm.

The magnitude of the minimum menu cost is much greater than that of the corresponding minimum extra advertising cost. For example, in case C, with $c_1 = 6.7$ and $k = 2.67$, the minimum menu cost is 15.5 per cent of the real payoff, while the minimum advertising cost is 3.7 per cent. If the supply is very inelastic ($c_1 = 30$) in this case, the minimum advertising cost is 14.6 per cent, while the minimum menu cost is 100 per cent, because in this case exit from the market is better than the no-adjustment strategy! In addition, the actual advertising cost is not likely to be small, whereas the menu cost must be quite small.

The second difference between the menu-cost approach and our predetermined-price approach is the existence of local shocks. Note that in the menu-cost framework the cost of no adjustment is the same for a given magnitude of demand shock, regardless of whether the shock is global or local. Suppose that the change in the money supply is very small, but there is a large local demand shock. Under these circumstances, it is evident that the firm facing menu costs will adjust its prices. By contrast, the analysis of the minimum extra-advertising cost $F^*$, which supports the predetermined-price equilibrium, shows that if $\sigma_m^2$ is very small $F^*$ is very small, even if $\sigma_u^2$ is large. We are thus likely to arrive at a predetermined-price equilibrium. As long as $\sigma_m^2$ is small, the average price does not change very much and becomes rather predictable, implying small gains from the perfect-information strategy. Consequently, the firm is likely to find the predetermined-price strategy attractive. This implies that the minimum menu cost that supports a no-adjustment equilibrium is substantially higher than Table 2.2 suggests, if there are sizable firm-specific demand shocks. By contrast, the minimum extra advertising cost that supports a predetermined-price equilibrium is still small in this case.

The foregoing discussion suggests two things. First, if the menu cost and the advertising cost are of the same magnitude, the relative strength of the two approaches as models of nominal price rigidity depends on the information available to the firm when determining its price. If the firm has some, albeit noisy, information about changes in demand, as in the model presented in this chapter, then the predetermined-price model is more plausible than the menu-cost model, because it allows *ex ante* price flexibility. However, if changes in demand are all unexpected, then the menu-cost model is likely to provide a more reasonable explanation of nominal price rigidity than the predetermined-price model. Second, if there are sizeable local demand shocks, as suggested by Okun (1981), the menu-cost argument of price rigidity collapses, while the predetermined-price argument still holds true.

### 3.4. *The Possibility of Multiple Equilibria*

We obtain small $F^*$ in Table 2.1 because of the strategic interdependence and induced externality that characterize an imperfectly competitive economy.[26] If all other firms take the imperfect-information (predetermined-price) strategy, then the average price becomes rigid with respect to $m$. This implies a small forecast error and reduces the attractiveness of the perfect-information strategy. Thus, a small $F$ is sufficient to induce a given firm to adopt the predetermined-price strategy, as long as $c_1$ and $k$ are not large.

The importance of the externality can be illustrated by the following thought experiment. Suppose that all other firms use the perfect-information strategy. The average price is then sensitive to $m$ (see (32) and (35)). This implies an increase in uncertainty about the average price, and thus increases the incentive to obtain accurate information about the average price. Thus, a large $F$ will be needed to prevent the firm from choosing the perfect-information strategy. In Table 2.3 we calculate the minimum extra advertising cost $F^{**}$ that prevents the firm from using the perfect-information strategy, *if all other firms are using it.*[27] Thus, $F^{**}$ is the minimum extra advertising cost that blocks the perfect-information equilibrium. This table shows that $F^{**}$ is larger than $F^{*}$ and increases rapidly as $c_1$ and $k$ increase.

An interesting finding shown in Tables 2.1 and 2.3 is that there is a range of $F$ in which both predetermined-price and perfect-information equilibria

TABLE 2.3. The Minimum Extra Advertising Cost that Blocks a Perfect-Information Equilibrium

Case A ($\sigma_m = 0.02$)

| $k$ | $c_1$ (%) | | | |
|---|---|---|---|---|
| | 0.24 | 3 | 6.7 | 30 |
| 2.67 | 0.064 | 0.127 | 0.228 | 0.459 |
| 6.7 | 0.623 | 1.782 | 3.373 | 6.854 |
| 15 | 3.674 | 11.081 | 20.204 | 37.413 |

Case B ($\sigma_m = 0.05$)

| $k$ | $c_1$ (%) | | | |
|---|---|---|---|---|
| | 0.24 | 3 | 6.7 | 30 |
| 2.67 | 0.402 | 0.790 | 1.420 | 2.832 |
| 6.7 | 3.829 | 10.632 | 19.303 | 35.839 |
| 15 | 20.859 | 52.002 | 75.600 | 94.654 |

Case C ($\tau_m = 0.2$)

| $k$ | $c_1$ (%) | | | |
|---|---|---|---|---|
| | 0.24 | 3 | 6.7 | 30 |
| 2.67 | 6.244 | 11.924 | 20.447 | 36.852 |
| 6.7 | 46.455 | 83.446 | 96.766 | 99.918 |
| 15 | 97.632 | 99.999 | 100.000 | 100.000 |

*Note*: The minimum extra advertising cost is measured as a percentage of the expected real payoff of the firm adopting the perfect-information strategy.
*Source*: This table is based on equations in Appendix C.

exist. This is the case if $F$ is in the range $(F^*, F^{**})$. This multiplicity of equilibria is often found in imperfectly competitive economies.[28]

## 4. INELASTIC SUPPLY, COMPETITION, AND NOMINAL PRICE RIGIDITY

In the previous section, it was shown that the predetermined-price (imperfect-information) equilibrium exists for a wide range of parameters. Thus, the imperfect-information monopolistically competitive equilibrium of Section 2 is robust with respect to parameter changes. In this section, I investigate the characteristics of the imperfect-information monopolistically competitive equilibrium in (18). I first compare the imperfect-information monopolistically competitive economy with the imperfect-information perfectly competitive economy studied by Lucas (1972; 1973) and others. I then take up the effect of increased competition on nominal price rigidity.

Let us first compare the imperfect-information equilibrium (32) with the perfect-information equilibrium (35). Both equilibria can be depicted graphically in 'the reaction curve' framework of Fi. 2.2 and 2.3. These figures are drawn for the case of $m = 1$. I use the following notations in these figures:

$\bar{e}(\bar{p}_u \mid \Omega) \equiv \int_u e(\bar{p}_u|\Omega)f(u)du$ (the average expectation about $\bar{p}_u$)

$\Delta\bar{p}_u \equiv \bar{p}_u - \bar{\bar{p}}_u$ (the response of $\bar{p}_u$ to $m$)

$\Delta\bar{e}(\bar{p}_u \mid \Omega) = \bar{e}(\bar{p}_u \mid \Omega) - \bar{\bar{p}}_u$ (the response of the average expectation).

where $\bar{\bar{p}}_u$ is the unconditional mean of $\bar{p}_u$ such that $\bar{\bar{p}}_u = \int_m \bar{p}_u g(m)dm$. Using these definitions, we can transform the optimal price formula (30) into the following 'average reaction function':

$$\Delta\bar{p}_u = \frac{c_1}{1+c_1k} + \left(1 - \frac{c_1}{1+c_1k}\right)\Delta\bar{e}(\bar{p}_u|\Omega). \tag{40}$$

This is analogous to the reaction function of the duopoly which depicts the way a given firm's price reacts to that of the other firm. Because the model is monopolistically competitive, and because information is imperfect, the other firm's price is replaced by expectations about the average price. In addition, the average is taken in order to cancel out the effect of the firm-specific disturbance $u$.

The basic difference between the imperfect-information equilibrium and the perfect-information equilibrium lies in the way $\Delta\bar{e}(\bar{p}_u \mid \Omega)$ is related to $\Delta\bar{p}_u$. In the perfect-information equilibrium, we have, by definition,

$$\Delta\bar{e}\ (\bar{p}_u|\Omega) = \Delta\bar{p}_u; \tag{41}$$

while in the imperfect-information equilibrium, we get

$$\Delta\bar{e}\ (\bar{p}_u|\Omega) = \theta\Delta\bar{p}_u; \tag{42}$$

Because of the possibility of local–global confusion, the average expectation about the average price is not as sensitive to the demand disturbance as the average price itself. This stickiness of the average expectation makes the imperfect-information (predetermined-price) average price less sensitive than its perfect-information counterpart and renders money non-neutral.

Figure 2.2 illustrates the point. In this figure the response of the average price is on the vertical axis, and that of the average expectation is on the horizontal axis. The line *AB* represents the reaction curve (40), which shows the response of the average price $\Delta\bar{p}_u$, given the response of the average expectation $\Delta\bar{e}(\bar{p}_u \mid \Omega)$. *OA* represents $c_1/(1 + c_1k)$, which is the weight of the firm's own demand condition in its price formula (30), while the slope *AB* represents the weight of the expected average price, $1 - [c_1 / (1 + c_1k)]$. The line *OC* is the 45° line, which represents the relationship between the average expectation and the actual average price under perfect information (41). The line *OD* is its imperfect-information counterpart (42). Because $\theta$ is less than unity, *OD* is always steeper than *OC*. The perfect-information equilibrium is the intersection $E^*$ ($\Delta\bar{p}_u = \Delta\bar{e}(\bar{p}_u \mid \Omega) = 1$) of *AB* and *OC*, while the imperfect-information equilibrium is *E* of *AB* and *OD*. From this figure it is evident that the imperfect-information response is less than unity.

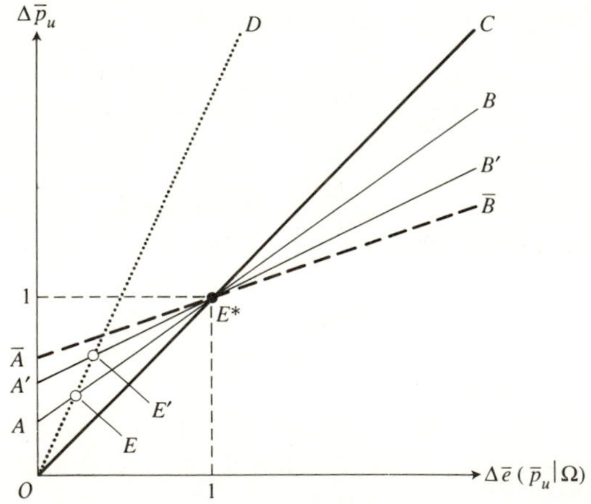


Fig. 2.2. Inelastic Supply

### 4.1. *Inelastic Supply and the Magnitude of Fluctuations: The Imperfect-Information Monopolistically Competitive Approach and the Imperfect-Information Perfectly Competitive Approach*

The above explanation of monetary non-neutrality is similar to the one in the well known imperfect-information perfectly competitive model of Lucas (1973). Both are based on local–global confusion. However, in the Lucas model confusion is between local equilibrium prices and the global average price, whereas in our model confusion is between local demand shocks and the global average demand shock. Moreover, the origin of imperfect information is different. In the model of Lucas, imperfect information is due to the assumption of the informational separation of local markets (the Phelps–Lucas islands); in the present model imperfect information is not assumed: it is an equilibrium phenomenon. Firms voluntarily choose imperfect information. The source of imperfect information is sluggish information diffusion and costly advertisement.

In addition to different sources of imperfect information, price behaviour in the two economies differs when supply is inelastic. Suppose that marginal costs are rapidly increasing ($c_1$ is large). This implies that supply is inelastic. In this case, it is well-known that perfectly competitive firms in Lucas's model will not want to change their production level. Thus, aggregate supply does not change, and thus changes in nominal demand are absorbed by price changes. By contrast, prices are sticky in the imperfect-information monopolistically competitive economy even if $c_1$ is large. Consequently, changes in nominal demand still have sizeable effects on output.

The effect of inelastic supply in the imperfect-information monopolistically competitive economy is illustrated in Fig. 2.2. In the figure, an increase in $c_1$ makes the $AB$ curve rotate clockwise around $E^*$. Thus, the new equilibrium $E'$ is above the old $E$, implying that prices become more flexible. However, the flexibility is usually small, even if $c_1$ is large. Note that $OA$ is $c_1 / (1 + c_1 k)$. Thus, $O\bar{A}$, the upper bound of $OA$, is $k^{-1}$, which is less than unity because $k > 1$; and even if $k$ is relatively small, it is still significantly smaller than unity. For example, if $k = 2.67$ and $\sigma_u = 2\sigma_m$ ($\theta = 0.2$), the upper bound of $\Delta\bar{p}_u$ is 0.42. In this economy, even if labour supply is inelastic, the monetary disturbance will induce a large fluctuation in the real variables.

The difference in price behaviour stems from the different assumptions about competition. In the model based on imperfect information and perfect competition, firms consider that they can sell any amount of output at the market price. They have perfect control over the quantities they sell. Thus, if $c_1$ is large they do not want to change their quantities, and they simply supply the same quantities. Prices absorb all fluctuations.

By contrast, firms in the imperfect-information (predetermined-price) economy are imperfectly competitive. Their sales depend not only on their prices but also on the average price, about which they do not have perfect information. Firms do not have perfect control over quantity. When $c_1$ is large, predetermined-price (imperfect-information) firms also have an incentive to keep their quantities constant, by keeping an appropriate relative price. However, firms must infer the average price that determines the location of the demand curve, relying only on partial information. This involves local–global confusion, so that expectations become sticky. Consequently, actual prices are sticky and quantities fluctuate, even if $c_1$ is large.

## 4.2. *Competition and Price Rigidity*

The imperfect-information monopolistically competitive economy also differs from other models in that competition makes prices rigid, rather than flexible. Suppose that $k$, the own-price elasticity of demand, is increased. This implies a smaller weight on the firm's own condition and a larger weight on the expected average price in the firm's price formula. This change is represented by a counter-clockwise rotation of $AB$ (equation (40)) around $E^*$ in Fig. 2.3, so that the new imperfect-information (predetermined-price) equilibrium $E'$ is below the old $E$. Thus, under imperfect information, increased competition reduces the sensitivity of prices to the demand disturbance $m$.

Under monopolistic competition, increased competition implies that the firm must shift weight from its own conditions to the expected average price in determining its price (see (30)). Because the expected price index is less sensitive to $m$ than the individual demand conditions, the shift implies stickier prices.[29]

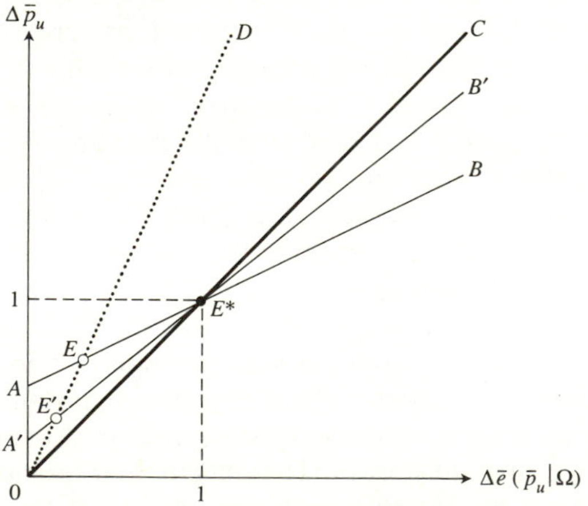


FIG. 2.3. Increased competition

## 5. IMPERFECT COMPETITION, IMPERFECT INFORMATION, AND SOCIAL WELFARE

In this section, I analyse social welfare and identify the source of inefficiency in the predetermined-price economy. In particular, I investigate the effect of imperfect competition and imperfect information on social welfare. I then analyse the effect of increased competition on social welfare in this economy.

The appropriate criterion for my analysis of social welfare, $W$, is the unconditional expected utility of the representative household, which owns firms and supplies labour to them; that is, $W = \int_m \int_u \Psi g(m) f(u) dm du$, where $m = \log M$, and $u = \log U$. I first characterize social welfare and the social optimum using the original framework of Section 2. Then, a convenient second-order approximation of social welfare is presented, and inefficiency arising from imperfect competition and imperfect information is identified. Finally, the effect of competition is analysed by employing the approximation.

### 5.1. *Social Welfare in the General Case*

Let us consider the representative household's utility $\Psi$ in the general case, where the $i$th firm's price is

$$P_i = \Xi M^{\delta} U_i^{\lambda}, \tag{43}$$

where $\Xi$, $\delta$, and $\lambda$ are positive real numbers. From (8) and (15) (see Appendix D), we then have

$$\Psi = n\frac{1}{\zeta} \bar{Y} - n (\bar{Y})^{1+c_1} \exp [\Gamma (\lambda)], \tag{44}$$

where

$$\bar{Y} = H_1 \frac{M}{\bar{P}^* (M, \Xi, \delta, \lambda)} = H_1 \frac{M}{\Xi M^{\delta} \exp[-z(\lambda)\sigma_u^2]} \tag{45}$$

and

$$\Gamma(\lambda) = \frac{1}{2} \left\{ (1+c_1)^2 (1-k\lambda)^2 - \frac{k}{k-1} (1+c_1) [1-(k-1)\lambda]^2 \right\} \sigma_u^2 . \tag{46}$$

The first term in (44) is the utility that originates from the consumption of goods and liquidity services. The utility from consumption of goods is equal to $n\bar{Y}$, while the utility from liquidity services is equal to $n[(1-\zeta)/\zeta)]\bar{Y}$ in equilibrium. The sum of the two is $n(1/\zeta)\bar{Y}$.

The second term in (44) represents disutility of labour which produces $n\bar{Y}$. To produce $n\bar{Y}$, the household gets a disutility of $n(\bar{Y})^{1+c_1}$.

$\Gamma(\lambda)$ in the second term of (44) represents the effect of product differentiation on production processes. Note that $\lambda$ is the sensitivity of the individual price $P_i$ to the idiosyncratic disturbance $U_i$. A change in this sensitivity affects the production level of individual firms and the disutility of labour of the representative household, which supplies labour to the firms, even if the average output $\bar{Y}$ is unchanged. The term $\Gamma(\lambda)$ represents this effect.

From (44), the unconditional mean of the representative household's utility $W$ is, from the property of log-normal distributions,

$$W[\bar{\bar{Y}},\ V(\log\ \bar{Y}),\ \Gamma(\lambda)]=n\frac{1}{\zeta}\bar{\bar{Y}}\ \exp\left[\frac{1}{2}V(\log\ \bar{Y})\right]$$

$$-n(\bar{\bar{Y}})^{1+c_1}\ \exp\left[\frac{1}{2}(1+c_1)^2V(\log\bar{Y})+\Gamma(\lambda)\right] \quad (47)$$

where $\bar{\bar{Y}}$ is the geometric average of $\bar{Y}$, such that $\log\bar{\bar{Y}}=\int_m \log\bar{Y}g(m)dm$, and where $V(\log\bar{Y})$ is the variance of $\log\bar{Y}$.

The social welfare function (47) shows that social welfare depends on three components: the 'normal' level of the average consumption index, $\bar{\bar{Y}}$; the volatility of the log of the average consumption index, $V(\log\bar{Y})$; and the effect of relative price dispersion, $\Gamma(\lambda)$.

## 5.2. *The Social Planner's Problem*

As a frame of reference, let us consider the 'social planner', who controls all the firms in the economy. He is informed of the behaviour of the representative consumer and the characteristics of the monetary disturbance. He takes them as given. Thus, the social planner knows the true values of $M$ and $U_i$ and determines the distribution of $P_i$ in order to maximize $W$. His task is to maximize (47) with respect to $(\Xi, \delta, \lambda)$ in (43).

Note that, because of (45), we have

$$\log\ \bar{Y}=\log H_1-\log\Xi+(1-\delta)\log M+z(\lambda)\sigma_u^2.$$

Consequently, we have

$$V\ (\log\bar{Y})=(1-\delta)^2\sigma_m^2.$$

Moreover, we obtain

$$\log\ \bar{\bar{Y}}=\log\ H_1-\log\Xi+z(\lambda)\sigma_u^2.$$

From this, it is evident that, if $\bar{\bar{Y}}$ is determined in addition to $\delta$ and $\lambda$, then $\Xi$ is uniquely determined. Thus, maximizing (47) with respect to $(\Xi, \delta, \lambda)$ is equivalent to maximizing $W(\bar{\bar{Y}}, (1-\delta)^2\sigma_m^2, \Gamma(\lambda))$ with respect to $(\bar{\bar{Y}}, \delta,$

$\lambda$). It is then straightforward to show that the socially optimum value of $(\bar{\bar{Y}}, \delta, \lambda)$ is

$$\bar{\bar{Y}} = \bar{\bar{Y}}^0 \equiv \exp\left\{\frac{1}{c_1}\left[\log \zeta^{-1} - \log(1+c_1) + (1+c_1k)z(\lambda^0)\sigma_u^2\right]\right\}$$

$$\delta = \delta^0 \equiv 1 \qquad (48)$$

$$\lambda = \lambda^0 \equiv \frac{c_1}{1+c_1k},$$

because we have $\Gamma(\lambda^0) = -(1+c_1k)z(\lambda^0)\sigma_u^2$ through some calculation. Thus, the optimum level of social welfare is $W^0 = W(\bar{\bar{Y}}^0, 0, \Gamma(\lambda^0))$.

### 5.3. *The Second-Order Approximation of the Deviation in Welfare from the Social Optimum*

The analysis in Section 2 has shown that we have $\Xi = \Phi_\theta$, $\delta = \rho_\theta$, and $\lambda = \rho_\theta$ in the predetermined-price (imperfect-information) economy. We use this to obtain

$$\begin{aligned}\log \bar{Y}_\theta &= \log H_1 + \log M - \log \bar{P}^*(\Phi_\theta, M, \rho_\theta, \rho_\theta)\\ &= \log H_1 + (1-\rho_\theta)\log M - \log \Phi_\theta + z(\rho_\theta)\sigma_u^2,\end{aligned}$$

which implies that $\log \bar{\bar{Y}}^\theta = \log H_1 - \log \Phi_\theta + z(\rho_\theta)\sigma_u^2$, where $\Phi_\theta$ is defined in (19) and $\rho_\theta$ in (20). Consequently, we have

$$\bar{\bar{Y}}_\theta = \exp\left\{-\frac{1}{c_1}\left[\log(1+c_1) + \log\frac{k}{k-1} + \omega\rho_\theta^2\,\theta\sigma_u^2 - (1+c_1k)z(\rho_\theta)\sigma_u^2\right]\right\}.$$

Social welfare in the imperfect-information monopolistically competitive economy is then given by

$$W_\theta = W\left[\bar{\bar{Y}}_\theta, (1-\rho_\theta)^2\sigma_m^2, \Gamma(\rho_\theta)\right].$$

Although the social welfare function, $W$, is nonlinear and complicated, there exists a convenient second-order approximation of the welfare around the social optimum (48) (see Appendix E). Using this approximation, we obtain a simple representation of the deviation in welfare from the social optimum, which we hereafter call the welfare loss. In the case of imperfect-information monopolistically competitive economy, we have a normalized welfare loss $(W_\theta - W^0)/W^0$, such that[31]

$$\frac{W_\theta - W^0}{W^0} \approx -\frac{1}{2}(1+c_1)\left[\left(1-\frac{\bar{\bar{Y}}_\theta}{\bar{\bar{Y}}^0}\right)^2 + (1-\rho_\theta)^2\sigma_m^2 + \frac{k(1+c_1k)}{c_1}(\rho_\theta - \lambda^0)^2\sigma_u^2\right], \qquad (49)$$

where

$$\frac{\bar{\bar{Y}}_\theta}{\bar{\bar{Y}}^0} = \exp\left\{\frac{1}{c_1}\left[-\log\zeta^{-1} - \log\frac{k}{k-1} - \omega\rho_\theta^2\,\theta\sigma_u^2 - (1+c_1k)\,(z(\lambda^0) - z(\rho_\theta))\sigma_u^2\right]\right\}. \quad (50)$$

Here ω is defined in (21).

### 5.4. *Imperfect Competition, Imperfect Information, and the Welfare Loss*

The welfare loss can be decomposed into three parts.

First, there is an insufficient level of liquidity services. Under the monopolistically competitive assumption in the strong form, firms do not take into account the effect of their prices on the price index. Consequently, firms ignore the effect of their price decisions on liquidity services through the price index. This causes inefficiency, and is represented by the first term in (50).

Second, we have non-competitive pricing. Social welfare is reduced by the non-competitive behaviour of firms. This loss appears in the second term in (50). Here, $k$, the degree of substitutability between products, represents the degree of competition.

Finally, all other terms in (49) and (50) are due solely to imperfect information.

Imperfect information affects social welfare in two ways. First, it reduces welfare by reducing the 'normal' level of the average consumption index. This effect is represented in the remaining two terms of (50). Second, imperfect information lowers social welfare by increasing the average disutility of labour by causing fluctuations in the average consumption index and the individual production level of differentiated products. This effect is shown in the second and third terms of (49).

Let us first consider the effect of imperfect information on the 'normal' level of the average consumption index $\bar{\bar{Y}}$. Imperfect information implies uncertainty about the average price in the firm's price decision. The firm's marginal benefit from a price increase ($\partial\hat{E}Y/\partial p_u$) is convex in the average price around the optimal $p_u$ if and only if $\omega > 0$.[32] Thus, if $\omega > 0$, which is likely as long as $c_1$ and $k$ are not too small, the expected marginal benefit is convex in the average price. Consequently, uncertainty about the average price increases the firm's price and, ultimately, the average price itself. (An intuitive explanation is as follows. Because shocks are mutiplicative, the negative effect of forecast errors on the firm's objective function is large when demand is strong. Taking this into account, the firm will increase its price in order to reduce demand when uncertainty about the average price increases.) In this case, the average price uncertainty decreases the 'normal' level of the average consumption index. This is represented by the third term in (50), because $\rho^2_\theta\theta\sigma_u^2 = V(\bar{p}_u|\Omega)$.

Imperfect information also reduces $\bar{\bar{Y}}$ by increasing the variability of relative prices. The fourth term in (50) represents this effect. The sign of this term is positive in most cases.[33] The excessive variability of the relative price implies the excessive variability in the consumption of individual products. This directly reduces the consumer's utility through the concavity of the utility function.[34]

Next, consider the effect of imperfect information on the aggregate disutility of labour. Imperfect information increases the volatility of the average consumption index. This induces volatility of labour inputs and reduces welfare. This effect is represented by the second term in (49), which is equal to $V(\log \bar{Y})$. In addition, imperfect information increases the volatility of relative prices, as explained above. The relative price variability induces the variability of labour demand, which also increases the disutility of labour. The third term in (49) shows this effect, because this term is proportional to $V[\log (P_u/\bar{P}_u) - \log (P_u/\bar{P}_u)^0]$, where $(P_u/\bar{P}_u)^0$ is the relative price at the social optimum $(\bar{\bar{Y}}^0, 0, \lambda^0)$.

## 5.5. *Competition and Welfare*

The conventional view about increased competition is that it increases social welfare. However, this does not necessarily hold true in the imperfect-information monopolistically competitive economy. Although increased competition always reduces the welfare loss arising from non-competitive behaviour (the second term in (50)), the effect of competition on the welfare loss arising from imperfect information is subtle and complicated. This is because increased competition (an increase in $k$) increases the volatility of output, as explained in the previous section.

Numerical analysis shows that the effect of increased competition depends crucially on the value of $c_1$.

In general if $c_1$ is small, increased competition decreases the welfare loss. Note that a small $c_1$ implies a near-constant marginal 'cost'. (In our bilateral-monopoly efficient-bargains framework, the marginal 'cost' depends on the marginal disutility of labour and returns to scale.) So a firm's expected relative price is close to a constant mark-up over the constant marginal cost. Then, the firm's nominal price is also close to a constant mark-up over the expected average price. Thus, the economy falls into a kind of a price-price spiral. Because every firm wants a mark-up over the average price, the average price goes up sharply. The larger the mark-up (that is, the less competitive the economy is), the higher the equilibrium average price and, ultimately, the smaller the equilibrium average consumption index. In this case, increased competition substantially reduces prices and decreases the welfare loss. By contrast, because the firm's price is insensitive to the demand condition $m$ arising from the near-constant marginal cost, the average price is also insensitive to $m$. Consequently, uncertainty about the average price is small, implying that the welfare loss arising from imperfect information is also small.

On the other hand, if $c_1$ is large, increased competition may increase, rather than decrease, the welfare loss. In this case, the welfare loss arising from imperfect information may dominate the loss arising from non-competitive behaviour. This is because the loss caused by forecast errors may be large when $c_1$ is large, compared with the loss caused by non-competitive behaviour. Because an increase in competition increases the volatility of output by enhancing price rigidity, its overall effect may be to increase the welfare loss.

Figure 2.4 illustrates this point. This figure shows that competition may increase the welfare loss even in a realistic range of parameters. In this figure, we assume $\zeta = 0.95$,[35] $c_1 = 6.7$, $\sigma_m = 0.05$, and $\sigma_u = 2\sigma_m$. Here, the value of $c_1 = 6.7$ is taken as an example of inelastic labour supply.[36] The vertical axis represents the normalized welfare loss $(W_\theta - W^0)/W^0$, where $W^0$ is the social optimum. The horizontal axis shows the degree of competitiveness, $k$. When $k$ is small, an increase in $k$ reduces the welfare loss by reducing the non-competitive mark-up. However, as $k$ becomes large, the rigidity-enhancing effect of increasing competition dominates the mark-up-reducing effect. Thus, an increase in competition becomes welfare-reducing for $k$ larger than 9 in this figure.

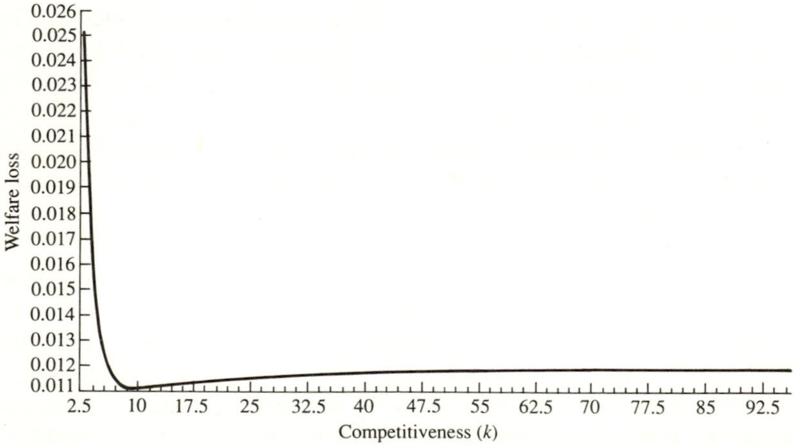


FIG. 2.4. Competition and welfare loss: the case of inelastic supply

## 6. CONCLUDING REMARKS

This chapter has shown that the imperfect-information (predetermined-price) equilibrium exists for a wide range of parameters even if the supply elasticity is not large. Although imperfect-information perfectly competitive models and menu-cost monopolistically competitive models fail to generate large fluctuations in output when the elasticity of supply is low, the predetermined-price model is capable of generating such fluctuations.

The outcome of this chapter can also be considered an example of the general principle that small nominal rigidity may produce large nominal rigidity when coupled with real rigidity. The argument was mentioned in Chapter 1. Here imperfect information is the source of real rigidity, and the imputed cost of frequent price changes arising from buyers' imperfect information is the source of nominal rigidity. However, it should be noted that simply having both kinds of rigidity is not sufficient to produce large nominal rigidity. As explained in Chapter 1, imperfect information alone can explain only a small part of the large nominal rigidity observed in the real economy; the same is true for price-adjustment costs. By combining them in a multiplicative shock framework, we are able to explain large nominal rigidity in this chapter.

The crucial elements of this chapter are (1) the information transmission process that generates the imperfect-information (predetermined-price) equilibrium; (2) the assumption of rational expectations (or, equivalently, the Bayesian Nash equilibrium); and (3) the assumption that the monetary information is not available to firms.

Let us first consider the information transmission process. We have assumed (*a*) sluggish information diffusion and (*b*) costly price advertisement, and in addition (*c*) that consumers do not actively search. The discussion in Chapter 1 suggests that (*a*) and (*b*) are prevalent in many consumer goods markets and some industrial markets, except for well organized commodity markets. Assumption (*c*) seems plausible for service markets, such as hotel and restaurant services, to a certain extent.[37] It is also likely to hold for products that consumers buy frequently. On the other hand, the argument may not be directly applicable to the markets of motor cars and large household appliances, in which many consumers seem to search actively,[38] but a slight modification of the model is sufficient to explain sticky prices in these markets (see Chapter 9). In this case, announcing the price in advance reduces the search cost of consumers, instead of the extra advertising cost of firms.

I make the assumption of rational expectations in this chapter (and throughout this book) because I am concerned with an 'expectational equilibrium' in which no economic agent has an incentive to change his behaviour, even when the true mechanism that generates the actual movement of economic variables becomes known to him. However, it may be worthwhile to examine the robustness of the results of this chapter when expectations are not rational.

The result of Section 4—that is, the effect of inelastic supply and competition on nominal price rigidity—does not depend on the rational expectations assumption. This is because the argument is essentially based on three claims: (1) expectations about the average are rigid compared with the actual average; (2) increased competition makes a firm's price more dependent on rigid expectations about the average; (3) buyers determine their purchase quantities. These claims are not particularly related to the rational expectations assumption. Thus, if (1)–(3) hold true, which seems a natural assumption in many markets, competition still enhances nominal rigidity, and we obtain large fluctuations in output even if supply is inelastic. By contrast, the results of Sections 3 and 5 depend on the rational expectations assumption. It is not clear at this stage that these results still hold true under expectation-formation processes other than the rational one.

Next, consider the assumption of lack of monetary information. Arguments similar to the one in this chapter are often subject to the criticism that the money supply and the price index are available at little cost in most industrialized economies. Thus, the counter-argument goes, a monetary non-neutrality argument of this kind cannot explain the persistent effect of money supply shocks, which in fact is the phenomenon that requires explanation. On this basis, the counter-argument questions the significance of the imperfect-information approach as a theory of nominal price rigidity. I will take up this issue in the next chapter.

Finally, a remark may be due about the difference between the effects of sluggish price adjustment and those of sluggish quantity adjustment. The simplest way to introduce sluggish quantity adjustment is to take the existence of a production period into account. If a non-negligible production period exists, the firm must determine its production quantities before it has perfect knowledge of the economy. This is another type of imperfect information in an imperfectly competitive economy. Imperfect information arising from a non-negligible production period is analysed in Nishimura (1988*c*), assuming instantaneous information transmission. The results, however, are not very much different from those obtained under perfect competition and perfect information.

# Appendix A: Computation of the Bayesian Nash Equilibrium

In this appendix, the Bayesian Nash equilibrium defined in (18) is computed. Let $P_i^E$ be the solution of the right-hand side of (18). From (13) and (17), we obtain, taking account of $\Omega_i = \{A_i\}$,

$$(P_i^E)^{(1+c_1k)} = \frac{(1+c_1)k}{k-1} H_1^{c_1}A_i^{c_1} \frac{E\{\,[\bar{P}^*\ (M, \Phi, \rho, \rho)\,]^{(1+c_1)\ (k-1)}|A_i\}}{E\{\,[\bar{P}^*\ (M, \Phi, \rho, \rho)\,]^{(k-2)}|A_i\}}$$

$$= \frac{(1+c_1)k}{k-1} H_1^{c_1}A_i^{c_1}\Phi^{1+c_1(k-1)} \exp\{-[1+c_1\,(k-1)\,]z(\rho)\sigma_u^2\}$$

$$\times \frac{E[M^{(1+c_1)\ (k-1)\rho}|A_i]}{E[M^{(k-2)\rho}|A_i]}. \tag{A$_1$}$$

Note that, under the assumption made in the text, the distribution of (log $M$, log $A_i$) is a multivariate normal distribution with mean (0, 0) and variance–covariance matrix $\Sigma$, such that

$$\Sigma = \begin{bmatrix} \sigma_m^2 & \sigma_m^2 \\ \sigma_m^2 & \sigma_m^2+\sigma_u^2 \end{bmatrix}.$$

Consequently, the distribution of log $M$ conditional on log $A_i$, log $M|$log $A_i$, is a normal distribution with $E(\log M|\log A_i) = \theta \log A_i$ and $V(\log M|\log A_i) = \theta\sigma_u^2$, where $\theta = \sigma_m^2/(\sigma_m^2 + \sigma_u^2)$. Therefore, using the properties of log-normal distributions, we obtain

$$\frac{E[M^{(1+c_1)\ (k-1)\rho}|A_i]}{E[M^{(k-2)\rho}|A_i]} = A_i^{[1+c_1(k-1)]\rho\theta} \exp\left(\omega\rho^2\theta\sigma_u^2\right),$$

where

$$\omega = {}^1\!/_2\,[(1+c_1)^2\ (k-1)^2-(k-2)^2].$$

From (18), $\Phi$ and $\rho$ must satisfy

$$\Phi A_i^\rho = P_i^E. \tag{A$_2$}$$

Consequently, we obtain

$$\left(\Phi\ A_i^\rho\right)^{1+c_1k} = \frac{(1+c_1)k}{k-1} H_1^{c_1}\Phi^{1+c_1(k-1)} A_i^{c_1+[1+c_1(k-1)]\rho\theta}$$

$$\times \exp\left\{\omega\rho^2\theta\sigma_u^2-[1+c_1(k-1)]z(\rho)\sigma_u^2\right\}.$$

Collecting the terms in the above expression, we obtain the equilibrium value of $\Phi$ and $\rho$. We have

$$\Phi = \Phi_\theta \equiv \left[\frac{(1+c_1)k}{k-1}\right]^{1/c_1} H_1\ \exp\left[\frac{1}{c_1}\omega\rho_\theta^2\theta\sigma_u^2 - \frac{1+c_1(k-1)}{c_1} z(\rho_\theta)\sigma_u^2\right]$$

and

$$\rho = \rho_\theta \equiv \frac{c_1}{1+c_1k-[1+c_1(k-1)]\theta}.$$

# Appendix B: The Menu-Cost Model

In this appendix, I formulate a menu-cost model and derive the minimum menu cost which supports a no-adjustment equilibrium.

In this menu-cost model I assume $u = 0$. There is no microeconomic real disturbance. Consequently, $x = h_1 + m$, $\sigma_u^2 = 0$, $\rho = 0$, and $v(\rho) = 0$. The firm's objective function Y is now

$$\begin{aligned} Y = {} & \exp[(1-k)(p_u-\bar{p}_u)+(h_1+m)-\bar{p}_u] \\ & - \exp\{(1+c_1)\;[-k(p_u-\bar{p}_u)+(h_1+m)-\bar{p}_u]\}. \end{aligned} \tag{A$_3$}$$

Suppose that all firms are initially in equilibrium. Then, the optimal price formula is

$$p_u = \frac{1}{1+c_1k}a^* + \frac{c_1}{1+c_1k}(h_1+m) + \left(1-\frac{c_1}{1+c_1k}\right)\bar{p}_u, \tag{A$_4$}$$

where $a^* = \log(1+c_1) + \log[k/(k-1)]$. Because we have $p_u = \bar{p}_u$ in equilibrium, we obtain

$$\bar{p}_u = \frac{1}{c_1}a^* + h_1 + m. \tag{A$_5$}$$

Next, $m$ is changed to $m' = m + \Delta$. However, assume that other firms do not adjust their prices. Then, we still have (A5). Thus, we obtain

$$(h_1+m')-\bar{p}_u = (h_1+m+\Delta)-\bar{p}_u = -(1/c_1)a^*+\Delta.$$

On the one hand, if the given firm does not change its price either, we have $p_u - \bar{p}_u = 0$. In this case, from (A3) we obtain

$$Y_{na} = \exp\left(-\frac{1}{c_1}a^*+\Delta\right) - \exp\left[(1+c_1)\left(-\frac{1}{c_1}a^*+\Delta\right)\right].$$

On the other hand, if the firm does adjust its price, its optimal price is given by

$$p_u = \frac{1}{1+c_1k}a^* + \frac{c_1}{1+c_1k}(h_1+m+\Delta) + \left(1-\frac{c_1}{1+c_1k}\right)\bar{p}_u.$$

Thus, we have $p_u - \bar{p}_u = [c_1/(1+c_1k)]\Delta$. Consequently, we obtain

$$Y_a = \exp\left(-\frac{1}{c_1}a^* + \frac{1+c_1}{1+c_1k}\Delta\right) - \exp\left[(1+c_1)\left(-\frac{1}{c_1}a^*\right) + \frac{1+c_1}{1+c_1k}\Delta\right] - F_m,$$

where $F_m$ is the menu cost. The minimum menu cost that supports a no-adjustment equilibrium is $F^*_m$, such that $\Upsilon_{na} = \Upsilon_a$.

# Appendix C: The Payoffs of the Predetermined-Price Strategy and the Perfect-Information Strategy When All Other Firms Adopt the Perfect-Information Strategy

In this appendix, I derive the payoff functions of the imperfect-information (predetermined-price) strategy and perfect-information strategy, *when all other firms adopt the perfect-information strategy*. Table 2.3 is based on these conditions.

The payoff is the unconditional expected value of the objective function$\Upsilon$: $R = \int_m \int_u \Upsilon g\ (m)\ f(u) dm du$, where

$$\Upsilon = \exp\,[v + (1 - k)\ (p_u - \bar{p}_u) + x - \bar{p}_u] \\ - \exp\,\{(1 + c_1)\,[-\,k\,(p_u - \bar{p}_u) + x - \bar{p}_u]\}.$$

Because all other firms adopt the perfect-information strategy, the average price $\bar{p}_u$ is determined by (35).

On the one hand, under the perfect-information strategy, the $p_u$ equation in (35) determines the firm's optimal price. Thus, the relative price is $p_u - \bar{p}_u = \rho^* u$. Similarly, we have

$$x - \bar{p}_u = r^* + m + u - [(b^*/c_1) + r^* + m] = \bar{\bar{d}}^* + u,$$

where $\bar{\bar{d}}^* = b^*/\ c_1$, $b^* = b(\rho^*,\ 0)$, and $r(\rho^*)$, = because of (35). Thus, the expected value of the objective function under the perfect-information strategy, $\hat{R}^P$, is

$$\hat{R}^P = \exp\,\{\,\bar{\bar{d}}^* + v^* + \tfrac{1}{2}[(1-k)\rho^* + 1]^2\sigma_u^2\} \\ -\exp\left\{(1+c_1)\,\bar{\bar{d}}^* + \tfrac{1}{2}(1+c_1)^2\,[(-k\rho^*+1)^2\sigma_u^2\,]\right\}, \qquad (A_6)$$

where $v^* = v(\rho^*)$.

On the other hand, if the firm adopts the imperfect-information (predetermined-price) strategy, it can no longer observe $\bar{p}_u$ in the sixth stage. However, because $\bar{p}_u$ is still determined by (35), we have

$$e(\bar{p}_u|\Omega) = (b^*/c_1) + r^* + \theta(x - r^*) \qquad \text{and} \qquad V(\bar{p}_u|\Omega) = \theta\sigma_u^2.$$

Thus, the optimal imperfect-information (predetermined-price) strategy price, which is denoted by $\hat{p}'_u$, is, from (30),

$$\hat{p}'_u = \frac{1}{1+c_1 k}\,b^{*\prime} + \frac{c_1}{1+c_1 k}\,x + \left(1 - \frac{c_1}{1+c_1 k}\right)e\ (\bar{p}_u|\Omega). \qquad (A_7)$$

where

$$b^{*'} = b^* + \omega V(\bar{p}_u | \Omega) = b^* + \omega\theta\sigma_u^2.$$

Consequently, because $e(\bar{p}_u|\Omega) = \bar{p}_u - (1-\theta)m + \theta u$, we obtain a relative price under the perfect-information strategy, such that

$$\hat{p}_u' - \bar{p}_u = \frac{1}{1+c_1 k}\omega\theta\sigma_u^2 - (1-\rho^*)(1-\theta)m + [\rho^* + (1-\rho^*)\theta]u. \qquad (A_8)$$

Here $\rho^* = c_1/(1+c_1 k)$ is used. Consequently, by substituting (A8) into Y, rearranging the terms, and integrating with respect to $u$ and $m$, we obtain the unconditional mean of the objective function of the firm under the imperfect-information (predetermined-price) strategy, $\hat{R}^I$, such that

$$\hat{R}^P = \exp\left(\bar{\bar{d}}^* + \frac{1-k}{1+c_1 k}\omega\theta\sigma_u^2 + v^* + \frac{1}{2}\left\{[\phi_1(1-\theta)]^2\sigma_m^2 + \left(\frac{1+c_1}{1+c_1 k} + \phi_1\theta\right)^2 \sigma_u^2\right\}\right)$$
$$- \exp\left((1+c_1)\bar{\bar{d}}^* - \frac{(1+c_1)k}{1+c_1 k}\omega\theta\sigma_u^2 + \frac{1}{2}\left\{[\phi_2(1-\theta)]^2\sigma_m^2 + \left(\frac{1+c_1}{1+c_1 k} - \phi_2\theta\right)^2\sigma_u^2\right\}\right) - F, \qquad (A_9)$$

where $\phi_1 = (1-k)(1-\rho^*)$, $\phi_2 = (1+c_1)k(1-\rho^*)$, and $F$ is the extra advertising cost. $F^{**}$ in Table 2.3 is defined as $F$, making $\hat{R}^I = \hat{R}^P$.

# Appendix D: Social Welfare in the General Case

In this appendix, I derive the social welfare function (44) in the general case of (43).

In the general case where $P_i = \Xi M^\delta U_i^\lambda$, we have $\bar{P}(\{P_i\}) = \bar{P}^*(M, \Xi, \delta, \lambda)$ using the same argument as in note 6 below. Then, from (8), we obtain

$$\Psi = n\left(\frac{1}{\zeta}\bar{Y}\right) - \sum_{i=1}^{n} L_i^u$$

where

$$\bar{Y} = H_1 \frac{M}{\bar{P}^*(M, \Xi, \delta, \lambda)}.$$

Next, consider the second term, which is the disutility of labour. Because $Q_i = L_i^{\phi}$, $1 + c_1 = \mu/\phi$, (9), and $P_i/\bar{P} = U_i^{\lambda} \exp\,[z(\lambda)\sigma_u^2]$, we obtain the following transformations:

$$\sum_{i=1}^{n} L_i^{\mu} = n\left(\frac{1}{n}\sum_{i=1}^{n} Q_i^{1+c_1}\right) = n\left\{\frac{1}{n}\sum_{i=1}^{n}\left[\left(\frac{P_i}{\bar{P}}\right)^{-k} \bar{Y}U_i\right]^{1+c_1}\right\}$$

$$= n\left(\frac{1}{n}\sum_{i=1}^{n} \{[U_i^{\lambda} \exp\,((\lambda)\sigma_u^2)]^{-k}\ \bar{Y}U_i\}^{1+c_1}\right)$$

$$= n\bar{Y}^{1+c_1} \exp\,[-(1+c_1)kz(\lambda)\sigma_u^2]\left[\frac{1}{n}\sum_{i=1}^{n} U_i^{(1-k\lambda)(1+c_1)}\right]$$

$$\approx n\bar{Y}^{1+c_1} \exp\,[-(1+c_1)kz(\lambda)\sigma_u^2]\left\{\int_u \exp\,[(1-k\lambda)\ (1+c_1)u]\ f(u)du\right\}.$$

Here we use the law of large numbers. We then have

$$\sum_{i=1}^{n} L_i^{\mu} = n\bar{Y}^{1+c_1} \exp\left[-(1+c_1)kz(\lambda)\ \sigma_u^2 + \frac{1}{2}(1-k\lambda)^2\ (1+c_1)^2\sigma_u^2\right]$$

$$= n\bar{Y}^{1+c_1} \exp\,[\Gamma(\lambda)],$$

where the definition of $z(\cdot)$ in (16) is utilized.

# Appendix E: The Second-Order Approximation of the Welfare Loss

We will prove (49) in this appendix. Note that, because $(\bar{\bar{Y}}, \delta, \lambda) = (\bar{\bar{Y}}^0, 1, \lambda^0)$ maximizes

$$W\left(\bar{\bar{Y}}, (1-\delta)^2\sigma_m^2, \Gamma(\lambda)\right) = n\frac{1}{\zeta}\bar{\bar{Y}} \exp\left\{\frac{1}{2}(1-\delta)^2\sigma_m^2\right\}$$

$$- n(\bar{\bar{Y}})^{1+c_1} \exp\left[\frac{1}{2}(1+c_1)^2\ (1-\delta)^2\sigma_m^2 + \Gamma(\lambda)\right]$$

we have

$$W_1 = n\frac{1}{\zeta} - (1+c_1)n\ (\bar{\bar{Y}}^0)^{c_1} \exp\,[\Gamma(\lambda^0)] = 0. \tag{A$_{10}$}$$

Here $W_i$ denotes the first derivative of the $i$th argument. Using this relation, we obtain

$$W^0 = n\frac{1}{\zeta}\,\bar{\bar{Y}}^0 - n(\bar{\bar{Y}}^0)^{1+c_1}\,\exp[\Gamma(\lambda^0)] = c_1\, n\,(\bar{\bar{Y}}^0)^{1+c_1}\,\exp\,[\Gamma(\lambda^0)]. \qquad (A_{11})$$

Next, consider the second-order Taylor expansion of $W$ with respect to $(\bar{\bar{Y}}, \delta, \lambda)$ around $(\bar{\bar{Y}}^0, 1, \lambda^0)$. It is straightforward to show that

$$W - W^0 = \frac{1}{2}\,[W_{11}\,(\bar{\bar{Y}}-\bar{\bar{Y}}^0)^2 + 2\sigma_m^2\,W_2\,(\delta-1)^2 + \Gamma''(\lambda^0)\,W_3\,(\lambda-\lambda^0)^2],$$

where

$$W_{11} = -\,c_1\,(1+c_1)n\,(\bar{\bar{Y}}^0)^{c_1-1}\,\exp\,[\Gamma(\lambda^0)];$$

$$W_2 = \frac{1}{2}\left\{\frac{n}{\zeta}\,\bar{\bar{Y}}^0 - (1+c_1)^2\,n\,(\bar{\bar{Y}}^0)^{1+c_1}\,\exp\,[\Gamma(\lambda^0)]\right\} =$$

$$-\frac{1}{2}\,c_1\,(1+c_1)\,n\,(\bar{\bar{Y}}^0)^{1+c_1}\,\exp\,[\Gamma(\lambda^0)];$$

$$W_3 = -\,n(\bar{\bar{Y}}^0)^{1+c_1}\,\exp\,[\Gamma(\lambda^0)];\ \text{and}\ \Gamma''(\lambda^0) = k\,(1+c_1)\,(1+c_1k).$$

Using $(A_{10})$ and $(A_{11})$, we obtain

$$\frac{W_\theta - W^0}{W^0} \approx -\frac{1}{2}(1+c_1)\left[\left(1-\frac{\bar{\bar{Y}}}{\bar{\bar{Y}}^0}\right)^2 + (\delta-1)^2\sigma_m^2 + \frac{k(1+c_1k)}{c_1}\,(\lambda-\lambda^0)^2\sigma_u^2)\right], \qquad (A_{12})$$

From this we obtain (49), because $W_\theta = W\,(\bar{\bar{Y}}_\theta,\,(1-\rho_\theta)^2\,\sigma_m^2,\,\Gamma(\rho_\theta))$.

# Notes

1. Newman (1978) surveyed a number of empirical studies about consumers' actual shopping behaviour and found that typically 40–60% of the buyers visited only one store, regardless of whether a non-durable or a durable product was purchased. A few illustrative percentages of one-store buyers are 22% for living room furniture, 49% for new cars and major household appliances, and 60–90% for cookware, towels and sheets, and toys. See also Katona and Mueller (1954). In many markets, consumers do not actively search for the best offer. Thus, the assumption of no active search is reasonable. The case in which consumers actively search for the best buy will be analysed in Ch. 9.

2. Moreover, it is often argued that the bilateral monopoly is a realistic labour-market assumption in many industrialized economies. Long-term employer–employee relationships are widely observed in the Japanese economy. Hall (1980) asserts that this assumption is also a plausible one for the short-run analysis of the US economy.

   It should be noted here that the result of this chapter does not depend on this particular assumption. Ch. 3's analysis of an economy with perfectly competitive labour markets, and Ch. 4's analysis of an economy with monopolistically competitive unions, where wages are predetermined with cost-of-living adjustments included, reveal that the effect of product-market monopolistic competition and imperfect information obtained under bilateral–monopoly labour markets holds true even there, with minor qualifications.
3. I assume away the possibility that firms renege on their price offers and ration their products. Such behaviour antagonizes customers and may be detrimental to the long-run profits. Thus, I implicitly assume that the cost of turning customers away is large. The presence of the cost of turning customers away is absolutely standard in operations research and inventories models (see Taha 1982: Ch. 12). This cost is also incorporated into oligopoly models (see Dixon 1989).
4. Suppose that the firm is allowed to conduct market research about demand, and to ask the household about the nominal demand for its product if its price is equal to the average price. The firm gets $H_1 A_i$ as an answer, where $H_1$ is known to the firm.
5. For various arguments to justify the Nash equilibrium concept, see Binmore and Dasgupta (1986).
6. Let $f^*(U)$ be the density function of the log-normal distribution from which $U_s$ ($s = 1, \ldots, n$) is drawn. Because $n$ is large, the number of firms having $U$ is approximately $nf^*(U)$. Since $\phi(A_s) = \Phi(MU_s)^\rho$, the log of the price index $\bar{P}\{[\phi(A_s)]:_{s=1,\ldots,n}\}$ is

$$\log\left(\bar{P}\{[\phi(A_s)]:_{s=1,\ldots,n}\}\right) = \frac{1}{1-k}\log\left[\sum_{s=1}^{n} U_s(\Phi M^\rho U_s^\rho)^{1-k}\frac{1}{n}\right]$$

$$\approx \log\Phi + \rho\log M + \frac{1}{1-k}\log\left[\int_0^\infty U^{1+(1-k)\rho} f^*(U)\, dU\right]$$

$$= \log\Phi + \rho\log M - z(\rho)\sigma_u^2.$$

   Here we utilize the property of the log-normal distribution such that $\log[E(U^h)] = hE(\log U) + \frac{1}{2}h^2V(\log U)$ for a real number $h$ (see Aitchison and Brown 1957).
7. On the one hand, because $p_u = \log\Phi + \rho\log M + \rho\log U$, we have $\bar{p}_u = \log\Phi + \rho\log M$. On the other hand, from (17) we have $\bar{p} = \log\Phi + \rho\log M - z(\rho)\sigma_u^2$. We combine these two relations to get the above relation.
8. The firm's expectations about the average price depend on other firms' expectations about the average price. Because the firm knows this, its expectations depend on expectations about other firms' expectations. The firm

knows that other firms also apply the same reasoning, and so its expectations depend on expectations about other firms' expectations about other firms' expectations; and so on without end. This is the infinite regress problem. For more about this problem, see the discussions in Frydman and Phelps (1983).

9. The firm's objective function is now

$$\hat{E}Y = \exp\,[v + x + (1-k)p_u]\ \hat{E}\exp\,[(k-2)\bar{p}_u]$$
$$-\exp\,[-(1+c_1)\,kp_u + (1+c_1)\,x]\ \hat{E}\exp\,[(1+c_1)\,(k-1)\bar{p}_u].$$

Because we assume $\bar{p}_u$ is normally distributed, we have, for an arbitrary $h$, $\log\,\hat{E}\exp\,(h\bar{p}_u) = h[e(\bar{p}_u\,|\,\Omega)] + \tfrac{1}{2}h^2[V(\bar{p}_u\,|\,\Omega)]$. Using this relation, the first-order condition of optimality can be transformed into the optimal price formula (30).

10. Let the firm assume $e(\bar{p}_u|\Omega) = J + K(x-r)$. Here $J$ and $K$, as well as ρ, are undetermined coefficients. Insert this into the individual optimal price formula (30) and average it over $u$. Apply $e(\cdot|\Omega)$ on both sides, taking account of $e(m\,|\,\Omega) = \theta(x-r)$ and $V(m\,|\,\Omega) = E\{[m - e(m\,|\,\Omega)]^2\} = \theta\sigma_u^2$. Collect terms in order to arrive at the expressions for $J$ and $K$. We then obtain $e(\bar{p}_u\,|\,\Omega) = (1/c_1)b + r + \rho_\theta[\theta(x-r)]$. Substitute this expression into the optimal price formula and average the resulting expression over $u$. We then have (32), where $\log\,\Phi = \tfrac{1}{c_1}b + r$. From this expression, it is easy to get $\rho = \rho_\theta$.

As for $V(\bar{p}_u\,|\,\Omega)$, apply $V(.\,|\,\Omega)$ on both sides of the $\bar{p}_u$ equation in (32). We then obtain $V(\bar{p}_u\,|\,\Omega) = \rho_\theta^2\theta\sigma_u^2$.

11. Let $\rho^*$ be the undermined coefficient such that $p_u - \bar{p}_u = \rho^*_u$ under perfect information. Substituting $e(\bar{p}_u|\Omega) = \bar{p}_u$ and $V(\bar{p}_u|\Omega) = 0$ into the optimal price formula (30), we have

$$p_u = \frac{1}{1+c_1k}b^* + \frac{c_1}{1+c_1k}(r^* + m + u) + \left(1 - \frac{c_1}{1+c_1k}\right)\bar{p}_u,$$

where $b^* = b(\rho^*, 0)$ and $r^* = r(\rho^*)$. Averaging $p_u$ over all $u$ and rearranging the terms, we obtain the result in the text. As for $\rho^*$, we immediately obtain

$$\rho^* = c_1/(1 + c_1k).$$

from the above relation.

It can easily be shown that this corresponds to the complete-information Nash equilibrium in the game described earlier.

12. It may not be appropriate to contrast the imperfect-information argument in this chapter with the menu-cost argument. Menu-cost models are, in a broad sense, models of nominal price rigidity based on the cost of changing prices. Because the incomplete-information argument in this chapter is based on the 'implicit' cost of changing prices arising from sluggish and costly information transmission, it belongs to the category of menu-cost models in a broad sense. However, in order to clarify the characteristics of the incomplete-information argument, we can compare it with a simple menu-cost argument, which takes literally and single-mindedly the argument developed in Mankiw (1985), Akerlof and Yellen (1985), and Blanchard and Kiyotaki (1987).

13. The analysis in this section is closely related to that of Ball and Romer (1989*a*). In their analysis, firms must choose *ex ante* whether to have flexible prices. They then derive conditions where no adjustment is a non-cooperative equilibrium. Because the choice between predetermined prices and perfect information can be considered as the choice between sticky prices and flexible ones, the formal setting of this section's model is identical to that of Ball and Romer (1989*a*). There are, however, two important differences. First, firms in my model have some (imperfect and noisy) information about the money supply, whereas in Ball and Romer firms have no information about the money supply at all. Second, there are local shocks in my model, but not in that of Ball and Romer. As will be shown later in this section, these differences lead to major differences between the predetermined-price approach and the menu-cost approach as a theory of nominal price rigidity.
14. Thus we assume that, if a firm chooses a predetermined-price strategy, it cannot later change its price. This assumption is made for analytic simplicity and is not crucial to the result of this chapter, namely, the plausibility of the predetermined-price equilibrium. In fact, if a predetermined-price firm is allowed to adjust its price (possibly only downward), then the predetermined-price strategy is more attractive than in the text, and the predetermined-price equilibrium is even more likely. However, this possibility introduces nonlinearity into our log-linear model, making an explicit characterization of the rational expectations equilibrium almost impossible.
15. The extension to the case of a positive advertising cost is straightforward.
16. The qualitiative characteristics of the model do not change even if we allow firms to have *some* noisy information about the average price, execpt that there is then a possibility of multiple expectational equilibria (see Ch. 7).
17. In one round of the information exchange, the association announces the average price of all firms in the previous round. The complete-information firms determine their prices based on the announced average price; the incomplete-information (price-pledge) firms do nothing. The association collects all price information at the end of this round, and announces the average price at the beginning of the next round. The process continues until the average price in one round is the same as that of the following round.
18. In terms of real profits, this takes the form of extra labour cost.
19. Substituting the above relations into Y, we obtain

$$Y = \exp\{v + [(1-k)\rho_\theta + 1]u + (1-\rho_\theta)m + \bar{\bar{d}}\}$$
$$- \exp\{(1+c_1)[(-k\rho_\theta + 1)u + (1-\rho_\theta)m + \bar{\bar{d}}]\}.$$

Taking the characteristics of the log-normal distribution into account, we obtain the result in the text.
20. Because the firm's objective function Y is concave in the relative price $p_u - \bar{p}_u$, at least at the optimal price, the excessive sensitivity of the relative price to $u$ decreases the value of the objective function. Moreover, the rigidity of the optimal price with respect to the general demand condition reduces the value of the objective function, because the firm would increase its profits by increasing its price more when demand is strong, and by decreasing its price more when demand is weak.

21. If $\sigma_u \to 0$, we have $\theta \to 1$, and $\rho_\theta \to 1$. Then it is straightforward to show that $F^* \to 0$. If $\sigma_m \to 0$, we have $\theta \to 0$, and $\rho_\theta \to c_1/(1 + c_1 k)$. Using these results, we can show that $F^* \to 0$ with some calculation.
22. If $c_1 \to 0$, then $(1 + c_1)/(1 + c_1 k) \to 1$, and $\rho_\theta \to 0$, so that $F^* \to 0$. If $k \to \infty$, then $(1 + c_1)/(1 + c_1 k) \to 0$, $\rho_\theta \to 0$, $(1 - k)\rho_\theta + 1 \to -1/(1 - \theta)$ and $-k\rho_\theta + 1 \to - 1/(1-\theta)$. Using this, it is evident that $F^*$ remains substantial.
23. The result does not depend on this particular choice of $\sigma_u$.
24. In a more sophisticated version of a menu-cost model in Ball and Romer (1989*a*), firms determine their prices *ex ante*, without having any information about the current state of the money supply and then decide whether to readjust prices when information about the money supply is eventually known. Thus, *ex ante* rigidity is assumed in their model.
25. The analysis of the menu-cost model and relevant formulas in Table 2.2 are presented in App. B.
26. See Ch. 3 for a discussion of the effect of strategic interdependence and induced externality on information acquisition in a monopolistically competitive economy.
27. Relevant formulas are found in App. C.
28. See e.g. Blanchard and Fischer (1989: Ch. 8) and Ball and Romer (1989*a*).
29. Ch. 5 extends this analysis to the case of correlated demand and supply shocks. In a partial equilibrium framework allowing correlated demand and cost disturbances, I show that if $k$ goes to infinity $\Delta\bar{p}_u$ approaches zero, implying completely rigid prices.
30. It can easily be shown that this social optimum is obtained if the economy is perfectly competitive under perfect information, provided we ignore utility from liquidity services. However, if we take the utility of the services of real balances into account, the optimality of perfect competition disappears. This is because perfect competition guarantees only production efficiency and does not optimize the utility from the services of real balances.
31. Numerical analysis shows that this formula gives a relatively good approximation as long as $\sigma_m^2$ and $\sigma_u^2$ are not large compared with $\bar{\bar{Y}}^0$.
32. Note that we have $\partial^2(\partial\hat{E}Y/\partial p_u)/\partial\bar{p}_u^2 > 0$ around the optimal $p_u$, if $\omega > 0$. If $c_1$ and $k$ are not small (that is if $(c_1 + 2)(k - 1) > 1$), then $\omega > 0$.
33. Note that we have $\partial z/\partial\lambda < 0$ as long as $1 > (k - 1)\lambda$ (see (16)). It is straightforward to show that $\rho_\theta > \lambda^0$ and $1 > (k-1)\lambda^0$. We also have $1 > (k-1)\rho_\theta$, if $1+c_1 > [1 + c_1(k - 1)]\theta$. The latter condition is satisfied if $\sigma_u^2$ is significantly larger than $\sigma_m^2$ (a small $\theta$), which is likely in the real world (see Okun 1981). Thus, in most cases we are likely to have $z(\lambda^0) > z(\rho_\theta)$. The increased relative-price variability arising from imperfect information reduces the average consumption index in such cases.
34. This term is subtle and dependent on the specification of preference disturbances $U_i$ in the utility function and their distribution properties.
35. In 1980s, the ratio of the base money to the sum of the base money and nominal GNP was around 0.95 in the USA.
36. This corresponds to the labour-supply elasticity often found in empirical studies of labour supply which assume wage-taking workers (see e.g. Killingthworth 1983).
37. It is not always possible to satisfy all demand because of physical limits.
38. See, however, Newman (1978).

# 3
# Externality in Information Acquisition and the Non-Neutrality of Money

## 1. INTRODUCTION

The purpose of this chapter is to construct a macroeconomic model where it is not individually worthwhile for firms to obtain (costly) information about monetary disturbances, but where the economy as a whole would be better off if firms all paid for and obtained the information. The economy would benefit because firms that acquire the information would provide a positive externality to consumers, who dislike fluctuations in consumption and leisure, because their price adjustments stabilize output.

If firms acquire information about monetary disturbances, then their prices are perfectly flexible with respect to these disturbances. Therefore real balances, and thus output, are stabilized. Output stabilization increases the utility of consumers, because it reduces fluctuations in consumption and work hours. Consequently, there is a substantial social gain from acquiring the information. However, when a firm considers whether or not to acquire information, it does not take this social gain from acquiring the information into consideration. Real balances depend on the general price level, which is beyond the control of any one firm. Because the firm cannot influence real balances, it ignores the gain from stabilizing them in its calculation of the private gain from acquiring the information. Thus, there is an externality in acquiring information, which causes the private and social gains therefrom to diverge.

If a firm acquires information about monetary disturbances, it can reduce forecast errors about the general price level. Its profits then increase, because the possibility of suboptimal production caused by forecast errors has been reduced. This increase in profits is the private gain from acquiring information.

In this chapter I argue that the private gain from acquiring information about monetary disturbances may be small under predetermined wages in a monopolistically competitive macroeconomic model similar to Weitzman (1985) and Blanchard and Kiyotaki (1987). In order to illustrate the argument in the framework of predetermined prices and wages, I consider an economy with the perfectly competitive labour market where wages are predetermined before prices are determined. In addition, I assume real wages are predetermined (nominal wages are perfectly indexed to the price level) in the labour market, because in this case we obtain monetary neutrality if all firms acquire information. I show that, if consumers' utility functions are sufficiently concave in consumption and leisure, and if, in addition, firms' technology exhibits constant returns to scale, then the private gain from acquiring information about monetary disturbances is negligible, while the social gain is substantial. Thus, the externality in information acquisition is capable of inducing the non-neutrality of monetary disturbances in a monopolistically competitive economy, where money is otherwise neutral. I make the predetermined real-wage assumption for expository simplicity. Qualitatively, the same result can be obtained under the bilateral–monopoly labour market assumption (labour as a quasi-fixed factor) of Chapter 2, and also under the union-controlled predetermined nominal wage assumption of Chapter 4.

The private gain from acquiring information depends on the predictability of the price level, and on the loss arising from forecast errors. Imperfect and noisy information about monetary disturbances implies sticky prices, because the firm is aware of the possibility of confusing local, firm-specific shocks with global, macroeconomic shocks. These sticky prices in turn mean that the general price level is more predictable in this case than in the case of flexible prices. This reduces the private gain from acquiring information. Moreover, the loss arising from forecast errors is smaller under constant marginal costs than under increasing marginal costs: this further reduces private gain. In fact, it will be shown that under these assumptions the price level becomes constant (that is, completely rigid with respect to monetary disturbances) and perfectly predictable, even though firms do not acquire information about monetary disturbances. Thus, firms do not gain at all from acquiring information about monetary disturbances. In this case, a very small cost of acquiring the information is sufficient to prevent firms from doing so. Thus, firms rationally choose to be imperfectly informed about monetary disturbances.

On the other hand, the social gain from acquiring the information would be large. Imperfect information leads to rigid prices, which in turn implies large fluctuations in consumption and leisure, and consumers dislike such fluctuations. From the point of view of a social planner, the economy ends up in a situation where insufficient information is built into price formation.

The argument in this chapter is closely related to the 'small-menu-cost' approach to price rigidity (Mankiw 1985; Akerlof and Yellen 1985; Blanchard and Kiyotaki 1987). Just as it is possible to show that a small menu cost associated with price adjustment may lead to large output movements because of price stickiness, it can also be shown that a small cost of acquiring information may lead to large output fluctuations because of imperfect information. In both cases the argument hinges on an externality that derives a wedge between the private and social costs of changing prices (in the one case) and acquiring information (in the other).

The point made in this chapter is important for macroeconomics. A common criticism of Lucas (1973) and similar perfectly competitive models that are based on imperfect information about the money supply is that producers can obtain the information at fairly low costs; if the gains from doing so are large, they will obtain the information. The imperfect-information monopolistically competitive model of Chapter 2 could be criticized on the same grounds. However, the results of this chapter show that this need not be the case under monopolistic competition: the private gains from information acquisition may be small, but the positive external effect in the monopolistically competitive economy is large.

The information-acquisition externality is also capable of resolving another problem of the imperfect-information perfectly competitive models. These models have the property that only unanticipated monetary disturbances influence the real economy. However, many empirical results show that anticipated monetary shocks also affect output.[1] In addition, the imperfect-information perfectly competitive models cannot explain the persistence of output movement found in time-series data without additional assumptions, because unanticipated shocks are not autocorrelated. The results of this chapter show that monetary disturbances are not neutral, because economic agents do not acquire information about them. In this case, all monetary shocks are 'unanticipated', in the sense used in the rational expectations literature, even if information about them is made public. Monetary disturbances have persistent effects on the economy as long as they are autocorrelated.

This chapter proceeds as follows. In Section 2, the model is laid out. Section 3 contains the major result of this chapter; here the social gain from information acquisition and private gain are defined and calculated under the assumption of constant returns to scale. Section 4 concludes the chapter.

## 2. THE MODEL

The model in this chapter is a slight modification of the one in Chapter 2. It differs from that one first in the household's preferences, in which the household is more risk-averse, and second in the labour market, in which labour inputs are homogeneous and the real wage is predetermined.

The economy consists of one representative consumer and $n$ firms. Each firm produces a specific good that is an imperfect substitute for the other goods. Because products are differentiated, each firm has some monopoly power in product markets. Thus, product markets are monopolistically competitive. Firms use labour inputs supplied by the consumer, and pay wages and dividends to the consumer. Firms do not retain profits.

As for labour markets, we assume predetermined real wages. It is assumed that the real wage is predetermined through full indexation of the nominal wage to the price level, and that firms are given the right to determine employment. Suppose that the labour market is competitive, like in Fischer (1977*b*) and Gray (1976), but assume first that the labour market is opened before the realization of monetary and preference shocks, and second that the real wage is determined there (that is, the nominal wage determined in the labour market is, implicitly or explicitly, fully indexed to the price level[2]). This predetermined real-wage assumption is made because monetary disturbances are neutral under the predetermined real-wage assumption if all firms acquire information about monetary disturbances and are perfectly informed about them. Thus, any monetary non-neutrality found in this economy does not stem from nominal rigidity in the labour market.[3] (The argument developed in this chapter, that firms rationally choose to be imperfectly informed about monetary disturbances, holds true for the case of predetermined nominal wages, but in this case monetary disturbances are, in a trivial sense, not neutral.) The firm maximizes its real profits, taking the real wage as given.

At the beginning of the period, the real wage is determined and then nature determines the money supply and preference disturbances. Then, firms obtain imperfect information about them, and determine their prices simultaneously. After all prices are offered, the household determines its consumption plan and purchases products.

### 2.1. *The Representative Household*

The representative household derives utility from consumption, real-money balances, and leisure. Its utility function $\Psi$ is the following composite of the CES and Cobb–Douglas functions:

$$\Psi \equiv \frac{1}{1-z}\left[D(n\bar{Y})^{\zeta}\left(\frac{\tilde{M}}{\bar{P}}\right)^{1-\zeta}\right]^{1-z} - \left(\sum_{i=1}^{n} L_i\right)^{\mu} \tag{1}$$

where $D$ is a normalization factor, such that $D = \zeta^{-\zeta}(1-\zeta)^{-(1-\zeta)}$; $n$ is the number of goods (and the number of firms); $\bar{Y}$ is the average consumption index defined below; $\tilde{M}$ represents the end-of-period nominal money holdings; $\bar{P}$ is the price level; and $\zeta$ is a parameter that satisfies $0 < \zeta < 1$. Real balances $\tilde{M}/\bar{P}$ are in the utility function, because real balances yield liquidity services. $L_i$ is the labour supplied to the $i$th firm, and $\sum_{i=1}^{n} L_i$ gives the total work hours of the representative household, thus, $(\sum_{i=1}^{n} L_i)^{\mu}$ represents the disutility of labour. I assume that $\mu > 1$.

The term $z$ in (1) represents the degree of the household's 'consumption-risk aversion' with respect to the composite of the average consumption index and real balances, $D(n\bar{Y})^{\zeta}(\bar{M}/\bar{P})^{1-\zeta}$, which is hereafter called the consumption composite. If $z>0$, the household dislikes fluctuations in the consumption composite. I assume $z>1$, so that the household is sufficiently consumption-risk-averse. In fact, this assumption can be relaxed without changing the result: see Section 4.

The average consumption index $\bar{Y}$ is defined as follows:

$$\bar{Y} = \bar{Y}(\{Q_i\}:_{i=1,\ldots,n}) \equiv [(\sum_{i=1}^{n} U_i^{1/k} Q_i^{(k-1)/k})/n]^{k/(k-1)} \tag{2}$$

where $Q_i$ is the consumption of the $i$th product. The parameter $k$ satisfies $k>1$.

$U_i$ represents the product-specific preference disturbance. I assume that $U_i$ is a draw from a log-normal distribution; that is, log $U_i$ is a draw from a normal distribution with mean zero and variance $\sigma_u^2$.

$\bar{P}$ is defined as the price level function associated with the average consumption index function $\bar{Y}$:

$$\bar{P} = \bar{P}(\{P_i\}:_{i=1,\ldots,n}) \equiv [(\sum_{i=1}^{n} U_i P_i^{1-k})/n]^{1/(1-k)}, \tag{3}$$

where $P_i$ is the price of the $i$th product.

The household's demand for each product and the demand for real balances are derived from the maximization of $\Psi$ with respect to $Q_i$ and $\bar{M}/\bar{P}$, subject to the following budget constraint:

$$\sum_{i=1}^{n} P_i Q_i + \bar{M} = B, \tag{4}$$

where $B$ is the beginning-of-period asset of the household.

Let us now consider $B$. The household obtains money from the government as transfer payments, as well as wage payments and dividends from firms. I assume, first, that the predetermined real wage is the same for all firms, and second, that firms are given the right to determine employment. For notational simplicity, the real wage is assumed to be unity. Then,

$$B = \sum_{i=1}^{n} (\bar{P}L_i + \bar{P}\Pi_i) + M,$$

where $\bar{P}L_i$ is the nominal-wage payment (that is, $L_i$ is the real-wage payment) of the $i$th firm, and $\bar{P}\Pi_i$ is the nominal dividend (that is, $\Pi_i$ is the real dividend) from the $i$th firm. It is assumed that firms do not retain profits, so $\bar{P}\Pi_i$ is the nominal profit of the $i$th firm. The beginning-of-period money holdings are equal to the money supply, $M$.

The money supply is a random variable. I assume that $M$ is a draw from a log-normal distribution; that is log $M$ is a draw from a normal distribution with mean zero and variance $\sigma_m^2$. log $M$ and log $U_i$ are independent.

### 2.2. *Demand Functions and the Household's Utility in Equilibrium*

The household knows all prices when it determines its consumption plan. Using the property of the CES and Cobb–Douglas functions, we can derive the demand $Q_i$ for the $i$th product and the demand for real balances $\tilde{M}/\bar{P}$. They are

$$Q_i = \left(\frac{P_i}{\bar{P}}\right)^{-k} \bar{Y} U_i, \tag{5}$$

where

$$n\bar{Y} = \xi\,(B/\bar{P}), \text{ and } (\tilde{M}/\bar{P}) = (1-\xi)\,(B/\bar{P}).$$

In order for the economy to be in monetary equilibrium, the money demand must be equal to the money supply. Thus, the end-of-period money holdings should be equal to the beginning-of-period money holdings; that is,

$$\tilde{M} = M \tag{6}$$

should be satisfied. Because of (5) and (6), we obtain from the monetary equilibrium condition

$$\bar{Y} = H_1 \frac{M}{\bar{P}}, \tag{7}$$

where

$$H_1 = [\xi/(1-\xi)]/(1/n).$$

Thus, in equilibrium the average demand is proportional to initial real-money holdings.

Substituting demand functions (5) and (7) into (1), we obtain the household's utility in equilibrium, such that

$$\Psi \equiv \frac{1}{1-z}\left(\frac{B}{\bar{P}}\right)^{1-z} - (\sum_i L_i)^{\mu} = \frac{1}{1-z}\left(\frac{n}{\zeta}\bar{Y}\right)^{1-z} - (\sum_{i=1}^{n} L_i)^{\mu}, \tag{8}$$

where $L_i$ is determined by firms.

### 2.3. *The Firms' Payoff Function*

Firms are indexed by $i$, $i = 1, \ldots, n$. The demand for the $i$th firm's product, $Q_i$, is, from (5) and (7),

$$Q_i = \left(\frac{P_i}{\bar{P}}\right)^{-k} \bar{Y} U_i = H_1 \left(\frac{P_i}{\bar{P}}\right)^{-k} \left(\frac{A_i}{\bar{P}}\right). \tag{9}$$

where

$$A_i = MU_i.$$

In order to produce output $Q_i$, the $i$th firm needs labour inputs. I assume that

$$L_i = GQ_i^{1+c_1}, \tag{10}$$

where $L_i$ is labour input, and $c_1 \geqslant 0$. Thus, I assume non-increasing returns to scale. $G$ is a normalization factor, such that

$$G = \frac{k-1}{(1+c_1)k} \exp\left\{[1+c_1(k-1)]\, \hat{z}\left(\frac{c_1}{1-c_1 k}\right) \sigma_u^2\right\}, \tag{11}$$

where

$$z(x) = \frac{[1-(k-1)x]^2}{2(k-1)}. \tag{12}$$

This normalization simplifies the expression of the equilibrium price level derived later.

The $i$th firm's nominal profit $\bar{P}\Pi_i$ is

$$\bar{P}\,\Pi_i = P_i Q_i - \bar{P} L_i = P_i Q_i - \bar{P} G Q_i^{1+c_1}, \tag{13}$$

because the real wage is unity.

The $i$th firm maximizes the real profit. From (9) and (13), the firm's payoff function is

$$\Pi_i = \Pi(P_i, \bar{P}, A_i) \equiv H_1 \left(\frac{P_i}{\bar{P}}\right)^{1-k} \frac{A_i}{\bar{P}} - G\left[H_1 \left(\frac{P_i}{\bar{P}}\right)^{-k} \frac{A_i}{\bar{P}}\right]^{1+c_1}. \tag{14}$$

In this chapter, as in Chapter 2, I make the strong form of the monopolistically competitive assumption that the number of firms (and the number of goods), $n$, is so large that the dependence of the price index $\bar{P}$ ($\{P_i\}$) on a particular $P_i$ is negligible. This implies that, in determining its price, the firm ignores the dependence of $\bar{P}$ on its own price $P_i$. Thus, the firm takes $\bar{P}$ as given under this strong form of a monopolistically competitive assumption.

### 2.4. *The Incomplete-Information Game*

When the firm determines its price, it gets information about $M$ and $U_i$. Let $\Omega_i$ be the information that the firm receives. We consider two cases. In the first case there is no monetary information: the firm can observe $A_i = MU_i$, but $M$ and $U_i$ are not independently observed. In this case, $\Omega_i = \{A_i\}$. In the second case there is monetary information: the firm can observe both $M$ and $A_i$. Here, the firm can correctly infer $U_i$ using the relation $A_i = MU_i$. Thus, $\Omega_i = \{M, U_i\}$ in the second case.

The firm's strategy is its price, and depends on information $\Omega_i$. Under the monopolistically competitive assumption in the strong form, the Bayesian Nash equilibrium of the incomplete-information game is defined as the set of policy functions $\{\phi_i(\Omega_i)\}_{i=1,\ldots,n}$, such that, for all $i = 1, \ldots, n$, $M \in [0, \infty)$ and $U_i \in [0, \infty)$,

$$E\left\{\Pi\left[\phi_i(\Omega_i),\ \bar{P}(\{\phi_s(\Omega_s)\}), A_i\right] \mid \Omega_i\right\} \geqq$$

$$E\left\{\Pi\left[P_i,\ \bar{P}(\{\phi_s(\Omega_s)\}),\ A_i\right] \mid \Omega_i\right\}$$

is satisfied for all $P_i \in [0, \infty)$. Note that the price index $\bar{P}(\{P_s\}:_{s=1,\ldots,n})$ is defined in (3).

As in Chapter 2, we consider the symmetric equilibrium, and restrict our attention to the case of log-linear policy functions. Thus, in the case of no monetary information where $\Omega_i = \{A_i\}$, we assume $\phi_j(\Omega_i) = \phi_k(\Omega_i) = \phi(\Omega_i) \equiv \Theta A_i^{\rho}$, for all $j$ and $k$ and for some real numbers $\Theta$ and $\rho$; in the case of monetary information where $\Omega_i = \{M, U_i\}$, we assume $\phi_j(\Omega_i) = \phi_k(\Omega_i) = \phi(\Omega_i) \equiv \Phi\, M^{\delta} U_i^{\lambda}$, for all $j$ and $k$ and for some real numbers $\Phi$, $\delta$, and $\lambda$.

As in Chapter 2, the monopolistically competitive assumption in the strong form, together with the symmetric and log-linear policy assumptions, simplifies the expression of the price index.[4] Let us define the following price-index function:

$$\bar{P}^*(M, \Phi, \delta, \lambda) \equiv \Phi M^{\delta} \exp\left[-z(\lambda)\, \sigma_u^2\right]. \tag{15}$$

where $z(\lambda)$ is defined in (12). Then, the price level in the case of no monetary information is

$$\bar{P}(\{\phi(A_s)\}:_{s=1,\ldots,n}) = \bar{P}^*(M, \Theta, \rho, \rho), \tag{16}$$

while the price level in the case that monetary information is freely available is

$$\bar{P} = (\{\phi(M, U_s)\}:_{s=1,\ldots,n}) = \bar{P}^*(M, \Phi, \delta, \lambda). \tag{17}$$

### 2.5. *The Symmetric, Log-Linear Policy, Monopolistically Competitive Bayesian Nash Equilibrium*

Under the above assumptions, the symmetric Bayesian Nash equilibrium of the incomplete information game is defined as follows.

First, in the case of no monetary information, where $\Omega_i = \{A_i\}$, the symmetric Bayesian Nash equilibrium is a policy function $\phi\ (A_i) = \Theta A_i^{\rho}$ such that

$$E\left\{\Pi\left[\phi(A_i),\ \bar{P}^*\ (M,\Theta,\rho,\rho),A_i\right]|A_i\right\} =$$

$$\underset{P_i \in (0,\infty)}{Max}\ E\left\{\Pi\left[P_i,\bar{P}^*\ (M,\Theta,\rho,\rho),A_i\right]|A_i\right\} \tag{18}$$

for all $M \in [0, \infty)$, and $U_i \in [0, \infty)$, where $A_i = MU_i$, and $\Theta$ and $\rho$ are real numbers.

Second, there is the case that monetary information is freely available where $\Omega_i = \{M,\ U_i\}$. Note that under the assumptions made earlier there is no uncertainty about the real profit, because the firm can correctly infer $\bar{P}^*\ (M,\ \Phi,\ \delta,\ \lambda)$ since $M$ is observable. Thus, the symmetric Nash equilibrium is a policy function $\phi(M,\ U_i) = \Phi\ M^{\delta}U_i^{\lambda}$ such that

$$\Pi\left[\phi(M,U_i),\ \bar{P}^*\ (M,\Phi,\delta,\lambda),A_i\right] =$$

$$\underset{P_i \in (0,\infty]}{Max}\ \Pi\left[P_i,\bar{P}^*\ (M,\Phi,\delta,\lambda),A_i\right], \tag{19}$$

where $\Phi$, $\delta$, and $\lambda$ are real numbers.

## 3. CO-ORDINATED INFORMATION ACQUISITION VS. NON-CO-OPERATIVE INFORMATION ACQUISITION

### 3.1. *Costly Acquisition of Information about the Money Supply*

Suppose that monetary information is initially not available. Thus, firms play the incomplete-information game with no monetary information. Then an government agency announces the money supply $M$. However, assume that, in order to use this information, the firm has to pay the cost of information before nature chooses $M$ and $U_i$. The firm has to commit itself in advance to constantly monitoring the money-supply figure, in order to utilize the money-supply information. Assume that $F$ units of labour input are needed to monitor constantly the money supply. Because the real wage is assumed to be unity, $F$ is also the firm's real information cost in the form of the real-wage payment for the monitoring activities.

We compare the following two cases. The first case is co-ordinated information acquisition: in this case, all firms agree to incur the information cost $F$. The second case is non-co-operative information acquisition: here, information acquisition becomes a game. We consider the symmetric equilibrium of the following information-acquisition game. In the first stage, firms simultaneously determine whether to incur $F$ in order to monitor constantly the money supply. In the second stage, nature chooses $M$ and $U_i$. In the third stage, the $i$th firm observes $A_i$. If the firm incurred $F$ in the first stage, it obtains perfect information about $M$ in the third stage; thus, its information is $\Omega_i = \{M, U_i\}$. If it did not incur $F$ in the first stage, its information is $\Omega_i = A_i$ in the third stage. In the fourth stage, all firms simultaneously choose $P_i$.

### 3.2. *The Net Social Gain from Information Acquisition*

The net social gain from information acquisition is defined as the difference in the unconditional expected utility of the representative household under co-ordinated information acquisition and under no information acquisition. If all firms acquire information, we have $\Omega_i = \{M, U_i\}$ for all $i$. If no firm acquires information, we get $\Omega_i = A_i$ for all $i$. Thus, the net social gain (NSG) from information acquisition is, from (8),

$$\mathrm{NSG} = E_{M,U_i}\left[\frac{1}{1-z}\left(\frac{n}{\zeta}\bar{Y}\right)^{1-z} - \left(\sum_{i=1}^{n} L_i + nF\right)^{\mu}\right]\Bigg|_{\Omega_i = \{M, U_i\}:\forall_i}$$

$$- E_{M,U_i}\left[\frac{1}{1-z}\left(\frac{n}{\zeta}\bar{Y}\right)^{1-z} - \left(\sum_{i=1}^{n} L_i\right)^{\mu}\right]\Bigg|_{\Omega_i = A_i:\forall_i} \tag{20}$$

Here $E_{M,\ U_i}$ is the expectation operator with respect to the random variables $M$ and $U_i$. Thus, if NSG $> 0$, it is socially desirable to acquire information about the money supply.

### 3.3. *The Net Private Gain from Information Acquisition*

In order to acquire monetary information, the firm must use $F$ labour inputs in order to monitor constantly the movement of the money supply. Thus, the cost of information acquisition for the firm is the additional wage payment to these workers, which is equal to $F$.

The net private gain from information acquisition is defined as the difference between a given firm's unconditional expected payoff[5] in the case where *only* this firm incurs $F$ (and thus *only* this firm has perfect information about $M$) and its unconditional expected payoff when no firm incurs $F$ (and thus no firm knows $M$). Under the monopolistically competitive assumption in the strong firm, the price level does not depend on the given firm's price. Thus, the price level in both cases is the same as in the case of no monetary information. However, if the firm incurs $F$, it has perfect information about $M$ as well as about $A_i$. Thus, from (14), the net private gain (NPG) from information acquisition is

$$\begin{aligned} \text{NPG} &= (E_{M,U_i}\Pi|_{\Omega_i=[M,U_i],\Omega_j=A_j:j\neq i} - F) - E_{M,u_i}\Pi|_{\Omega_i=A_i:V_i} \\ &= \left( E_{M,U_i}\left\{ H_1\left(\frac{P_i}{\bar{P}}\right)^{1-k}\frac{A_i}{\bar{P}} - G\left[H_1\left(\frac{P_i}{\bar{P}}\right)^{-k}\frac{A_i}{\bar{P}}\right]^{1+c_1} - F\right\}\bigg|_{\Omega_i=[M,U_i],\Omega_j=A_j:j\neq i}\right) \\ &\quad - \left( E_{M,U_i}\left\{ H_1\left(\frac{P_i}{\bar{P}}\right)^{1-k}\frac{A_i}{\bar{P}} - G\left[H_1\left(\frac{P_i}{\bar{P}}\right)^{-k}\frac{A_i}{\bar{P}}\right]^{1+c_1}\right\}\bigg|_{\Omega_i=A_i:V_i}\right) \end{aligned} \tag{21}$$

If NPG $< 0$, then the given firm will choose not to incur the information cost $F$. In this case, the no-information-acquisition strategy is optimal for the firm, given that all other firms adopt it: that is, the no-information-acquisition strategy is a symmetric Nash equilibrium strategy of the information-acquisition game described earlier.

### 3.4. *Is a Small Information Cost Sufficient to Cause Insufficient Information Acquisition?*

We are concerned with the case in which the gross private gain from acquiring information, $E_{M,U_i}\Pi|_{\Omega_i=\{M,U_i\},\ \Omega_j=A_j:j\neq i} - E_{M,U_i}\Pi|_{\Omega_i=A_i}$, is very small, so that a very small cost $F$ of constantly monitoring the money supply is sufficient to prevent firms from incurring the information cost (NPG is negative), while, on the other hand, the net social gain from acquiring information (NSG) is substantial. In such an economy information is acquired in insufficient amounts.

In the following, I investigate whether a macroeconomic equilibrium is characterized by insufficient information acquisition under plausible conditions. My answer is affirmative. I show that, if the production technology of firms exhibits constant returns to scale, then the private gain is zero in the monopolistically competitive macroeconomic model of the previous section. Thus, a very small cost of monitoring the money supply is sufficient to prevent firms from acquiring the money-supply information. However, the resulting fluctuation in the average consumption index lowers the representative household's utility. Thus, acquiring the information would result in a large social gain.

### 3.5. *The Case of Constant Returns to Scale*

Suppose that the technology of firms exhibits constant returns to scale, so that $c_1 = 0$. In this case, from (14) we have

$$\Pi\,(P_i, \bar{P}, A_i) = H_1 \left(\frac{P_i}{\bar{P}}\right)^{1-k} \frac{A_i}{\bar{P}} - GH_1 \left(\frac{P_i}{\bar{P}}\right)^{-k} \frac{A_i}{\bar{P}}\,. \tag{22}$$

### 3.6. *The Net Social Gain from Information Acquisition under Constant Returns to Scale*

In order to calculate the net social gain, we must first find the Bayesian Nash equilibrium of the case where there is no monetary information and of that where monetary information is available.

In the first case, if technology is subject to constant returns to scale and there is no monetary information ($\Omega_i = A_i$), prices become completely rigid with respect to the monetary disturbance as well as to the product-specific disturbances. To see this, recall that the policy function has the form $P_i = \Theta A_i^{\rho}$. I shall show that $(\Theta, \rho) = (H_1, 0)$ is a Bayesian Nash equilibrium.

From (22), (16), and the equilibrium definition (18), we obtain the equilibrium condition such that

$$P_i = \frac{k}{k-1}\, G\, \frac{E\,\{\,[\bar{P}^*\,(M, \Theta, \rho, \rho)]^{k-1} | A_i\,\}}{E\,\{\,[\bar{P}^*\,(M, \Theta, \rho, \rho)]^{k-2} | A_i\,\}}\,. \tag{23}$$

Because $M$ is log-normally distributed, so is $\bar{P}^*\,(M, \Theta, \rho, \rho)$. Consequently, we obtain

$$P_i = \left(\frac{k}{k-1} G\right) E[\bar{P}^*(M, \Theta, \rho, \rho) | A_i]$$

$$\times \exp\left\{\frac{1}{2}\,[(k-1)^2 - (k-2)^2]\; V\,[\bar{P}^*\,(M, \Theta, \rho, \rho) | A_i]\right\}. \tag{24}$$

It is easy to show that $P_i = H_1$ satisfies the above expression, because we have $G = [(k-1)/k] \exp [z(0)\, \sigma_u^2]$ from (11) in the case of constant returns to scale ($c_1 = 0$), and $\bar{P}^* (M, H_1, 0, 0) = H_1 \exp [-z(0)\, \sigma_u^2]$ from (15).

The complete rigidity of the price index can be explained in the following way. The equilibrium condition (24) implies that the firm's optimal price should be exactly as elastic to the change in $M$ as the expected price conditional on $A_i$. However, this is not possible if $P_i$ is sensitive to $A_i$, that is, if $\rho > 0$. Because of the possibility of local–global confusion, a 1 per cent change in $A_i$ arising from the change in $M$ induces a change of less than 1 per cent in the expectation of $M$ conditional on $A_i = MU_i$. Consequently, if $\rho > 0$, a 1 per cent change in $M$ would induce a $\rho$ per cent change in $P_i$, but this would induce a change of less than $\rho$ per cent in the expected price index conditional on $A_i$, which violates the equilibrium condition. Thus, we have $\rho = 0$ in equilibrium.

Because prices are completely rigid in this equilibrium, the monetary disturbance is absorbed by the fluctuation in the average consumption index. From (7), we have

$$\bar{Y}|_{\Omega_i = A_i : V_i} = M \exp [z(0)\sigma_u^2] \tag{25}$$

in the case of no monetary information. The average consumption index fully reflects the change in the money supply.

In contrast to the above, if firms use monetary information ($\Omega_i = \{M, U_i\}$), prices become completely flexible with respect to the monetary distrubance, although they are rigid with respect to the product-specific disturbances. In this case, the policy function has the form $P_i = \Phi M^\delta U_i^\lambda$. From (22) and the equilibrium definition (19), we obtain the equilibrium condition such that

$$P_i = \frac{k}{k-1} G\bar{P}^* (M, \Phi, \delta, \lambda). \tag{26}$$

It is fairly straightforward to show that $\Phi = H_1$, $\delta = 1$, and $\lambda = 0$ satisfy the above equation, because $G = [(k-1)/k] \exp [z(0)\, \sigma_u^2]$ and $\bar{P} (M, H_1, 1, 0) = H_1 M \exp [-z(0)\, \sigma_u^2]$. Consequently, they constitute a Nash equilibrium.

Since prices are completely flexible with respect to the monetary disturbance, the average consumption index is insulated from the monetary disturbance. We have

$$\bar{Y}|_{\Omega_i = \{M, U_i\} : V_i} = \exp [z(0)\sigma_u^2]. \tag{27}$$

Let us now consider the utility of the representative household. I will analyse it in the following way. I first show that the representative household's utility $\Psi$ (ignoring the disutility $nF$ of the information-acquiring activities) depends solely on the log of the average consumption index, $\log \bar{Y}$. I then show that the household's utility is strictly concave in

$\log \bar{Y}$. Using (25) and (27), I show that $\log \bar{Y}$ in the case of no information acquisition is a mean-preserving spread of $\log \bar{Y}$ in the case of co-ordinated information acquisition. The representative household's utility (ignoring the disutility $nF$ of the information-acquiring activities) will be shown to be unambiguously higher in the case of co-ordinated information acquisition than in the case of no information acquisition. Thus, as long as $nF$ is small, there will be a substantial positive net social gain.

From (9) we have

$$L_i = GQ_i = G\left(\frac{P_i}{\bar{P}}\right)^{-k} \bar{Y} U_i$$

under constant returns to scale, and thus from (8), ignoring the disutility of the information-acquiring activities, we obtain

$$\Psi = \frac{1}{1-z}\left(\frac{n}{\zeta}\bar{Y}\right)^{1-z} - (\bar{Y})^{\mu}\left[G\sum_{i=1}^{n}\left(\frac{P_i}{\bar{P}}\right)^{-k} U_i\right]^{\mu}.$$

Note that we have $P_i/\bar{P} = \exp[z\ (0)\ \sigma_u^2]$ in the case of no monetary information, because $P_i = H_1$ is its Bayesian Nash equilibrium. Similarly, we have $P_i/\bar{P} = \exp[z\ (0)\ \sigma_u^2]$ in the case of monetary information, because $P_i = H_1 M$ is its Nash equilibrium. Consequently, we obtain

$$\Psi = \frac{1}{1-z}\left(\frac{n}{\zeta}\bar{Y}\right)^{1-z} - (\bar{Y})^{\mu} Z.$$

regardless of whether $\Omega_i = A_i$ for all $i$ or $\Omega_i = \{M, U_i\}$ for all $i$, where $Z$ is a constant such that

$$Z = (Gn)^{\mu} \exp[-\mu k z(0)\sigma_u^2]\left(\frac{1}{n}\sum_{i=1}^{n} U_i\right)^{\mu}$$

$$= (Gn)^{\mu} \exp\left\{\mu[-kz(0) + \tfrac{1}{2}]\ \sigma_u^2\right\}.$$

Here the law of large numbers is employed for $U_i$. Thus, we get the representative household's utility in the log form:

$$\Psi = \frac{1}{1-z}\exp\left[(1-z)\log\left(\frac{n}{\zeta}\right) + (1-z)\log\bar{Y}\right] - \exp[\mu\log\bar{Y}]Z. \quad (28)$$

From (28), the second derivative of $\Psi$ with respect to $\log \bar{Y}$ is

$$\delta^2\Psi/\partial(\log\bar{Y})^2 = (1-z)\exp\left[(1-z)\log\left(\frac{n}{\zeta}\right) + (1-z)\log\bar{Y}\right] - \mu^2\exp(\mu\log\bar{Y})Z$$

(29)

which is negative as long as $\mu > 1$ and $z > 1$. Thus, the representative household dislikes fluctuations in the log of the aggregate consumption index, $\log \bar{Y}$.

Note that $\log \bar{Y} = \log H_1 + \log M - \log \bar{P}$. On the one hand, because prices become completely sticky in the case where no firm acquires monetary information, we have $\log \bar{Y} = \log M + z(0)\ \sigma_u^2$ from (25), which makes for a fluctuating average consumption index. On the other hand, if all firms acquire monetary information, the price level is perfectly flexible with respect to the money supply, so that we get a completely stable average consumption index, $\log \bar{Y} = z\ (0)\ \sigma_u^2$, from (27). This implies that the average consumption index in the case of no information acquisition is a mean-preserving spread of the average consumption index in the case of co-ordinated information acquisition, because $E\ (\log M) = 0$, and $V\ (\log M) = \sigma_m^2$. Consequently, the representative household's utility (excluding the disutility of the information-acquiring activities) is higher in co-ordinated information acquisition than in no information acquisition. Thus, there is a positive net social gain from acquiring information through the stabilization of the average consumption index, as long as the disutility of information-acquiring activities is small.

### 3.7. *The Net Private Gain from Information Acquisition under Constant Returns to Scale*

Next, consider the net private gain from information acquisition under constant returns to scale. Recall that the net private gain is the difference between the firm's unconditional expected payoff in the case where *only* this firm incurs $F$ (and thus only this firm has perfect information about $M$) and the case where *no* firm incurs $F$ (and thus no firm knows $M$).

Under constant returns to scale, the firm's payoff, ignoring the cost of information acquisition, is, from (22) and (9),

$$\Pi\ (P_i, \bar{P}, \bar{Y} U_i) = \left[ \left( \frac{P_i}{\bar{P}} \right)^{1-k} - G \left( \frac{P_i}{\bar{P}} \right)^{-k} \right] \bar{Y} U_i.$$

Because under the monopolistically competitive assumption in the strong form the price level does not depend on the firm's price, the firm cannot influence the average demand $\bar{Y}$. Consequently, the private gain from acquiring information is the gain from reducing suboptimal production arising from forecast errors by improved forecasting of the price level. However, as explained earlier, if the other firms do not acquire information, the price level is constant and completely insensitive to the money supply. In this case the firm can correctly infer the price level even when it has no information about the money supply. Thus, even if the firm obtains information about the money supply, this information is redundant in estimating the price level. Therefore, information about the money supply is of no value to the firm if other firms do not also acquire it. Consequently, the private gain from acquiring information is zero under constant returns to scale.

### 3.8. *Insufficient Information Acquisition under Constant Returns to Scale*

Suppose that the variance of log $M$ is large, and that only a very small labour input $F$ is needed to acquire information about the money supply. Then, $nF$ in (20) is negligible. As shown by the foregoing argument, the net social gain is substantial in this case, so acquiring money supply information is socially desirable. However, because the private gain is zero, no information acquisition is a Nash equilibrium of the non-cooperative information-acquisition game. Consequently, the economy suffers from the insufficient information acquisition of firms.

## 4. CONCLUDING REMARKS

In this chapter we have shown that (1) if the representative household's utility function is sufficiently concave in consumption and leisure ($z > 1$ and $\mu > 1$), and (2) if firms' technology exhibits constant returns to scale ($c_1 = 0$), then the net private gain from acquiring information about monetary disturbances is negative, while the net social gain is substantial, in a monopolistically competitive economy where (3) real wages are predetermined (nominal wages are perfectly indexed to the price level) and firms determine their employment. In this economy, monetary disturbances have real effects on output, because firms choose not to acquire information about them. However, output fluctuations reduce social welfare.

The argument of this chapter depends on assumptions (1), (2), and (3) above. Let us briefly discuss the effect of relaxing these assumptions.

The assumption that $z > 1$ can be relaxed without changing the qualitative results of this chapter, as long as $\mu$ is sufficiently large. This is evident from (29), in which $\Psi$ is concave in log $\bar{Y}$ even when $z < 1$ as long as the second term dominates the first. A large $\mu$ implies a large absolute value of the second term.

The constant-returns-to-scale assumption can also be relaxed without changing the qualitative results, as long as the degree of decreasing returns to scale, $c_1$, is not large. The appendix of this chapter presents the Bayesian Nash equilibrium for the case of no monetary information and the case where monetary information is available. It is shown that the sensitivity of the price level to monetary disturbances is small in the case of no monetary information, provided $c_1$ is small. Then, by using the same argument as in the case of constant returns to scale, it can be shown that the private gain from information acquisition is small, while the social gain is substantial. (Because of the complexity of the equilibrium values of $\Theta$ and other variables, we have to resort to a numerical analysis in the case of $c_1 > 0$.) However, if $c_1$ is large, then the private gain becomes large.

Next, let us consider the assumption of predetermined real wages. This can be replaced by the assumption of predetermined nominal wages without changing the qualitative results of this chapter. Moreover, a qualitatively similar result is also obtained in the framework of short-run immobility of labour and efficient wage bargains, as in Chapter 2 (see Nishimura 1988*d*). As long as the marginal cost of production is nearly constant, the social gain is substantial, whereas the private gain is small.

However, if wages and prices are determined simultaneously, then the argument in this chapter may not hold true. This is because in this case wages convey information about monetary disturbances, which firms take into account in determining their prices.

The result obtained in this chapter has another implication for the rational expectations hypothesis. Empirical studies on expectations reveal a discrepancy between the economist's version of rational expectations and the actual expectations of the public. Many studies using survey data find that people do not seem to use all available information.

Figlewski and Wachtel (1981) examined the full set of individual responses in Livingston's survey on inflationary expectations, and found that the data were inconsistent with the hypothesis of rational expectations, as that concept is customarily defined.[6] Similar results were obtained by B. Friedman (1980) for the Goldsmith–Nagan survey of interest rates.[7] Lovell (1986) surveyed empirical studies on expectations about sales, inventories, prices, and wages, and concluded that commonly invoked rational expectations are inconsistent with his findings.[8]

This chapter suggests that, in an economy where acquiring and processing information involves cost, agents may rationally choose seemingly 'irrational' behaviour, in that they form their expectations without using all available information. Thus, the seemingly irrational expectations found in empirical studies may in fact be rational if the cost of acquiring and processing information is properly taken into account.

# Appendix: Equilibrium Characterization in the General Case

## A1. *The Case of No Monetary Information*

Let $P_i^{NM}$ be the solution of the right-hand side of (18). From (14) and (16) we obtain

$$(P_i^{NM})^{1+c_1 k} = \frac{(1+c_1)k}{k-1} \; GH_1^{c_1} A_i^{c_1} \; \frac{E\{[\bar{P}^*(M,\Theta,\rho,\rho)]^{(1+c_1)(k-1)} | A_i\}}{E\{[\bar{P}^*(M,\Theta,\rho,\rho)]^{(k-2)} | A_i\}}$$

$$= \frac{(1+c_1)k}{k-1} \; GH_1^{c_1} A_i^{c_1} \Theta^{1+c_1(k-1)} \exp\{-[1+c_1(k-1)]z(\rho)\sigma_u^2\} \times \frac{E[M^{(1+c_1)(k-1)\rho} | A_i]}{E[M^{(k-2)\rho} | A_i]}. \tag{A$_1$}$$

Note that under the assumption made in the text, the distribution of (log $M$, log $A_i$) is a multivariate normal distribution with mean (0, 0) and variance–covariance matrix $\Sigma$, such that

$$\Sigma = \begin{bmatrix} \sigma_m^2 & \sigma_m^2 \\ \sigma_m^2 & \sigma_m^2 + \sigma_u^2 \end{bmatrix}.$$

Consequently, the distribution of log $M$ conditional on log $A_i$, log $M|$ log $A_i$, is a normal distribution with $E[\log M|\log A_i]=\theta \log A_i$ and $V[\log M|\log A_i]=\theta\sigma_u^2$, where $\theta = \sigma_m^2/(\sigma_m^2 + \sigma_u^2)$. Therefore, we obtain

$$\frac{E[M^{(1+c_1)(k-1)\rho} | A_i]}{E[M^{(k-2)\rho} | A_i]} = A_i^{[1+c_1(k-1)]\rho\theta} \exp(\omega\rho^2\theta\sigma_u^2),$$

where

$$\omega = \tfrac{1}{2}[(1+c_1)^2(k-1)^2 - (k-2)^2].$$

From (18), $\Theta$ and $\rho$ must satisfy

$$\Theta A_i^{\rho} = P_i^{NM}. \tag{A$_2$}$$

Consequently, we obtain

$$(\Theta A_i^{\rho})^{1+c_1 k} = \frac{(1+c_1)k}{k-1} \; GH_1^{c_1} \Theta^{1+c_1(k-1)} A_i^{c_1 + [1+c_1(k-1)]\rho\theta} \times \exp\{\omega\rho^2\theta\sigma_u^2 - z(\rho)[1+c_1(k-1)]\sigma_u^2\}.$$

Collecting terms in the above expression, we obtain the equilibrium value of $\Theta$ and $\rho$. Because of (11), we have

$$\Theta = H_1 \exp\left\{\left(\frac{1}{c_1}\omega\rho^2\theta\sigma_u^2\right) - \frac{1+c_1(k-1)}{c_1}\left[z(\rho) - z\left(\frac{c_1}{1+c_1 k}\right)\right]\sigma_u^2\right\},$$

and

$$\rho = \frac{c_1}{1 + c_1 k - [1 + c_1(k-1)]\theta}.$$

A2. *The Case where Monetary Information is Freely Available*

Let $P_i^M$ be the solution of the maximization of the right-hand side of (19). From (14) and (17) we obtain

$$(P_i^M)^{1+c_1 k} = G \frac{(1+c_1)k}{k-1} H_1^{c_1} A_1^{c_1} [\bar{P}^*(M, \Phi, \delta, \lambda)]^{1+c_1(k-1)}. \tag{A3}$$

From (19), $\Phi$, $\delta$, and $\lambda$ must satisfy

$$\Phi M^{\delta} U_i^{\lambda} = P_i^M. \tag{A4}$$

We then have

$$\Phi = H_1;\ \delta = 1;\ \text{and}\ \lambda = \frac{c_1}{1 + c_1 k}.$$

# Notes

1. See e.g. Blanchard and Fischer (1989: Ch. 7) for a compact survey of the literature.
2. Alternatively, the labour union controls the labour market but for some reason must determine its real wage before monetary and preference disturbances are realized.
3. In addition, this assumption is a convenient short-cut for describing at least the non-unionized part of the US economy, where there is no systematic relationship between real wages and output and where firms determine employment. There is a sizeable literature about real-wage rigidity during a business cycle in the USA. In a recent example, Blanchard and Fischer (1989: Ch. 1) report very little correlation between economy-wide real wages and output.
4. Because the case of no monetary information is a special case of monetary information with the additional constraint $\delta = \lambda$ $(= \rho)$, I first derive the price index for the case where monetary information is available. The price index in the case of no monetary information is obtained in a similar way.

   Let $f(U)$ be the density function of the log-normal distribution from which $U_s$ $(s = 1, \ldots, n)$ is drawn. Because $n$ is large, the number of firms having $U$ is approximately $nf(U)$. Since $\phi(M, U_s) = \Phi M^{\delta} U_s^{\lambda}$, the log of the price index

$\bar{P}\ (\{\phi(M,\ U_s)\}:_{s\,=\,1,\,\ldots\,,\,n})$ is

$$\log\,[\bar{P}(\{\phi(M,U_s)\}:_{s\,=\,1,\,\ldots\,,\,n})] = \frac{1}{1-k}\log\left[\sum_{s=1}^{n} U_s\,(\Phi M^{\delta}\,U_s^{\lambda})^{1-k}\,\frac{1}{n}\right]$$

$$\approx \log\Phi + \delta\log M + \frac{1}{1-k}\log\left(\int_0^{\infty} U^{1+(1-k)\lambda}\,f(U)\,dU\right)$$

$$= \log\Phi + \delta\log M - z(\lambda)\,\sigma_u^2$$

Here the property of the log-normal distribution is utilized.

5. Because all firms are symmetric, the unconditional payoff is the same for all firms.
6. See also Pesando (1975). Caskey (1985) suggested that these seemingly irrational expectations may be interpreted as an adaptive learning process from incorrect prior distributions. If these expectations are in fact involved in a learning process, and if they converge to rational expectations rather rapidly, then for practical purposes they can be considered to be rational. However, convergence is not always guaranteed. For more details about learning and rational expectations, see Cyert and DeGroot (1974), Frydman and Phelps (1983), Townsend (1978, 1983), Bray and Savin (1986), and Fourgeaud *et al.* (1986).
7. There are, however, some strong objections to interpreting the survey data as being the actual expectations of the market: see Mishkin (1981).
8. Other evidence is found in the studies of expectations in experimental economics. See Williams (1987) for a survey of the literature.

# 4

# Indexation and Imperfect Insulation from Nominal Disturbances

## 1. INTRODUCTION

In the previous two chapters, we examined the macroeconomic consequences of product-market monopolistic competition under imperfect information. This chapter investigates the macroeconomic implications of labour-market monopolistic competition under imperfect information. Following the literature of labour contracts and indexation (see Fischer 1977b and Gray 1976), I assume labour contracts with predetermined nominal wages and a cost-of-living adjustment. These 'long-run' wage contracts are often observed in industrialized economies and are rationalized by the existence of substantial negotiation costs.

In this chapter I shall analyse the effects of wage indexation. They are very different under monopolistic competition than under perfect competition. Full indexation completely insulates the economy from nominal shocks if labour markets are perfectly competitive (see Fischer 1977*b* and Gray 1976).[1] However, under monopolistic competition full indexation does not insulate the economy from nominal shocks at all. Complete insulation is achieved by less than full indexation. Under monopolistic competition in labour markets, full indexation causes price uncertainty to reduce the unconditional mean of output, whereas under perfect competition, full indexation renders the output level independent of price uncertainty. Moreover, these characteristics of labour-market monopolistic competition do not depend on the degree of competition among labour unions. Thus, the economy with monopolistically competitive labour markets does not converge to the economy with perfectly competitive labour markets, even if the competition in labour markets is very strong.

This chapter is organized as follows. A macroeconomic model with differentiated products and differentiated labour is presented in Section 2. (A choice-theoretic microfoundation of the model is given in the Appendix to this chapter.) In order to concentrate on labour markets, I assume product markets to be perfectly competitive under perfect information. By contrast, labour markets are monopolistically competitive under imperfect information. One labour union controls one type of labour input and determines its wage rate. Labour markets are subject to imperfect information because of the nature of the assumed labour contracts. The general solution to the union's decision problem and the resulting labour-market equilibrium are described in this section.

In Sections 3–5, I consider such special issues as the implications of full indexation, the degree of indexation that insulates the economy from nominal shocks, and the effects of price uncertainty on output under indexation. In Section 3, it is shown that full indexation does not insulate an economy that has monopolistically competitive unions from nominal shocks, although it completely insulates an economy having perfectly competitive labour markets. Moreover, under full indexation the monopolistically competitive economy has a *negative* correlation between money and output.

The rate of cost-of-living adjustment that insulates the monopolistically competitive economy is derived in Section 4. The rate is less than unity and depends on the convexity of preferences and technology. If the elasticity of the marginal cost of production and that of the marginal disutility of labour are large, then complete insulation is achieved by a small rate of cost-of-living adjustment. I also show that the monopolistically competitive economy has a positive money–output correlation only if the actual rate is smaller than the rate that provides complete insulation.

In Section 5, I investigate the effect of price uncertainty on the unconditional mean of output (this may be considered as the normal level of output) under monopolistic competition. In an economy with monopolistically competitive labour unions, if the actual rate of cost-of-living adjustment is smaller than the rate that provides complete insulation, price uncertainty decreases wages, and thus increases the unconditional mean of output; otherwise, price uncertainty increases wages and decreases the unconditional mean of output. These results are compared with those obtained for perfectly competitive labour markets.

In Section 6 I consider alternative specifications of monopolistically competitive unions. The objective function of the unions in Sections 3–5 is derived from a specific assumption about the preferences of consumers and workers; in this section I investigate whether the results of Sections 3–5 are dependent on this particular assumption. I analyse two types of union behaviour which are commonly assumed in the literature. It is shown that the results of Sections 3–5 still hold under these more conventional specifications.

Section 7 concludes this chapter with some remarks about its implications for wage rigidity in business-cycle theory.

## 2. MACROECONOMIC MODEL WITH MONOPOLISTICALLY COMPETITIVE UNIONS

Consider an economy with differentiated products and differentiated labour. The model is based on Blanchard and Kiyotaki (1987). I incorporate disturbancces in product demand, labour supply, and production technology into their model. In the following I analyse the reduced-form model based on product- and labour-demand functions. The explicit analysis of its microfoundation is relegated to the appendix of this chapter.

Throughout this chapter, I assume perfect competition and perfect information in product markets. By contrast, labout markets are monopolistically competitive under imperfect information. Following Fischer (1977*b*), I assume (1) that labour markets open before product markets; (2) that wage contracts are signed in these labour markets, and (3) that employment is determined by firms after product markets open.[2] We assume that one union controls one type of labour input and determines its wage rate. In the following analysis, all variables are in logarithms if not otherwise stated. (Thus, for example, the average price in this section is the log of the geometric average price.)

### 2.1. *Wage Contracts*

I assume that the following wage contracts, which include a cost-of-living adjustment, are signed in the labour markets:

$$w = f + t\bar{p}, \tag{1}$$

where $w$ is the *ex post* wage of individual labour, $f$ is its base wage, $\bar{p}$ is the average price, and $t$ is the exogenous cost-of-living adjustment parameter, satisfying $1 \geqslant t \geqslant 0$. The union determines the base wage $f$. The degree of indexation, $t$, is assumed to have been determined in the past. Then the average *ex post* wage $\bar{w}$ is given by

$$\bar{w} = \bar{f} + t\bar{p}, \tag{2}$$

where $\bar{f}$ is the average base wage.

### 2.2. *Product Markets*

The demand for individual products is given by

$$q = -\,k\,(p - \bar{p}) + \bar{y} + u, \tag{3}$$

where $k > 1$ is the own-price elasticity of product demand, $p$ is the product's price, $\bar{y}$ is the average product demand, and $u$ is the product-specific demand disturbance.

The average product demand is[3]

$$\bar{y} = m - \bar{p}, \tag{4}$$

where $m$ is the economy-wide nominal money-supply disturbance. The disturbances $m$ and $u$ are assumed to be normally distributed, satisfying $Em = Eu = Emu = 0$, $Em^2 = \sigma_m^2$, and $Eu^2 = \sigma_u^2$. I assume perfect information in product markets, so that both $m$ and $u$ are observable.

The firm employs all types of labour in order to produce one type of product. The labour cost to the individual firm is given by

$$c = \bar{w} + l \tag{5}$$

where

$$l = -\log(c_1 + 1) + (c_1 + 1)q.$$

Here $\bar{w}$ is the average wage determined in (2), and $l$ is the labour-input index of the firm. The term $c_1$ is the elasticity of the labour-input index to output. I assume $c_1 > 0$, which implies decreasing returns to scale. The term $-\log\ (c_1+1)$ is a convenient normalization factor.

The firm's real profit is

$$\exp\ (\pi) = \exp\,(-\,\bar{p})\,[\exp\ (p)\ \exp\ (q) - \exp\ (c)]. \tag{6}$$

The firm maximizes (6) with respect to $q$, subject to (5) and (1). This determines the supply of products, $q^s$. It is straightforward to show from the first-order condition of optimality that the supply is given by

$$q^s = \frac{1}{c_1}(p - \bar{w}) = \frac{1}{c_1}(p - t\bar{p} - \bar{f}). \tag{7}$$

From $q = q^s$, the equilibrium price is

$$p = (1+c_1k)^{-1}\ \{[t + c_1(k-1)]\ \bar{p} + \bar{f} + c_1m + c_1u\}. \tag{8}$$

Consequently, the average price is

$$\bar{p} = \frac{\bar{f}}{1 - t + c_1} + \delta^* m \tag{9}$$

where

$$\delta^* = \frac{c_1}{(1 - t + c_1)}.$$

## 2.3. *Labour Markets*

The demand for an individual labour input has the form

$$n = -\ r(w - \bar{w}) + (\bar{n} + v), \tag{10}$$

where $r$ is the own-wage elasticity of labour demand, satisfying $r > 1$; $\bar{n}$ is the average labour demand; and $v$ is the type-specific labour-demand disturbance. The disturbance $v$ stems from productivity disturbances in the production function. The composite $(\bar{n} + v)$ in (10) is the individual real-labour-demand condition, which determines the location of the individual labour-demand curve.

The average labour demand $\bar{n}$ is given by[4]

$$\bar{n} = -\log\ (c_1 + 1) + (c_1 + 1)\ \bar{y}. \tag{11}$$

Thus, we have the following individual labour demand:

$$n = -\ r(w - \bar{w}) - \log\ (c_1 + 1) + (c_1 + 1)\ (m - \bar{p}) + v. \tag{12}$$

A worker supplying one type of labour has the following objective function:

$$\exp\ (\psi) = \exp\ (w - \bar{p})\ \exp\ (n) - \exp\ (z). \tag{13}$$

Here, $z$ represents the disutility of labour such that

$$z = -\log (z_1 + 1) + (z_1 + 1)\, n + \beta, \tag{14}$$

where $z_1$ is the elasticity of the marginal disutility of labour. Here we assume that $z_1 > 0$, which implies increasing marginal disutility. The term $-\log (z_1 + 1)$ is a normalization factor. The term $\beta$ is the individual labour-supply disturbance, which consists of the economy-wide labour-supply disturbance, $s$, and the labour-input-specific supply disturbance, $x$. We have

$$\beta = s + x. \tag{15}$$

The random variables $v$, $s$, and $x$, together with $m$, are assumed to have the following characteristics: random variables $v$, $s$, and $x$ are normally distributed, satisfying $Ev = Es = Ex = Emv = Esx = Ems = Emx = Evx = Esv = 0$; $Ev^2 = \sigma_v^2$; $Es^2 = \sigma_s^2$; and $Ex^2 = \sigma_x^2$. I assume that $\sigma_s^2$ is sufficiently large compared with $\sigma_m^2$.[5]

## 2.4. *The Union's Decision Problem*

I assume that the union's objective function is the same as that of its workers. Thus, the union maximizes $\hat{E}\{\exp(\psi)\}$ with respect to $f$, where $\hat{E}$ is the expectation operator with respect to the union's subjective distribution of $\bar{p}$. The union is endowed with rational expectations. It assumes that $\bar{p}$ is normally distributed with mean $e(\bar{p}|\Omega_u)$ and variance $V(\bar{p}|\Omega_u)$, where $e(\bar{p}|\Omega_u)$ is the linear least-squares regression of $\bar{p}$ on the information $\Omega_u$ available to the union, and $V(\bar{p}|\Omega_u)$ is its error variance.

Let us now consider the union's information set $\Omega_u$ at the time it determines its base wage. I assume that the union can observe the average base wage $\bar{f}$. In addition, the union is assumed to know the individual labour-supply disturbance $\beta$. However, I assume that the union has only imperfect knowledge about the individual real-labour condition $(\bar{n} + v)$ in (10). I also assume that the following individual *nominal*-labour-demand disturbance $\xi$ is observed by the union:[6]

$$\xi = (c_1 + 1)m + v. \tag{16}$$

Although $\beta$ and $\xi$ are observed, the union cannot observe $s$, $x$, $m$, and $v$ independently. Thus, $\Omega_u$ includes $\beta$, $\xi$, and $\bar{f}$.

The optimal base-wage formula derived from the first-order condition is

$$f = \frac{z_1 r}{1 + z_1 r}\left(\bar{f} + \frac{\hat{a}_u + \beta + z_1\,\xi}{z_1 r}\right) + \left(1 - \frac{z_1 r}{1 + z_1 r}\right)[1 - t - z_1(c_1 + 1)]\,e(\bar{p}|\Omega_u), \tag{17}$$

where

$$\hat{a}_u = a_l^* + \log\frac{r}{r-1} - \frac{1}{2}[1 - t - z_1(c_1 + 1)] \times [(z_1 + 2)(c_1 + 1) + (1 - t)]\,V(\bar{p}|\Omega_u), \tag{18}$$

in which

$$a^*_l = -z_1 \log (c_1+1). \tag{19}$$

The above optimal base-wage formula implies that, if $1 - t - z_1(c_1 + 1) > 0$, then the base wage goes up when $e(\bar{p}|\Omega_u)$ is increased; otherwise, an increase in the expected price lowers the base wage. Because we have

$$z_1\xi - z_1(c_1+1)e(\bar{p}|\Omega_u) = z_1(c_1+1)e(m-\bar{p}|\Omega_u) + z_1 e(v|\Omega_u).$$

(17) can be rewritten as

$$f = \frac{z_1 r}{1+z_1 r}\left(\bar{f} + \frac{\hat{a}_u+\beta}{z_1 r}\right) + \left(1 - \frac{z_1 r}{1+z_1 r}\right)[(1-t)e(\bar{p}|\Omega_u) + z_1(c_1+1)e(m-\bar{p}|\Omega_u) + z_1 e(v|\Omega_u)]. \tag{20}$$

On the one hand, because the real wage is proportional to the reciprocal of the average price, its increase clearly puts upward pressure on the base wage for a given level of employment. This effect is represented by the first term in the square brackets in (20). On the other hand, an increase in the average price implies a decrease in aggregate demand through a reduction in real balances, so that the base wage must be cut in order to maintain employment. The second term in the brackets in (20) shows this effect. The relative magnitudes of these conflicting forces determine whether or not an increase in the expected price raises the base wage.

If the marginal disutility of labour increases rapidly as output increases (if $z_1(c_1+1)$ is large), the union gives the highest priority to employment stability. The incentive to reduce the base wage then dominates the incentive to increase it. Thus, an increase in $e(\bar{p}|\Omega_u)$ decreases the base wage. In this case the union is more concerned with the level of employment than with the base wage (i.e., it is an employment-concerned union). By contrast, if $z_1(c_1 + 1)$ is small the union puts more weight on the base wage than on employment (i.e., it is a base-wage-concerned union).

In addition to $z_1$ and $c_1$, the degree of indexation ($t$) also determines whether the union is employment-concerned or base-wage-concerned. If $t$ is increased, pressure on the base wage to maintain the real wage is decreased. The union then has more leeway in maintaining the level of employment. Thus, the overall effect depends on the sign of $1 - t - z_1(c_1 + 1)$. If this is positive, then the union is base-wage-concerned; otherwise, it is employment-concerned. Note that, in the case of full indexation ($t = 1$), the union is unambiguously employment-concerned.

Using the above structure of the economy and the information contained in $\xi$ in (16), the union can calculate $e(\bar{p}|\Omega_u)$ from (9):

$$e(\bar{p}\,|\,\Omega_u) = \frac{\bar{f}}{1-t+c_1} + \delta^*\phi\xi, \tag{21}$$

where

$$\phi = (c_1+1)\sigma_m^2/[(c_1+1)^2\sigma_m^2+\sigma_v^2]. \tag{22}$$

We then obtain the following average-price and quantity equations for the economy:

$$\bar{p} = \Xi\,(\hat{a}_u) + \Upsilon_u(t)m + \Theta s;$$
$$\bar{y} = -\Xi(\hat{a}_u) + [1-\Upsilon_u(t)]m - \Theta s, \tag{23}$$

where

$$\Xi\,(\hat{a}_u) = \frac{\hat{a}_u}{c_1+z_1+c_1z_1}, \tag{24}$$

$$\Upsilon_u(t) = 1 - \frac{[1-t-z_1(c_1+1)]\,[1-\phi(c_1+1)]c_1}{(1-t+c_1)\,(c_1+z_1+c_1z_1)}, \tag{25}$$

and

$$\Theta = \frac{1}{c_1+z_1+c_1z_1}. \tag{26}$$

## 2.5 *Monopolistic Competition and Perfect Competition*

It may be worthwhile at this point to compare monopolistically and perfectly competitive labour markets. Because of the predetermined wage, $\bar{p}$ cannot be observed by workers in perfectly competitive labour markets. However, except for $\bar{p}$, information is perfect. The worker can observe $\beta$, $f$, and $\bar{f}$, and these are thus included in the worker's information set $\Omega_w$.

The worker maximizes $\hat{E}\{\exp(\psi)\}$ with respect to $n$ (see (13)), where $\hat{E}$ is the expectation operator with respect to the worker's subjective distribution of $\bar{p}$. The worker is also endowed with rational expectations. He assumes that $\bar{p}$ is normally distributed with mean $e(\bar{p}|\Omega_w)$ and variance $V(\bar{p}|\Omega_w)$.

From the first-order condition of optimality, competitive labour supply is given by

$$n^s = \frac{1}{z_1}\left[f-(1-t)\,e(\bar{p}\,|\,\Omega_w) + \frac{1}{2}\,(1-t)^2V(\bar{p}\,|\,\Omega_w) - \beta\right]. \tag{27}$$

This shows that the labour supply depends on the expected real wage $e(w - \bar{p}|\Omega_w) = f - (1 - t)e(\bar{p}|\Omega_w)$. Thus, an increase in the expected price always reduces the labour supply. From $n = n^s$, the equilibrium base wage in a local labour market is

$$f = \frac{z_1 r}{1 + z_1 r}\left(\bar{f} + \frac{\hat{a}_w + \beta}{z_1 r}\right)$$
$$+ \left(1 - \frac{z_1 r}{1 + z_1 r}\right)[(1-t)e(\bar{p}|\Omega_w) + z_1(c_1+1)(m-\bar{p}) + z_1 v], \quad (28)$$

where

$$\hat{a}_w = a_l^* - \frac{1}{2}(t-1)^2 V(\bar{p}|\Omega_w). \quad (29)$$

Consequently, an increase in the worker's expected price unambiguously increases the base wage in the perfectly competitive case.

The average-price and quantity equations under perfect competition are:

$$\bar{p} = \Xi(\hat{a}_w) + \Upsilon_w(t)m + \Theta s;$$
$$\bar{y} = -\Xi(\hat{a}_w) + [1 - \Upsilon_w(t)]\, m - \Theta s, \quad (30)$$

where

$$\Upsilon_w(t) = 1 - \frac{(1-t)c_1[1 - t + c_1 - (1-t)\,\theta\, z_1\,(c_1+1)]}{(1-t+c_1)^2\,(c_1 + z_1 + c_1 z_1)}, \quad (31)$$

in which

$$\theta = \frac{z_1\,(c_1+1)\,(1-\delta^*)\,\sigma_m^2}{[z_1(c_1+1)\,(1-\delta^*)]^2\sigma_m^2 + z_1^2\sigma_v^2}.$$

Under perfect competition the worker considers only the real wage, whereas the union is concerned about the position of the 'local' labour-demand curve as well as the real wage. Because an increase in the expected price lowers the expected real wage, the perfectly competitive worker reduces his labour supply. Thus, the perfectly competitive equilibrium base wage increases if the expected price increases.

An increase in the expected price, however, reduces the expected aggregate demand through the real-balance effect. Since aggregate demand is a major component of local labour demand, the union must take into account this demand-reducing effect of an increase in the general price level, in addition to its effect on the real wage. Thus, the overall effect of an increase in the expected price on the equilibrium base wage is ambiguous under monopolistic competition, depending on the relative magnitudes of the real-wage effect and the local labour-demand effect.

Using the results obtained in this section, I shall consider three special issues in the following sections. Section 3 analyses the implications of full indexation. Section 4 derives the degree of indexation which insulates the economy from nominal shocks. Section 5 explains the interrelationship between the degree of indexation and the effect of price uncertainty on the unconditional mean of output.

## 3. DOES FULL INDEXATION INSULATE THE ECONOMY FROM NOMINAL DISTURBANCES?

In this section I analyse the case of full indexation ($t = 1$). I shall show that in a monopolistically competitive economy the monetary disturbance affects real variables even under full indexation, while full indexation completely insulates a perfectly competitive economy. The main reason for the difference between the two cases is that under monopolistic competition the union is concerned about the position of local labour demand as well as the real wage, and hence forms expectations about the local shock as well as the aggregate nominal shock (general price level); on the other hand, under perfect competition the worker considers only the real wage and forms expectations only about the general price level. Full indexation makes the real wage and aggregate demand independent of the nominal shock. Thus, full indexation insulates the perfectly competitive economy. By contrast, in the monopolistically competitive economy, the union must still infer the local shock. Because the available information $\xi$ (in (16) ) does not give the union perfect information about $v$, there is the possibility of local–global confusion. This leads to imperfect insulation under full indexation.

Under full indexation, the average price and the demand for labour are, respectively,

$$\bar{p} = \frac{\bar{f}}{c_1} + m;$$

$$n = -r(f-\bar{f}) - \log(c_1+1) - \left(1+\frac{1}{c_1}\right)\bar{f} + v. \qquad (32)$$

Let us first consider perfectly competitive labour markets. Under full indexation, the worker's objective function is simply

$$\exp(\psi) = \exp(f+n) - \exp[-\log(z_1+1)+(z_1+1)n+\beta]. \qquad (33)$$

Thus, full indexation eliminates uncertainty. Then, from (28), the equilibrium base wage is

$$f = (1+z_1 r)^{-1}\left[a^*_l + z_1\left(r - \frac{c_1+1}{c_1}\right)\bar{f} + z_1 v + \beta\right]. \qquad (34)$$

Consequently, from (30), the average base wage and the average output are

$$\bar{f} = \left[1+\frac{z_1(c_1+1)}{c_1}\right]^{-1}(a_l^*+s);$$

$$\bar{p} = \Xi\,(a_l^*)+m+\Theta s. \qquad (35)$$

Thus, full indexation makes the average base wage independent of $m$. Because the average price is completely flexible with respect to $m$ for a given $\bar{f}$, full indexation insulates the economy from the monetary disturbance.

In the monopolistically competitive case, the union's objective function under full indexation is

$$\exp(\psi) = \exp\left[f-r(f-\bar{f})-\log(c_1+1)-\left(1+\frac{1}{c_1}\right)\bar{f}+v\right]$$
$$-\exp\left\{-\log(z_1+1)\right.$$
$$\left.+(z_1+1)\left[-r(f-\bar{f})-\log(c_1+1)-\left(1+\frac{1}{c_1}\right)\bar{f}+v\right]+\beta\right\}. \qquad (36)$$

This shows that, although full indexation eliminates uncertainty about the real wage and aggregate demand, uncertainty about the local shock $v$ remains. The local shock $v$ must be inferred from $\xi$.

The optimal base wage is, from (20),

$$f = (1+z_1 r)^{-1}\left[\hat{a}_u+z_1\left(r-\frac{c_1+1}{c_1}\right)\bar{f}+z_1 e(v\,|\,\Omega_u)+\beta\right], \qquad (37)$$

where

$$\hat{a}_u = a_l^* + \log\frac{r}{r-1} + \frac{1}{2}\left[(z_1+1)^2-1\right]V(v\,|\,\Omega_u).$$

Because $e(v\,|\,\Omega_u) = [1-(c_1+1)\phi]\xi$, we obtain

$$\bar{f} = \left[1+\frac{z_1(c_1+1)}{c_1}\right]^{-1}\{\hat{a}_u+z_1[1-(c_1+1)\phi](1+c_1)m+s\}. \qquad (38)$$

Thus, under full indexation, the average base wage is no longer independent of $m$. It increases if $m$ increases.

The dependence of $\bar{f}$ on $m$ stems from local–global confusion in the monopolistically competitive union. Unlike the worker in a perfectly competitive labour market, the monopolistically competitive union must form expectations about the local condition $v$ relying on $\xi$. Because an increase in $\xi$ is accompanied by an increase in $m$ on average, an increase in

$m$ raises the average forecast of $v$. Consequently, the average wage $\bar{f}$ increases when $m$ increases; the average wage $\bar{f}$ and the money supply $m$ are positively correlated.

The dependence of the base wage on the monetary disturbance implies that the economy is imperfectly insulated from it. From (23), we obtain

$$\bar{p} = \Xi\,(\hat{a}_u) + \left(1 + \frac{z_1(1+c_1)\,[1-(c_1+1)\phi]}{c_1+z_1+c_1 z_1}\right)m + \Theta s. \qquad (39)$$

Thus, the monetary disturbance affects output under full indexation in an economy with monopolistically competitive unions.

The direction of the monetary effect, however, is different from that in other models of non-neutral money. We obtain a negative money–output correlation instead of a positive one. Because of perfect competition and perfect information in product markets, the average price is perfectly flexible with relation to the monetary disturbance for a given $\bar{f}$. (The coefficient of $m$ in (32) is unity.) Then the positive correlation between $\bar{f}$. and $m$ explained earlier makes the average price excessively sensitive to $m$. (The coefficient of $m$ in (39) is larger than unity.) Thus, local-global confusion under full indexation produces a negative money–output correlation.

## 4. COMPLETE INSULATION

In this and the following sections, I investigate the effect of money on real variables under the general wage contract (1). In this section I derive the rate of cost-of-living adjustment, $t^*$, that insulates the economy from nominal disturbances. In the next section I analyse the effect of price uncertainty on the unconditional mean of real variables.

It is straightforward to show that the level of output is independent of $m$ if

$$t = t^* \equiv 1 - z_1(1 + c_1), \qquad (40)$$

because $Y_u(t^*) = 1$. from (25). Thus, $t^*$ is the rate of cost-of-living adjustment that completely insulates the economy from the monetary disturbance.

Although $\xi$ is always observable, it does not give the union perfect information about shocks ($m$ and $v$). Since $m$ and $v$ influence the base wage (and hence the average price) in different ways, the observable $\xi$ provides the union with only partial information about the average price. This is essential for the results in Section 3. Complete insulation, however, is ensured by the choice of an indexation parameter which makes the local wage independent of the average price. In this way, imperfect information about $m$ and $v$ does not preclude insulation from the nominal shock. Thus, if $t = t^*$, we have $1 - t - z_1(1 + c_1) = 0$, which makes the optimal base wage independent of $e(\bar{p}|\Omega_u)$ (see (17) ). Then (20) shows that the base wage depends on $z_1(c_1 + 1)e(m|\Omega_u) + z_1 e(c|\Omega_u)$. However, we have

$$\begin{aligned} &z_1(c_1 + 1)e(m|\Omega_u) + z_1 e\,(v|\Omega_u) \\ &= z_1 e\,[(c_1 + 1)\,m + v|\Omega_u] \\ &= z_1 e\,(\xi|\Omega_u) = z_1\xi. \end{aligned}$$

Here imperfect information about $m$ and $u$ is of no consequence, because $m$ and $u$ influence the base wage only through the observable $\xi$.

Because $z_1 > 0$ and $c_1 > 0$, $t^*$ is always smaller than unity. Thus, complete insulation requires less than full cost-of-living adjustment. Moreover, if $z_1$ and $c_1$ are large, $t^*$ is small. In the extreme case, if $z_1\,(1 + c_1) > 1$, $t^*$ is negative. In this case, complete insulation requires a *negative* rate of cost-of-living adjustment.

The sign of the correlation between money and output depends on whether $t$ is greater or smaller than $t^*$. The reason for this can be explained by comparing the cases of imperfect and perfect information in labour markets.

If information is perfect in labour markets, money is neutral. Under perfect information, the individual base wage is

$$f = \frac{z_1 r}{1 + z_1 r}\left(\bar{f} + \frac{\hat{a}^*_u + \beta + z_1\xi}{z_1 r}\right) + \left(1 - \frac{z_1 r}{1 + z_1 r}\right)[1 - t - z_1(c_1 + 1)]\bar{p}, \quad (41)$$

where

$$\hat{a}^*_u = a^*_l + \log\,[r/(r-1)]. \quad (42)$$

Consequently, the average price is

$$\bar{p} = \Xi\,(\hat{a}^*_u) + m + \Theta s. \quad (43)$$

Under perfect information in labour markets, the base wage $f$ is always adjusted in such a way as to make $\bar{p}$ just offset any change in $m$. Under imperfect information, however, the actual average price $\bar{p}$ in the above formula is replaced by the union's expectations $e(\bar{p}|\Omega_u)$. Because of the possibility of local–global confusion, $e\,(\bar{p}|\Omega_u)$ is more rigid than $\bar{p}$; that is, $e\,(\bar{p}|\Omega_u)$ is less sensitive to $m$ than $\bar{p}$ is.

If $t < t^*$, or, equivalently, $1 - t - z_1\,(c_1 + 1) > 0$, the union is base-wage-concerned. Then, *ceteris paribus*, an increase in the average price increases the base wage. Suppose that $m$ is increased, so that $\bar{p}$ also increases. However, under imperfect information, the expected average price increases less than the actual average price. This implies that base wages do not increase as much under imperfect information as under perfect information where the actual average price is observable. Consequently, the average price $\bar{p}$ determined by these base wages does not increase as much under imperfect as under perfect information. A symmetric argument can be applied to a downward movement in $m$. Thus, $\bar{p}$ becomes less sensitive to $m$ than in the case of perfect information where money is neutral, and we obtain a positive correlation between money and output.

By contrast, if $t > t^*$ (if $1 - t - z_1 (c_1 + 1) < 0$), the union is employment-concerned. Then, *ceteris paribus*, an increase in the average price decreases the base wage. In this case the rigidity of expectations has the opposite effect on the base wage. Again, suppose that $m$ is increased so that $\bar{p}$ also increases. Because the expected average price increases less than the actual average price, the base-wage-reducing effect of the average price is smaller under imperfect than under perfect information. Thus, the base wage increases more under imperfect than under perfect information. So the average price determined by base wages increases more under imperfect than under perfect information where money is neutral. Thus, money and output are negatively correlated.

## 5. INDEXATION AND THE EFFECT OF PRICE UNCERTAINTY

In this section, I shall show that indexation influences the way price uncertainty affects the 'normal' level of output, and that the effect of indexation is different under monopolistic competition than under perfect competition.[7]

In an economy with monopolistically competitive unions, an increase in the variance of the monetary disturbance affects the unconditional mean of output by increasing price uncertainty. From (23), we obtain

$$\bar{y}|_{m=s=0} = -\Xi\ (\hat{a}_u). \tag{44}$$

Because $\partial\hat{a}_u/\partial V\,(\bar{p}|\Omega_u) \neq 0$ (except in the case where $1 - t - z_1 (c_1 + 1) = 0$), and $\partial\Xi/\partial\hat{a}_u > 0$, we have $\partial[\bar{y}|_{m\,=\,s\,=\,0}]/\partial V\,(\bar{p}|\Omega_u) \neq 0$. Thus uncertainty about the *absolute* price level affects the unconditional mean of output.

The unconditional mean of output can be considered the 'normal' level of output. The argument in the previous paragraph implies that monetary variance affects the normal level of output. However, the direction of the effect depends on the degree of indexation $t$. If $t$ is small so that the union is base-wage-concerned (if $1 - t - z_1 (c_1 + 1) > 0$), increased uncertainty about the average price increases the normal level of output. By contrast, if $t$ is large so that the union is employment-concerned (if $1 - t - z_1 (c_1 + 1) < 0$), the increased uncertainty decreases the normal level of output.

Whether price uncertainty increases or decreases the normal level of output depends on the concavity/convexity of the first derivative of the objective function exp ($\psi$) with respect to the decision variable $f$. The first derivative is

$$\frac{\partial \exp(\psi)}{\partial f} = (1-r)\exp\{(1-r)f - \log(c_1+1) + \xi + r\bar{f} - [1-t-(c_1+1)]\bar{p}\} + r\exp\{(z_1+1)[-rf - \log(c_1+1)+\xi] + \beta + (z_1+1)r\bar{f} - (z_1+1)(c_1+1)\bar{p}\}. \quad (45)$$

Consequently, around $f=f^*$, which is the solution of $\partial \exp(\psi)/\partial f = 0$, we obtain.

$$\frac{\partial^2}{\partial \bar{p}^2}\left(\frac{\partial \exp(\psi)}{\partial f}\right) = [1-t-z_1(c_1+1)]\,[(z_1+2)(c_1+1)+(1-t)]\Delta, \quad (46)$$

where

$$\Delta = (1-r)\exp\{(1-r)f^* - \log(c_1+1) + \xi + r\bar{f} - [1-t-(c_1+1)]\bar{p}\} < 0,$$

because $r > 1$. If $1-t-z_1(c_1+1) > 0$, then the first derivative is concave in $\bar{p}$. Thus, uncertainty about $\bar{p}$ decreases the marginal benefit of the base-wage increase, so that the optimal base wage is reduced. Because a reduction in the base wage implies an increase in output, price uncertainty increases the normal level of output if $1-t-z_1(c_1+1) > 0$. A symmetric result is obtained if $1-t-(c_1+1) < 0$. In this case, price uncertainty decreases the normal level of output. Specifically, under full indexation ($t=1$), price uncertainty unambiguously decreases the normal level of output.[8]

It may be worthwhile to compare monopolistically competitive labour markets with perfectly competitive labour markets. Recall that competitive labour supply is determined by (27). This is a familiar Lucas supply function if $t = 0$. The usual practice is to ignore the variance term in (27);[9] however, this conceals the importance of the effect of price uncertainty on labour supply.[10] Using this labour supply function, we obtain the normal level of perfectly competitive output as

$$\bar{y}|_{m=s=0} = -\Xi(\hat{a}_w), \quad (47)$$

where

$$\hat{a}_w = a_l^* - \frac{1}{2}(t-1)^2 V(\bar{p}|\Omega).$$

Thus, an increase in price uncertainty does not influence the normal level output under full indexation ($t=1$). Under less-than-full indexation, price uncertainty unambiguously increases the normal level of output.

The first derivative of the worker's objective function with respect to his decision variable $n^s$ is

$$\frac{\partial \exp(\psi)}{\partial n^s} = \exp\,[f-(1-t)\,p+n^s]-\exp[(z_1+1)n^s+\beta]. \qquad (48)$$

Consequently, we have

$$\frac{\partial^2}{\partial \bar{p}^2}\left(\frac{\partial \exp(\psi)}{\partial n^s}\right) = (1-t)^2 \exp\,[f-(1-t)p+n^s]>0. \qquad (49)$$

Thus, the first derivative is strongly convex in $\bar{p}$ if $t<1$. Under less-than-full indexation, price uncertainty unambiguously increases the marginal benefit of labour supply. Consequently, the labour supply increases, which reduces the equilibrium base wage and hence increases the equilibrium output.[11]

## 6. ALTERNATIVE SPECIFICATIONS OF LABOUR UNION BEHAVIOUR

The objective function used for the unions in the previous sections is not so usual in recent union literature, although it can be derived as the utility of its members (see the Appendix to this chapter). In this section I shall analyse the more conventional objectives of unions and discuss whether the same results would be obtained under such objectives. The case of full indexation will be considered.

Following Oswald (1985), consider two major specifications of union preferences. The first approach adopts the Stone–Geary functional form:

$$\exp(\psi)=[\exp(w-\bar{p})-\exp(\hat{h})]^b\,[\exp(n+\beta)-\exp(\hat{n})]^d, \qquad (50)$$

where $0<b<1$, and $0<d<1$. Here $\hat{h}$ and $\hat{n}$ are the 'reference' levels of real wages and employment, respectively. As in the previous sections, $\beta$ represents a shock in the union preference function. The second specification of union preferences is expected utility under the possibility of random layoffs; that is,

$$\exp(\psi) = \exp\,[g(w-\bar{p})]\,\exp(n-\hat{l})\,\exp(\beta) + \exp(\hat{z})\,[1-\exp(n-\hat{l})\,\exp(\beta)], \qquad (51)$$

where $0<g<1$. Here $\exp\,[g(w-\bar{p})]$ is the utility of an employed worker, $n$ is the number of employed workers, $\hat{l}$ is the membership of the union, and $\exp(\hat{z})$ is the utility of an unemployed worker. Thus $\exp(n-\hat{l})$ is the probability of employment if layoffs are randomly distributed, as long as the constraint $n\leqslant\hat{l}$ is not binding. Here again, $\beta$ represents a shock in the union preference function.[12]

Let us first consider the case of the Stone–Geary union preferences given by (50). Suppose that exp $(\hat{h})=0$, and $b > dr$. Then, the optimal base wage is approximately[13]

$$f = \frac{1}{r}\left\{\log \frac{b-dr}{b} - \log(1+c_1) + \left[r - \left(1+\frac{1}{c_1}\right)\right]\bar{f} + \beta - \hat{n} + e(v|\Omega_u)\right\}. \quad (52)$$

Because $e(v|\Omega_u)$ appears in the base-wage formula, full indexation does not insulate the economy. A qualitatively similar result is also obtained in the general case where exp $(\hat{h})$ and exp $(\hat{n})$ are both greater than zero. Thus, the results in the previous section hold true under this specification of union preferences.

Next, in the case of the expected-utility specification (51), the union's optimal base wage is approximately

$$f = \frac{1}{g}\log\frac{r}{r-g} + \frac{1}{g}\hat{z} \quad (53)$$

Because $f$ is independent of $e(v|\Omega_u)$, full indexation completely insulates the economy.

This complete-insulation result, however, stems from the rather restrictive assumption that the constraint $n \leqslant \hat{l}$ is never binding. In this case, the union's utility (51) is linear in labour supply. This property is essential to obtain complete insulation.[14]

If we allow the constraint $n \leqslant \hat{l}$ to be binding in some cases,[15] the union's objective function is

$$\exp(\psi) = \exp(\hat{z}) + \exp\{g(w-\bar{p})\}\{\min[1, \exp(n-\hat{l})\exp(\beta)]\}. \quad (54)$$

This shows that the union's utility is generally strictly concave in labour supply, even under the random-layoff scheme. In general we obtain incomplete insulation for utility functions which are strictly concave in labour supply. Thus, except for the case where the union is certain that $n$ will always be less than $\hat{l}$, insulation is likely to be incomplete.

## 7. CONCLUDING REMARKS: LABOUR–MARKET MONOPOLISTIC COMPETITION AND WAGE RIGIDITY

In this chapter we have compared an economy having monopolistically competitive labour markets with one having perfectly competitive labour markets in the framework of predetermined wages. It has been shown that full indexation may not insulate the monopolistically competitive economy from nominal disturbances, although it completely insulates the perfectly competitive economy. Price uncertainty has also been shown to influence the determination of nominal wages, and hence output.

Monopolistic competition in labour markets, however, makes prices more sensitive to nominal demand shocks than perfect competition. Because of this property, output is negatively correlated with money under full indexation. Thus, for complete insulation under monopolistic competition there must be less than full indexation. In this sense, monopolistic competition in labour markets is not likely to contribute to the observed rigidity of prices and wages with relation to nominal shocks. This result is in sharp contrast to the effect of monopolistic competition in product markets discussed in Chapters 2 and 3.[16] These chapters showed that monopolistic competition in product markets does indeed contribute to the rigidity of prices with relation to nominal shocks.

However, monopolistic competition in labour markets does make wages, and hence prices, rigid with relation to nominal shocks if the informational separation of monopolistically competitive unions is introduced as an additional source of imperfect information. In this case the average wage is assumed to be unobservable. Local–global confusion then makes individual wages less sensitive to labour-demand conditions and, ultimately, to aggregate nominal-demand conditions. Consequently, prices become insensitive to nominal shocks. This type of labour maket is analysed in Nishimura (1986*b*). It is shown there that, if competition among labour unions is strong, the rigidity-enhancing effect of monopolistic competition dominates the flexibility-enhancing effect.

Finally, it may be worthwhile to make a remark about the rational expectations assumption in the analysis of this chapter. The assumption that unions have information about the structure of the economy may seem a heroic assumption at first glance. However, what we need in the analysis is not complete knowledge, but some reliable knowledge about firms and other unions. (Uncertainty surrounding such knowledge can be treated by adding observation errors.) Under imperfect competition, knowledge about customers and rivals is vital. In this case, it is reasonable to assume that unions have some reliable knowledge about firms and other unions. Thus, in such an economy this assumption is not so unreasonable.

# Appendix: A Macroeconomic Model with Differentiated Products and Differentiated Labour Inputs

The model presented in this appendix is an extension of the microfoundation model found in Section 2 of Chapter 2. There are two differences between the model presented below and the model in Chapter 2. First, in the microfoundation model of Chapter 2, I assume bilateral–monopoly labour markets, in which labour inputs are firm-specific. In the model presented below, labour inputs are not firm-specific, although they are differentiated. Second, the model in Chapter 2 assumes that product markets are monopolistically competitive, while in this chapter they are perfectly competitive.

The model here is based on that of Blanchard and Kiyotaki (1987). The difference between my approach and theirs lies in my explicit formulation of disturbances in product demand, labour supply, and production processes. In addition, as in Chapter 2, I assume that one representative household supplies all types of labour. This is unlike Blanchard and Kiyotaki, who assume many households, each of which controls one type of labour. However, this representative-household assumption is made only for expository simplicity, and my results do not depend on it.

In this model events occur in the following way. Nominal wages are indexed to the price index. The degree of indexation is assumed to have been determined in the past. At the beginning of the period, nature chooses a particular realization of the money-supply disturbance, preference disturbances, technology disturbances, and labour-supply disturbances. Then, labour unions determine the base wage for their particular kind of labour input, relying on imperfect information about the disturbances, and without knowing what prices firms will set. After the labour unions determined their base wages, information about all disturbances becomes known to firms. Being perfectly informed about the disturbances, firms then determine their prices. Finally, the representative household determines its consumption plan and purchase products.

## A1. *The Representative Household*

Suppose that there are $n_1$ kinds of products and $n_2$ kinds of labour inputs. There is one household which supplies labour to the firms and owns their stocks. Specifically, let us assume that the representative household's utility function is

$$\Psi = D(n_1\bar{Y})^{\zeta}\left(\frac{\bar{M}}{\bar{P}}\right)^{1-\zeta} - n_2(\bar{N}^s)^{\mu}, \qquad (A_1)$$

where $D$ is the normalization factor, such that $D=\zeta^{-\zeta}(1-\zeta)^{-(1-\zeta)}$, in which $0<\zeta<1$; $\bar{Y}$ is the average-consumption index; $\bar{M}$ represents the end-of-period nominal money holdings; $\bar{P}$ is the price index associated with $\bar{Y}$; and $\bar{N}^s$ is the average-labour-supply index.

The average-consumption index is

$$\bar{Y} = \left[ \left( \sum_{i=1}^{n_1} U_i^{1/k} \, Q_i^{(k-1)/k} \right) / n_1 \right]^{k/(k-1)}, \tag{A2}$$

where $Q_i$ is the consumption of the *ith* product and $U_i$ is the product-specific preference disturbance. I assume $k > 1$. I also assume that log $U_i$ is a draw from a normal distribution with mean zero and variance $\sigma_u^2$. The corresponding price index is

$$\bar{P} = \left[ \left( \sum_{i=1}^{n_1} U_i \, P_i^{1-k} \right) / n_1 \right]^{1/(1-k)}, \tag{A3}$$

where $P_i$ is the price of the $i$th product. $\bar{N}^s$ is the average-labour-supply index such that

$$\bar{N}^s = \left\{ \left[ \sum_{j=1}^{n_2} \Delta_j \, (N_j^s)^{\mu} \right] / n_2 \right\}^{1/\mu}, \tag{A4}$$

where $N_j^s$ is the supply of the $j$th labour input. The term $\Delta_j$ in (A4) represents the labour-supply disturbance, which we assume consists of the economy-wide disturbance $S$ and the labour-input-specific disturbance $X_j$.

$$\Delta_j = S \, X_j.$$

I assume that log $S$ is a draw from a normal distribution with mean zero and variance $\sigma_s^2$, and that log $X_j$ is a draw from a normal distribution with mean zero and variance $\sigma_x^2$.

The representative household's demand for each product is derived from the maximization of $\Psi$ with respect to the level of consumption of each product and the level of real balances subject to the budget constraint

$$\sum_{i=1}^{n_1} P_i \, Q_i + \bar{M} = B, \tag{A5}$$

where

$$B = \sum_{j=1}^{n_2} W_j \, N_j^s + \sum_{i=1}^{n_1} \bar{P} \, \Pi_i + M.$$

Here, $M$ represents the beginning-of-period money holdings, $W_j$ is the wage of the $j$th labour input, and $\Pi_i$ is the real profit of the $i$th firm. (Thus, I assume that firms do not retain their profits.) $M$ is a random variable, and log $M$ is a draw from a normal distribution with mean zero and variance $\sigma_m^2$. $M$, $U_i$, $S$, and $X_j$ are mutually independent.

Using the property of the CES and Cobb–Douglas functions, we can derive the demand $Q_i$ and the demand for real balances. They are

$$Q_i = \left( \frac{P_i}{\bar{P}} \right)^{-k} \bar{Y} U_i, \quad n_1 \bar{Y} = \zeta \frac{B}{\bar{P}} \text{ and } \frac{\bar{M}}{\bar{P}} = (1-\zeta) \frac{B}{\bar{P}}. \tag{A6}$$

Substituting these into (A1), we obtain the representative household's utility, such that

$$\Psi \equiv \frac{B}{\bar{P}} - n_2 (\bar{N}^s)^{\mu} = \frac{1}{\bar{P}} \left( \sum_{j=1}^{n_2} W_j N_j^s + \sum_{i=1}^{n_1} \bar{P}\, \Pi_i + M \right) - \sum_{j=1}^{n_2} \Delta_j (N_j^s)^{\mu}. \quad (A_7)$$

## A2. *Wage Contracts*

The wage is indexed to the price index. I assume

$$W_j = F_j (\bar{P})^t , \quad (A_8)$$

where $F_j$ is the base wage of the $j$th labour input, and $t$ is the degree of cost-of-living indexation. The degree $t$ is exogenously given.

## A3. *The Monopolistically Competitive Assumption in the Strong Form*

As in Chapter 2, I assume that $n_1$ and $n_2$ are sufficiently large, so that the dependence of $\bar{P}$ on a particular $P_i$, and that of $\bar{W}$ on particular $W_j$, can be ignored. Thus, unions in labour markets do not consider $\bar{W}$ to be influenced by their own $W_j$.

## A4. *Product Markets*

I assume perfect competition and perfect information in product markets. The firm is a price-taker, and all prices and wages are known. Without loss of generality, I assume that one product is produced by one firm.

Here we first discuss the firm and then equilibrium.

The production function of the firm is

$$Q_i^s = (n_2 \bar{L}_i)^{\phi}, \quad (A_9)$$

where $\bar{L}_i$ is the average-labour-input index, which is defined as

$$\bar{L}_i = \left[ \left( \sum_{j=1}^{n_2} V_j^{1/r} L_{ij}^{(r-1)/r} \right) / n_2 \right]^{r/(r-1)}.$$

Here $L_{ij}$ is the $j$th labour input of the $i$th firm. The parameters in (A9) satisfy $r > 1$ and $0 < \phi < \mu$. Thus, the production function is a composite of the CES and Cobb–Douglas functions.

$V_j$ represents the productivity disturbance specific to the $j$th labour input log $V_j$ is a draw from a normal distribution with mean zero and variance $\sigma_v^2$. $V_j$ is independent of $M$, $U_i$, $S$, and $X_j$.

The firm maximizes its real profit with respect to its decision variables, $Q_i^s$ and $L_{ij}$. The firm's objective function is

$$\Pi_i = \frac{1}{\bar{P}} (P_i Q_i^s - C_i), \quad (A_{10})$$

where $C_i$ is the total wage payment such that

$$C_i = \sum_{j=1}^{n_2} W_j L_{ij}, \tag{A11}$$

in which $W_j$ is the wage of the $j$th labour input.

As is well known, this maximization takes two steps. The first is to minimize the total wage payment, $C_i$ in (All), by taking $Q_i^s$ as given. This yields

$$L_{ij} = \left(\frac{W_j}{\bar{W}}\right)^{-r} (\bar{L}_i)\ V_j \text{ and } C_i = \sum_{j=1}^{n_2} W_j\ L_{ij} = \bar{W} n_2\ \bar{L}_i = \bar{W}\ (Q_i^s)^{1/\phi}. \tag{A12}$$

Here $\bar{W}$ is the wage index corresponding to the labour-input index $\bar{L}_i$, such that

$$\bar{W} = \left[\left(\sum_{j=1}^{n_2} V_j\ W_j^{(1-r)}\right)/n_2\right]^{1/(1-r)}. \tag{A13}$$

Because of (A8), we have

$$\bar{W} = \bar{F}\ (\bar{P})^t, \tag{A14}$$

where $\bar{F} = [(\sum_{j=1}^{n_2} V_j F_j^{(1-r)}/n_2]^{1/(1-r)}$.

The second step is then to maximize

$$\frac{1}{\bar{P}}\ [P_i\ Q_i^s - \bar{W}\ (Q_i^s)^{1/\phi}] \tag{A15}$$

with respect to $Q_i^s$. This maximization determines the supply of the $i$th product, $Q_i^s$, so that

$$Q_i^s = (constant) \left(\frac{P_i}{\bar{W}}\right)^{1/c_1}. \tag{A16}$$

where $c_1 = (1/\phi) - 1$.

The equilibrium conditions in product markets consist of the monetary-equilibrium condition $\bar{M} = M$, and the individual-market-equilibrium conditions $Q_i^s = Q_i$.

Because the firm does not retain profits, from the monetary equilibrium condition we obtain

$$\bar{Y} = \frac{1}{n_1}\left(\frac{\zeta}{1-\zeta}\right)\frac{M}{\bar{P}}. \tag{A17}$$

Thus, the average demand is proportional to the initial real money holdings.

### A5. *Labour Markets*

Labour markets open before product markets. Thus, the participants in the labour markets have only imperfect information about the condition of the product markets. However, the firm is given the right to determine its employment level after product markets open. Let us first consider the monopolistically competitive case. Then, the perfectly competitive case is presented as a frame of reference.

First, let us look at labour demand. Let $N_j$ be the demand for the $j$th labour input, such that $N_j = \Sigma_{i=1}^{n_1} L_{ij}$. Define the average labour demand index $\bar{N}$ as

$$\bar{N} = \frac{1}{n_2} \sum_{i=1}^{n_1} (Q_i^s)^{1/\phi}. \tag{A$_{18}$}$$

From (A9) and (A12), we then obtain

$$N_j = \left(\frac{W_j}{\bar{W}}\right)^{-r} (\bar{N})\, V_j \quad \text{and} \quad n_2 \bar{W} \bar{N} = \sum_{i=1}^{n_1} \sum_{j=1}^{n_2} W_j\, L_{ij}. \tag{A$_{19}$}$$

Thus, $n_2 \bar{W} \bar{N}$ represents the total wage payments in the economy.

In the monopolistically competitive case, the supply of one type of labour is controlled by one union. The union controlling the $j$th labour input sets the base-wage rate $F_j$ in order to maximize the utility of the representative household (A7).

In determining $F_j$, the union does not know $\bar{P}$. The union is assumed to know the base-wage index $\bar{F}$, the individual labour-supply condition $\Delta_j$, and the following individual nominal-labour-demand condition:

$$\Xi_j = M^{1/\phi} V_j.$$

The meaning of the individual nominal-labour-demand condition is discussed in the text. The union cannot independently observe $M$, $U_i$, $S$, $X_j$, and $V_j$. Thus, the union's information is $(\bar{F}, \Delta_j, \Xi_j)$.

Consequently, the $j$th union's objective is to maximize the representative household's utility (A20):

$$\hat{E}\, \Psi = \hat{E}\, \frac{1}{\bar{P}} (W_j N_j) - \Delta_j\, N_j^{\mu} + D'', \tag{A$_{20}$}$$

with respect to $F_j$, subject to the labour-demand function (A19), where $\hat{E}$ is the expectation operator with respect to the union's subjective distribution of $\bar{P}$ based on the available information $(\bar{F}, \Delta_j, \Xi_j)$, and $D''$ is the term given to the union.

Let us now look at the case of perfectly competitive labour markets. The supply of the $j$th labour input is determined by the representative household. Let us assume that the household maximizes its utility with respect to this labour input, taking decisions about other labour inputs as given.

When it determines the supply of the $j$th labour input, the household does not know $\bar{P}$. It is assumed that the household has information about $\Delta_j$, $F_j$, and $\bar{F}$.

The supply of the $j$th labour input, $N_j^s$, is the solution of the maximization of the following expected utility (A20) with respect to $N_j^s$. Here $\hat{E}$ is the expectation operator with respect to the household's subjective distribution of $\bar{P}$ based on the available information $(\Delta_j, F_j, \bar{F})$. Then, the equilibrium is determined by $N_j^s = N_j$.

## A6. *Approximation*

As in the microfoundation model of Chapter 2, it is possible to get the exact log-linear formula of behavioural equations by using the law of large numbers and the property of long-normal distributions. However, the resulting expressions are too cumbersome to analyse, as they do not add any economic insights. Thus, retaining the above structure of the model, I use the long-linear approximation of the aggregate indices $\bar{P}$, $\bar{W}$, and $\bar{N}$. In the following, let the lower-case term be the log of the corresponding upper-case term; for example, $\bar{p} = \log \bar{P}, p_i = \log P_i$, etc. Consequently, from (A3) we have

$$\bar{p} = \{1/(1-k)\} \left( \log \{(1/n_1) \sum_{i=1}^{n_1} \exp (u_i) \exp [(1-k)\, p_i]\} \right).$$

Take the first-order Taylor expansion of this expression around $u_i = 0$ and $p_i = 0$ for all $i$. From this we obtain

$$\bar{p} = \frac{1}{n} \sum_{i=1}^{n_1} p_i,$$

because

$$\frac{1}{n_1} \sum_{i=1}^{n_1} u_i = Eu_i = 0.$$

Here we use the law of large numbers. Similar procedures on (A13), (A2), and (A18) yield

$$\bar{w} = \frac{1}{n_2} \sum_{j=1}^{n_2} w_j, \quad \bar{y} = \frac{1}{n_1} \sum_{i=1}^{n_1} q_i, \quad \text{and} \quad \bar{n} = \frac{1}{\phi} \left( \frac{1}{n_1} \sum_{i=1}^{n_1} q_i \right) = \frac{1}{\phi} \bar{y}.$$

These approximations amount to assuming away the influence of the distribution of relative prices and relative wages on the price index, the wage index, the consumption (output) index, and the labour-demand index. By using these approximations, ignoring the constant terms, and adding the normalization factors ($-\log (c_1 + 1)$ and $-\log (z_1 + 1)$), we get the log-linear log-normal model in the text with $c_1 = (1/\phi) - 1$ and $z_1 = \mu - 1$.

# Notes

1. For various aspects of wage indexation, see Dornbusch and Simonsen (1983).
2. Although such contracts are widely observed, they are *ex post* inefficient under imperfect information (Barro 1977). The analysis of this chapter, like other studies assuming this type of contract, depends on the existence of this inefficiency. However, the use of predetermined wage contracts may be justified under asymmetric information between the firm and the union, because contingent wage contracts are not incentive-compatible if the union cannot observe product-market conditions.
3. The formulation in this chapter neglects the macroeconomic effect of the distribution of relative prices, $p - \bar{p}$. This greatly simplifies the analysis, without substantially changing the results. See the appendix to this chapter.

4. The average labour demand $\bar{n}$ is equal to the average labour input, $\bar{l}$. From (5), we have $\bar{n} = \bar{l} = -\log (c_1 + 1) + (c_1 + 1)\bar{q}$. From this and the fact that $\bar{y} = \bar{q}$, we obtain the expression in the text.
5. Formally, I assume that $\sigma_s^2$ is much greater than $\sigma_m^2$, so that the average base wage, which is observable in the labour markets, gives little information about $m$. This assumption is made only for the sake of analytic simplicity. The results of this chapter do not depend on this rather unrealistic assumption. The main results of the chapter hold with little modification, as long as $\sigma_s^2$ is positive; however, the derivation of rational expectations in general cases becomes complicated, because we must consider information about $m$ contained in $\bar{f}$.
6. It should be noted here that the qualitative result in this chapter depends on the imperfect knowledge of the individual real-labour-demand condition $(\bar{n} + v)$, and is not dependent on this particular specification of information.
7. To put it more precisely, I here consider the unconditional mean of the *log* of output.
8. See Froyen and Waud (1987), and the references cited there for empirical studies on the relationship between price uncertainty and real output. The results are inconclusive, although many studies support the hypothesis of the negative effect of price uncertainty on real output.
9. Usually, $\log E \exp(x)$ is approximated by $Ex$.
10. See Persson (1979) and Azariadis (1981). See also Leland (1972) for general results.
11. However, the effect of uncertainty on the long-run level of output is generally ambiguous in models allowing the intertemporal substitution effect.
12. The way $\beta$ enters the utility functions (50) and (51) is only one of many possible ways of describing labour-supply disturbances. The results of this section hold true under various specifications, as long as $\beta$ influences the optimal base wage.
13. Let $\hat{E}f(v) = 0$ be the first-order condition of optimality, where $\hat{E}$ is the expectation operator with respect to the union's subjective distribution of $v$. If $\hat{E}f(v)$ is approximated by $f(\hat{E}v)$, then we obtain the base-wage formula in the text. This method yields a relatively good approximation for the short-run behavioural equations, though it may give misleading results in analysing the effect of price variability on the normal level of output, as explained earlier in the discussion of the Lucas supply function.
14. In fact, even in the framework of the previous sections, we obtain complete. insulation if the union's utility is linear in labour supply. $t^*$ is equal to unity if $z_1$ is equal to zero.
15. Under the assumption that $m$ and $v$ are log-normally distributed, there always exists the possibility of a very large labour demand. In this case, the constraint $n \leqslant l$ is likely to be binding.
16. See also Ch. 5. Andersen (1985) has also analysed the rigidity of prices in incompletely informed product markets.

# PART II

# PRICING, INVESTMENT, AND COMPETITION

# 5

# Cost-Based Prices: Competition and Price Behaviour under Correlated Shocks in Demand and Supply

## 1. INTRODUCTION

Prices of produced goods in the United States and other industrialized economies are mostly insensitive to shifts in demand, except for prices of so-called auction market goods, such as agricultural products.[1] On the other hand, they respond rather quickly to cost changes, especially wage changes. Various measures of demand pressure, such as the degree of capacity utilization and the capital–output ratio, have been included in price equations in econometric studies, but in many cases they have failed to yield significant results.[2] Although these studies have been criticized, for example for inadequate treatment of simultaneity, no evidence in favour of a strong effect of demand shifts on prices, given cost conditions, has been presented for non-auction-market goods.

Cost-based prices are inconsistent with perfect competition, except in the trivial case of a flat supply curve. Under perfect competition, prices are determined at the intersection of the demand and supply curves. A shift of the demand curve, as well as that of the supply curve, should affect the price.

The first purpose of this chapter is to present an explanation of these widely observed cost-based prices, based on the behaviour of prices in a monopolistically competitive industry with predetermined prices which is subject to both demand and supply disturbances. In a monopolistically competitive industry, one firm's optimal price depends on the other firms' prices, or the average price as their stand-in, as well as on its own conditions. In an industry that has imperfectly informed consumers, a firm is often forced to determine its price before it has information about the average price (see Chapter 2). The firm is assumed to form its expectations about the average price rationally, in the sense that it uses all available information. The argument of this chapter depends on this imperfect information about the average price.

Okun (1981) suggested that cost-based prices may emerge if cost disturbances are rather uniform, while demand disturbances are heterogeneous. This chapter confirms his conjecture in a monopolistically competitive industry with predetermined prices.[3] If cost disturbances are rather uniform among firms and demand and cost disturbances are correlated, then imperfect information makes the industry's average price more sensitive to cost conditions and less responsive to demand conditions. The reason is informational. Under the above two informational assumptions, local cost information provides more information about macroeconomic conditions of demand and cost than does local demand information. Thus, firms depend more on local cost information than on local demand information in determining their prices. Consequently, prices are responsive to cost disturbances and insensitive to demand disturbances if the industry is monopolistically competitive.

The second purpose of this chapter is to investigate the robustness of Chapter 2's result that competition enhances price rigidity, in the general framework of correlated shocks in demand and cost. In Chapter 2 it was demonstrated that, if *only* demand shocks are present, increased competition decreases, rather than increases, the sensitivity of prices with respect to demand shocks. The welfare analysis in Chapter 2 also showed that, because of this price-rigidity-enhancing effect, increased competition does not always improve welfare. However, when both demand and supply shocks are considered, their correlation should be explicitly taken into account. Production of one type of product usually requires other types of products as inputs. Thus, production is usually characterized by a complicated input–output relationship. Through this relationship, demand shocks and supply shocks may be correlated. For example, when the demand for passenger cars is strong because of generally favourable economic conditions, it is likely that the supply of rolled steel materials (which are used in the production of passenger cars) will also be tight. Such a correlation is likely to influence price behaviour.

In this chapter I show that increased competition still makes prices rigid in the general framework. However, the relationship between increased competition and price rigidity is looser in the model of correlated demand and supply shocks than in the model where only demand shocks exist. It is not true that an increase in competition always reduces price flexibility in the correlated-shock case; however, increased competition *ultimately* reduces price flexibility. Specifically, I show that, if the industry becomes very competitive (in the sense that the price elasticity of individual demand is close to infinity), the industry's average price becomes completely insensitive to temporary disturbances. By contrast, the average price adjusts to permanent changes as if it were the perfectly competitive price.

The plan of this chapter is as follows. In Section 2, the model is presented, and an explicit average-price formula is derived in a general imperfect-information case. In order to make analysis simple, a log-linear model is assumed. This log-linear model can be derived from the microfoundation model of Chapter 2, in which competitiveness is determined by consumers' preferences (the parameter of their CES utility functions). An alternative microfoundation model, in which competitiveness depends on the number of firms in the industry, is presented in the Appendix to this chapter. In section 3 the main results of this chapter are obtained by using the average-price formula derived in Section 2. Section 4 contains remarks about the implications of this study for the macroeconomic literature.

## 2. CORRELATED DEMAND AND SUPPLY SHOCKS IN A MONOPOLISTICALLY COMPETITIVE INDUSTRY

Consider an industry with $n$ monopolistically competitive firms facing downward-sloping demand curves. The firms are homogeneous except for disturbances in demand and cost. Throughout this chapter, all variables are in logarithms.

The demand for a firm's product is, in logarithmic form,

$$q = -m(p - \bar{p}) + (g - b\bar{p}) + \alpha, \tag{1}$$

where $p$ is the firm's price, $\bar{p}$ the average price in the industry, $q$ the demand for the firm's product, and $g$ a positive constant. The price elasticity of individual demand is $m$, while $b$ is the elasticity of the average demand with respect to the average price. I assume $m > b \geq 1$, so that individual demand is more elastic than average demand. Here $m$ represents the degree of competition among firms in this industry, while $b$ can be considered the degree of competition among industries; $\alpha$ is the demand disturbance affecting the demand for the firm's product.

The cost function of the firm is, in logarithmic form,

$$c = c_0 - \log(c_1 + 1) + (c_1 + 1)q + \beta, \tag{2}$$

where $c$ is the total cost to the firm producing $q$, and $c_0$ and $c_1$ are numbers satisfying $c_0 > 0$ and $c_1 > -1$.[4] Thus, this model allows the case of increasing returns to scale with $c_1 < 0$. I assume that $1 + c_1 b > 0$ and $1 + c_1 m > 0$, which ensure the existence of the optimal price for the firm maximizing its profits. The cost disturbance $\beta$ may reflect production uncertainty and input-price uncertainty.

I assume that the firm knows the functional forms of (1) and (2), as well as the constants $g$, $m$, $b$, $c_0$, and $c_1$.[5] I also assume that the firm has perfect information about the individual disturbances $\alpha$ and $\beta$.[6]

The individual demand disturbance $\alpha$ consists of two unobservable disturbances. One is the industry-wide disturbance, which influences all firms in the industry equally; the other is the firm-specific disturbance. Thus, we have

$$\alpha = d + u, \tag{3}$$

where $d$ is the industry-wide demand disturbance and $u$ the firm-specific one. Disturbances $d$ and $u$ are normally distributed random variables satisfying $Ed = Eu = 0$; $Ed^2 = \sigma_d^2$; $Eu^2 = \sigma_u^2$; and $Edu = 0$.

Similarly, $\beta$ has the form

$$\beta = s + w. \tag{4}$$

Here $s$ is the industry-wide cost disturbance and $w$ the firm-specific one. Their distributions are normal and have the following properties: $Es = Ew = 0$; $Es^2 = \sigma_s^2$; $Ew^2 = \sigma_w^2$; and $Esw = 0$.

The industry-wide disturbances may be positively correlated with each other, while the firm-specific disturbances are assumed to be mutually independent: $Esd = \sigma_{sd} > 0$, and $Ewd = Eus = Ewu = 0$. The firm is assumed to know the properties of the disturbances, although $d$, $u$, $s$, and $w$ are not directly observable.[7]

The number of firms, $n$, is sufficiently large that the average of the firm-specific disturbance $u$ is approximated by the mathematical expectation of $u$, $Eu$ $(= 0)$, through the law of large numbers. Similarly, the average of $w$ can be approximated by $Ew$ $(= 0)$. Moreover, because $n$ is large, firms ignore the dependence of the average price $\bar{p}$ on their own $p$ (the strong monopolistically competitive assumption). The average-demand function, which is the average of the demand functions of the individual firms, is then, in logarithmic form,

$$\begin{aligned} \bar{q} = \textstyle\int_{u,w} q\, f(u,\ w)\ du dw &= -\ m\,(\bar{p} - \bar{p}) + (g - b\bar{p}) + d \\ &= (g - b\bar{p}) + d, \end{aligned} \tag{5}$$

where $f(u, w)$ is the density function of $(u, w)$. Similarly, the average cost function, which is the average of the cost functions of the individual firms, is, in logarithmic form,

$$\bar{c} = \textstyle\int_{u,w} c\, f(u,w)\ du dw = c_0 - \log\,(c_1 + 1) + (c_1 + 1)\bar{q} + s. \tag{6}$$

The firm maximizes its profits $\exp(\pi) = \exp(p)\exp(q) - \exp(c)$ by choosing an appropriate price, taking (1)–(6) as given.[8] Thus, the firm is a price-maker and a quantity-taker. This implies that the firm does not ration its products.

### 2.1. *Perfect Information*

As a frame of reference, let us first consider the case in which $\bar{p}$ is known at the time the firm determines its own $p$. If price information from all firms is instantaneously transmitted to all consumers in the market, the firm can change its price after observing other firms' prices without confusing its own customers and potential buyers. In equilibrium the firm has no incentive to change its price, as the average price in the market is known. This is, in short, the perfect-information case.

In the perfect-information case, there is no uncertainty on the side of the firm. The optimal price for the firm satisfies the first-order condition of optimality, $\partial \exp(\pi)/\partial p = 0$. Thus, we have, in logarithmic form,

$$p - \log[(m/(m-1)] = c_0 + c_1 q + \beta. \tag{7}$$

Substituting (1) into (7) and rearranging terms, we obtain

$$p = (1 + c_1 m)^{-1} \ [a^* + (c_0 + \beta) + c_1 \ (g + \alpha) + (m - b) \ c_1 \bar{p}], \tag{8}$$

where

$$a^* = \log \ [m/(m-1)]. \tag{9}$$

This is the optimal pricing formula for the firm. It can easily be shown that (8) also satisfies the second-order condition of optimality.

The average price $\bar{p}$ is derived from (8). Taking the average of both sides of (8) and rearranging terms, we have

$$\bar{p} = (1 + c_1 b)^{-1} \ [a^* + (c_0 + s) + c_1(g + d)]. \tag{10}$$

This equation shows that changes in the unobservables $s$ and $d$ influence $\bar{p}$ in the same way as changes in $c_0$ and $g$, about which the firm has perfect information.

## 2.2. *Imperfect Information*

If it takes time to transmit current information about firms to consumers, the perfect-information price adjustment cannot take place, as explained in Chapters 1 and 2. We then assume that prices are predetermined, in the sense that all the firms in the industry must advertise their prices simultaneously at the beginning of each period, in order to inform their customers and potential buyers that they are in business in the current period, and that they must keep these advertised prices during the period, in order to avoid confusion among consumers.

The expected profit of the firm observing the demand disturbance $\alpha$ and the cost disturbance $\beta$ is, from (1) and (2).

$$\begin{aligned}\hat{E} \exp(\pi) = \hat{E}\big(&\exp(p) \exp[-m(p-\bar{p}) + (g-b\bar{p}) + \alpha] \\ &- \exp\{c_0 - \log(c_1+1) + (c_1+1)[-m(p-\bar{p}) + (g-b\bar{p}) + \alpha] + \beta\}\big),\end{aligned} \tag{11}$$

where $\hat{E}$ is the expectation operator with respect to $\bar{p}$, based on the firm's subjective distribution of $\bar{p}$. The first-order condition of maximizing $\hat{E}$ exp $(\pi)$ with respect to $p$ is

$$\begin{aligned}(1+c_1 m)\, p = {} & \log[m/(m-1)] \\ & - \log\{\hat{E}\exp[(m-b)\bar{p}]/\hat{E}\exp[(c_1+1)(m-b)\bar{p}]\} \\ & + (c_0 + \beta) + c_1 g + c_1 \alpha.\end{aligned} \tag{12}$$

Under our assumptions, it can easily be shown that the second-order condition of optimality is satisfied.

Equation (12) determines the firm's optimal price. It depends crucially on the firm's subjective estimates of $\exp[(m-b)\bar{p}]$ and exp $[(c_1+1)(m-b)\bar{p}]$. They are determined by the firm's expectations about the average price $\bar{p}$, summarized in its subjective distribution of $\bar{p}$.

The firm is endowed with rational expectations. The derivation of rational expectations is the same as in Chapters 2–4. However, it may be worth while explaining the expectation-formation process in more detail in this model, because the firm's recognition of the correlation between demand and cost disturbances, and its effect on the firm's pricing, play a crucial role in obtaining the major results in this chapter.

Let $\Omega$ be the information available to the firm. We have $\Omega = \{\alpha, \beta\}$. The firm is assumed to expect that the distribution of $\bar{p}$ is normal with mean $e(\bar{p}|\Omega)$ and variance $V(\bar{p}|\Omega)$, where $e(\bar{p}|\Omega)$ is the linear least-squares regression of $\bar{p}$ based on $\Omega$, and $V(\bar{p}|\Omega)$ is its error variance.

Under the foregoing expectations assumption, condition (12) can be transformed into

$$(1+c_1 m)p = \log[m/(m-1)] + \tfrac{1}{2} c_1 (c_1+2)(m-b)^2 V(\bar{p}|\Omega) + (c_0+\beta) + c_1(g+\alpha) + c_1(m-b)e(\bar{p}|\Omega), \qquad (13)$$

because $\log E[\exp(hx)] = hEx + \tfrac{1}{2} h^2 V(x)$ for a normal random variable $x$ (see e.g. Maddala 1977). Let us define $a$ such that

$$a = \log[m/(m-1)] + \tfrac{1}{2} c_1 (c_1+2)(m-b)^2 V(\bar{p}|\Omega). \qquad (14)$$

The term $a$ is constant as long as the parameters of the demand and cost functions, as well as the variances and covariances of $s$, $d$, $w$, and $u$, do not change.

Substituting (14) into (13) and rearranging the terms in (13), we obtain

$$p = (1+c_1 m)^{-1}[a + c_0 + \beta + c_1(g+\alpha) + c_1(m-b)e(\bar{p}|\Omega)], \qquad (15)$$

which is the optimal pricing formula under imperfect information.

Every firm assumes that other firms form expectations about the average price as a linear combination of the observed values of $\alpha$ and $\beta$, say

$$e(\bar{p}|\Omega) = H + J\alpha + K\beta. \qquad (16)$$

Here, $H$, $J$, and $K$ are the undetermined coefficients. Under this assumption, the firm estimates the average price in the following way.

Inserting (16) into (15) and averaging over all firms, the firm gets $\bar{p}$ as a linear function of $s$ and $d$:

$$\bar{p} = (1+c_1 m)^{-1}[a + c_0 + s + c_1(g+d) + c_1(m-b)(H + Jd + Ks)].$$

Consequently, the firm's forecast $e(\bar{p}|\Omega)$ is given by

$$e(\bar{p}|\Omega) = (1+c_1 m)^{-1}\{a + c_0 + e(s|\Omega) + c_1[g + e(d|\Omega)] + c_1(m-b)[H + Je(d|\Omega) + Ke(s|\Omega)]\}.$$

Here, $e(d|\Omega)$ and $e(s|\Omega)$ represent the firm's forecasts for $d$ and $s$ based on its information $\Omega$. These forecasts are the linear least-squares regressions on information $\Omega = \{\alpha, \beta\}$. Using the method of linear least-squares regression (see e.g. Sargent (1979: 203–14) ), the firm has

$$e\,(d|\Omega) = \xi_1\beta + \xi_2\alpha \quad \text{and} \quad e(s|\Omega) = \theta_1\beta + \theta_2\alpha, \tag{17}$$

where

$$\xi_1 = [(1 + r_\beta^2)\,(1 + r_\alpha^2) - \rho^2]^{-1}\,(\rho/r_m)\,r_\alpha^2;$$
$$\xi_2 = [(1 + r_\beta^2)\,(1 + r_\alpha^2) - \rho^2]^{-1}\,(1 + r_\beta^2 - \rho^2);$$
$$\theta_1 = [(1 + r_\beta^2)\,(1 + r_\alpha^2) - \rho^2]^{-1}\,(1 + r_\alpha^2 - \rho^2);$$
$$\theta_2 = [(1 + r_\beta^2)\,(1 + r_\alpha^2) - \rho^2]^{-1}\,\rho r_m\, r_\beta^2.$$

Here the following definitions are utilized:

$r_m^2 \quad = \sigma_s^2/\sigma_d^2$ : variance ratio of the industry-wide cost to the industry-wide demand

$r_\alpha^2 \quad = \sigma_u^2/\sigma_d^2$ : variance ratio of the firm-specific demand to the industry-wide demand

$r_\beta^2 \quad = \sigma_w^2/\sigma_s^2$ : variance ratio of the firm-specific cost to the industry-wide cost

$\rho \quad = \sigma_{sd}/\sigma_s\sigma_d$ : correlation of the industry-wide cost to the industry-wide demand

It is evident that the correlation between $s$ and $d$ is an important determinant of the expectations. The firm's expected average price is then

$$\begin{aligned} e(\bar{p}|\Omega) = (1 + c_1 m)^{-1}\,\{&a + c_0 + \theta_1\beta + \theta_2\alpha + c_1\,(g + \xi_1\beta + \xi_2\alpha) \\ &+ c_1(m - b)\,[H + J\,(\xi_1\beta + \xi_2\alpha) + K(\theta_1\beta + \theta_2\alpha)]\}. \end{aligned} \tag{18}$$

Because all firms are identical except for $\alpha$ and $\beta$, and other firms use the same expectation-formation process, (16) and (18) must be the same. Consequently, by collecting terms, we obtain

$$H = (1 + c_1 b)^{-1}\,(a + c_0 + c_1 g); \tag{19}$$
$$K = \Phi^{-1}\{(1 + c_1 b)\,(1 - \rho^2) + (1 + c_1 m)\,[1 + c_1\,(\rho/r_m)]\,r_\alpha^2\}; \tag{20}$$
$$J = \Phi^{-1}\,[c_1\,(1 + c_1 b)\,(1 - \rho^2) + (1 + c_1 m)\,(\rho r_m + c_1)\,r_\beta^2]; \tag{21}$$

where

$$\begin{aligned} \Phi = {} & (1 + c_1 m)\,(1 + c_1 b)\,(r_\alpha^2 + r_\beta^2) + (1 + c_1 m)^2\, r_\alpha^2\, r_\beta^2 \\ & + (1+c_1 b)^2\,(1 - \rho^2). \end{aligned} \tag{22}$$

### 2.3. *The Average Price under Imperfect Information*

Substituting the expected-price formulas ((16)–(21)) into the individual optimal pricing formula (15), we obtain

$$p = (1+c_1 b)^{-1}\ (a+c_0+c_1 g) + \phi_d\ \alpha + \phi_s\ \beta \tag{23}$$

where

$$\phi_d = \Phi^{-1}\ c_1\ [(1+c_1 b)\ (r_\alpha^2 + r_\beta^2 + 1-\rho^2) + (1+c_1 m)\ r_\alpha^2\ r_\beta^2 + (m-b)\ (\rho r_m + c_1)\ r_\beta^2]$$

and

$$\phi_s = \Phi^{-1}\ [(1+c_1 b)\ (r_\alpha^2 + r_\beta^2 + 1-\rho^2) + (1+c_1 m)\ r_\alpha^2\ r_\beta^2 + \{1+c_1\ (\rho/r_m)\}\ (m-b)\ c_1\ r_\beta^2]$$

Consequently, we obtain

$$\bar{p} = (1+c_1 b)^{-1}\ (a+c_0+c_1 g) + \phi_d d + \phi_s s. \tag{26}$$

Using (26), we can easily show that (16) is actually the linear least-squares regression of $\bar{p}$ on $\alpha$ and $\beta$. Thus, the expectations are rational (consistent). The error variance $V(\bar{p}|\Omega) = V\{\bar{p} - e(\bar{p}|\Omega)\}$ can also be calculated from (26) and (16).

The imperfect-information average-price formula, (26), is different from the perfect-information average-price formula (10) in two respects. First, uncertainty caused by imperfect information makes the unconditional mean of the average price $\bar{\bar{p}}$ ($\bar{p}$ when $d = 0$) higher than in the perfect–information case. Equations (26), (14), (10), and (9) imply

$$\bar{\bar{p}}|_{\text{incomplete information}} - \bar{\bar{p}}|_{\text{complete information}} > 0.$$

Second, the elasticity of the average price to the unobserved demand shock $d$ (the supply shock $s$), $\phi_d$ ($\phi_s$), is generally different from the elasticity to the observed change in $g$ ($c_0$), $(1 + c_1)^{-1}c_1$ $[(1 + c_1 b)^{-1}]$, although they are the same under perfect information. In the next section, the determinants of the elasticity of the average price will be investigated.

## 3. COST-BASED PRICES, PRICE RIGIDITY, AND COMPETITION

### 3.1. *Uniform Cost Disturbances and Cost-Based Prices*

It is often argued that cost changes are rather uniform in a given industry, while demand disturbances vary considerably among firms. In this subsection I analyse the average-price behaviour when cost changes are uniform ($r_\beta = \sigma_w/\sigma_s \to 0$). Other parameters ($r_\alpha$, $r_m$, $\rho$, $m$, and $b$) are held constant.

Let us consider the firm's estimates of $d$ and $s$. From (17), if $r_\beta \to 0$, we obtain $\theta_1 \to 1$, $\theta_2 \to 0$, $\xi_1 \to (1 + r_\alpha^2 - \rho^2)$ $(\rho/r_m)r_\alpha^2$, and $\xi_2 \to (1 + r_\alpha^2 - \rho^2)$ $(1 - \rho^2)$. Consequently, we have

$$e(s|\Omega) \to \beta, \tag{27}$$

and

$$e(d|\Omega) \to \{(1 + r_\alpha^2 - \rho^2)(\rho/r_m)r_\alpha^2\}\beta + (1 + r_\alpha^2 - \rho^2)(1 - \rho^2)\alpha. \quad (28)$$

When cost changes are almost uniform ($r_\beta \to 0$), $\beta$ itself is a good estimate of $s$. In addition, $\beta$ provides important information about $d$. This is because $s$ is correlated with $d$, and $\beta$ is a good estimate of $s$. Consequently, $e(d|\Omega)$ depends on $\beta$, as well as on $\alpha$.

Using (24), (25), and (26), we obtain the average price in the case of uniform cost disturbances;

$$\bar{p} \to (1 + c_1 b)^{-1}(a + c_0 + c_1 g) + \phi^*_d\, d + \phi^*_s\, s, \quad (29)$$

where

$$\phi^*_d = (1 + c_1 b)^{-1} c_1 - W^{-1} c_1^2 (m - b) r_\alpha^2 \quad (30)$$

and

$$\phi^*_s = (1 + c_1 b)^{-1} + W^{-1} c_1^2 (m - b)(\rho/r_m) r_\alpha^2, \quad (31)$$

in which

$$W = (1 + c_1 b)\,[(1 + c_1 b)(1 - \rho^2) + (1 + c_1 m)\, r_\alpha^2]. \quad (32)$$

Because under our assumptions $W > 0$, we obtain a positive temporary cost sensitivity, $\phi^*_s > 0$, whether $c_1 > 0$ (decreasing returns) or $c_1 < 0$ (increasing returns). Because an increase in $s$ means an increase in $\beta$ on average, it results in an increase in the individual optimal price, directly through an increase in the individual marginal cost and indirectly through an increase in the individual estimate of the average price. Consequently, the average price is raised.

The sign of temporary demand sensitivity $\phi^*_d$, however, depends on the sign of $c_1$. Rearranging the terms in (30) yields

$$\phi^*_d = W^{-1}(1 + c_1 b)(r_\alpha^2 + 1 - \rho^2)\, c_1. \quad (33)$$

Thus, we have $\phi^*_d < 0$ if and only if $c_1 < 0$. If the marginal cost is decreasing, an increase in $d$ implies that other firms reduce their prices. A firm observing an increased $\alpha$ decreases its expected average price. Consequently, the firm lowers its price because of its decreased marginal cost and lower expected average price. Since an increase in $d$ means an increase in $\alpha$ on average, the average price is reduced. The opposite is true if $c_1 > 0$.

Let us now compare the imperfect-information case with the perfect-information case. From (30) and (31), we have

$$\phi^*_d < (1 + c_1 b)^{-1} c_1 \quad (34)$$

and

$$(1 + c_1 b)^{-1} < \phi^*_s. \quad (35)$$

Because $(1 + c_1 b)^{-1} c_1$ and $(1 + c_1 b)^{-1}$ are, respectively, the demand sensitivity and cost sensitivity in the perfect-information case (see (10)), (34) and (35) imply that imperfect information makes the average price more sensitive to temporary cost changes and less responsive to temporary demand changes in the case of uniform cost changes.

Sensitivities $\phi^*_d$ and $\phi^*_s$ depend on $m$, the degree of competitiveness. When the industry is more competitive ($m$ increases), the average price responds more to temporary cost changes ($\partial\phi^*_s/\partial m > 0$) but less to temporary demand changes ($\partial\phi^*_d/\partial m < 0$). This is because individual prices become more sensitive to $e(\bar{p}|\Omega)$, which depends more on $\beta$ than on $\alpha$.

To summarize, under uniform cost disturbances, imperfect information makes the industry average price more sensitive to temporary cost conditions and less responsive to temporary demand conditions. Increased competition among firms strengthens these tendencies and makes prices more cost-based than before. Table 5.1 shows the comparative-statics result with respect to other determinants of $\phi^*_d$ and $\phi^*_s$.

TABLE 5.1 Effects on the Demand and Cost Sensitivities of the Average Price

| | $\phi^*_d$ | $\phi^*_s$ |
|---|---|---|
| $m$ | − | + |
| $r^2_\alpha$ | − | + |
| $r_m$ | 0 | − |
| $\rho$ | − | − |

Under imperfect information, firms must estimate the average price by relying on their observations of their own demand and cost conditions. In this case, uniform cost disturbances and diverse demand disturbances imply that their observations of cost provide more information about the average price than do their observations of demand. Consequently, their individual prices depend more on cost conditions, and so does the industry average price.

### 3.2. *Competition and Price Rigidity*

In the case of correlated demand and supply shocks, the average price under imperfect information in (26) is a complicated function of the degree of competitiveness, $m$. Thus, in general, we cannot obtain a definite result about the effect of increased competition on price rigidity, namely, the sign of $\partial\phi_d/\partial m$ and $\partial\phi_s/\partial m$. However, the following analysis shows that increased competition ultimately makes prices rigid.

Let us assume that $r^2_\alpha$, $r^2_\beta$, $r_m$ and $\rho$ take on finite values, and let us then analyse the behaviour of the average price when the degree of competition $m$ goes to infinity. That is, let us investigate the case in which economic disturbances are held constant, and only competitiveness moves to its limit. We shall also assume decreasing returns to scale, $c_1 > 0$, because, first, the case of constant returns to scale is a trivial case in which $p$ is independent of $m$, and second, if $c_1 < 0$ (increasing returns), then $m \to +\infty$ violates the assumption that $1 + c_1 m > 0$.

In the case that $m \to +\infty$, we obtain $\phi_d \to 0$ and $\phi_s \to 0$ from (24) and (25). This shows that the average price in the industry is completely sticky in the face of temporary industry-wide fluctuations in demand and cost. This implies that, in the case of imperfect information, competition ultimately makes the average price sticky, rather than flexible, with respect to temporary changes in industry-wide conditions, even though the average price is perfectly flexible with respect to changes in $c_0$ and $g$, i.e. the permanent changes in industry-wide conditions.

The relationship between competitiveness and price rigidity in the case of correlated demand and supply shocks can be explained in the following way. Suppose that firms respond to individual temporary demand and cost disturbances. Then, the average price is also responsive to industry-wide temporary disturbances, which are the average of the individual disturbances. However, because firms have only imperfect information about industry-wide conditions, most firms in the industry fail to predict the actual average price correctly, even though on the average their forecasts are correct in a rational expectations equilibrium. Note that in a very competitive industry, where the price elasticity of individual demand is very large, a price higher than the actual average price can hardly attract positive demand, while a lower price induces a large demand which the firm cannot satisfy profitably. Thus, the existence of forecast errors implies that most firms suffer a large loss. This contradicts the notion of an equilibrium. Keeping this in mind, firms in the industry expect that other firms will not respond to temporary disturbances. Thus, their estimates of the average price are insensitive to temporary conditions. Consequently, in a very competitive industry, individual optimal prices become sticky with respect to temporary disturbances, and so does the actual average price.

## 4. CONCLUDING REMARKS

This chapter has investigated the log-linear model of a monopolistically competitive industry subject to correlated disturbances in demand and cost. It has been shown that if (a) cost disturbances are rather uniform and (b) disturbances in demand and cost are correlated, imperfect information makes the average price more sensitive to temporary cost conditions and less responsive to temporary demand conditions. It is often argued that (a) and (b) hold in many consumer goods markets, as well as in industrial markets. The results in Section 4 thus suggest that monopolistic competition and imperfect information might be an important determinant of the asymmetric price behaviour (demand-insensitive, cost-responsive prices) found in many econometric studies on price behaviour.

It has also been shown in this chapter that, although firms form rational expectations about industry-wide disturbances based on observed individual disturbances, competition ultimately makes the average price insensitive to temporary shocks in demand and cost under imperfect information, even if these shocks are correlated. Thus, the implication that competition reduces price flexibility obtained in Chapter 2 holds true in the general case.

The idea that permanent observed changes in economic conditions have a different impact on aggregate economic variables than do temporary unobservable ones has been extensively explored in the macroeconomic literature in the last decade (see e.g. Brunner *et al.* 1980, 1983). The model of monopolistic competition under imperfect information and stochastic disturbances developed in this chapter provides these macro-oriented models with the necessary microfoundations.

# Appendix: Competitiveness in an Industry with Differentiated Products: The Own-Price Elasticity and the Number of Firms

This appendix presents the structure of consumer preferences that leads to the following demand functions for differentiated products:

$$Q_j = (P_j/\bar{P}_j)^{-n} \, (\bar{P}_j)^{-1} \, G \, U_j,$$

or, in logarithm (the lower-case variable is the log of the upper-case variable),

$$q_j = -\, n(p_j - \bar{p}_j) + (g - \bar{p}_j) + u_j. \qquad (A_1)$$

Here $n$ is the number of firms in the industry, $Q_j$ is the demand at the $j$th firm, $\bar{P}_j$ is the appropriately defined average price of firms other than the $j$th one, and $G$ is a constant. In words, the number of firms is exactly equal to the own-price elasticity of demand.

There is a popular notion (at least among laymen) that an increased number of firms makes the market more competitive. However, we also have constant-elasticity models, such as that of Dixit and Stiglitz (1977), which are also popular (at least among theorists) in describing product differentiation. In the latter, the elasticity is based on the preference of the representative consumer's utility (the parameter in the CES utility function) and is assumed to be independent of the number of firms. My aim here is to reconcile these two approaches.

This appendix follows Sattinger (1984), who in turn depends on Houthakker's results (1974). I consider disturbances in preferences, while Sattinger does not.

A1. *Consumer Preferences*

There are two types of goods. The first is the composite commodity (possibly real balances), which is considered to be homogeneous. The second is that of a monopolistically competitive industry with $n$ differentiated products.

The utility function for the $i$th consumer is assumed to be

$$\Psi_i = W_i^{1-\gamma} Z_i^{\gamma}, \qquad 0 < \gamma < 1, \tag{A2}$$

in which $W_i$ is the amount of the composite commodity, and $Z_i$ is the level of satisfaction the consumer receives from the consumption of the industry's products. Let

$$Z_i = \sum_{j=1}^{n} R_{ij} Z_{ij}, \tag{A3}$$

where

$$R_{ij} = U_j^{1/(n-1)} \bar{R}_{ij}.$$

Here, $Z_{ij}$ is the amount of the $j$th firm's products consumed by the $i$th consumer, and $R_{ij}$ is the level of satisfaction received by the consumer consuming the unit quantity of the $j$th firm's products. $R_{ij}$ has two components: $\bar{R}_{ij}$ (the parameter) and $U_j$ (the disturbance). Thus, the disturbances in preferences are assumed to be the same for all consumers.

Let us take the composite good as a numeraire. Let $P_j$ be the (relative) price of the $j$th firm's products. The budget constraint of the $i$th consumer is

$$W_i + \sum_{j=1}^{n} P_j Z_{ij} = Y_i, \tag{A4}$$

where $Y_i$ is the exogenously determined income of the $i$th consumer. I assume that $Y_i$ is the same for all consumers.

The preferences of the consumer described above have two distinctive features. First, because of our Cobb–Douglas specification of the utility function, the expenditure on the products of this monopolistically competitive industry has a constant share in the total expenditure. This characteristic avoids the cumbersome aggregation problem, which otherwise makes the following analysis very complicated. As will become clear, I do not assume homogeneous consumers. Thus, avoiding the aggregation problem is crucial in the following discussion.

Second, (A2) and (A3) show that the products in this monopolistically competitive industry are perfect substitutes for one another. Consequently, the $i$th consumer buys only one firm's products with a maximum value of $R_{ij}/P_j$, if no tie occurs. Let $j^*(i)$ be such a $j$. Then the $i$th consumer buys $\gamma Y_i/P_{j^*(i)}$ of the $j^*(i)$th firm's products. The immediate consequence of this characteristic is that consumers must be heterogeneous in order to have well-behaved demand functions. This perfect-substitute assumption with heterogeneous consumers may be more realistic than the oft-made assumption of homogeneous consumers buying a little of everything in the industry (see Chapter 2, Spence 1976; Dixit and Stiglitz 1977).

In this model, the heterogeneity of consumers is specified in a continuous way. It is defined implicitly in terms of the distribution of the parametric satisfaction levels $\bar{R}_{ij}$. The values of $\bar{R}_{ij}$ are assumed to be independently and identically distributed. Let $F(x)$ be its cumulative distribution and $f(x)$ its density. Then, $F(x)$ is the proportion of consumers with $\bar{R}_{ij}$ less than or equal to $x$. The proportion of consumers with $\bar{R}_{ij} \leq x_j$, for $j = 1, \ldots, n$, is $\prod_{j=1}^{n} F(x_j)$.

### A2. *Demand Functions*

Let us now construct the demand function faced by the $j$th firm. The purchasers of the $j$th firm's products are those for whom $R_{ij}/P_j > R_{ik}/P_k$, or, equivalently, for whom $\bar{R}_{ij}/(P_j U_j^{-1/(n-1)}) > \bar{R}_{ik}/(P_k U_k^{-1/(n-1)})$ for all $k \neq j$. Consider all consumers having an $\bar{R}_{ij}$ that is equal to a particular number $x$. Their density is equal to $f(x)$. Among them, those consumers whose values of $\bar{R}_{ik}$, $k \neq j$, satisfy $\bar{R}_{ik}/(P_k U_k^{-1/(n-1)}) < x/(P_j U_j^{-1/(n-1)})$ actually purchase the $j$th firm's products. Their proportion is given by

$$\prod_{k \neq j} F[(xP_k U_k^{-1/(n-1)})/(P_j U_j^{-1/(n-1)})].$$

Integrating this over $x$ yields the proportion of all consumers purchasing product $j$:

$$s_j = \int_x \{ \prod_{k \neq j} F[(xP_k U_k^{-1/(n-1)})/(P_j U_j^{-1/(n-1)})]\} f(x)\, dx. \tag{A5}$$

Consequently, letting $Y$ be the aggregate level of income, the demand for the $j$th firm's product is

$$Q_j = s_j \gamma\, Y/P_j. \tag{A6}$$

### A3. *The Assumption of Uniform Distribution and the Derivation of (A1).*

Let us further assume that $\bar{R}_{ij}$ is uniformly distributed in [0, 1]. In this case, its cumulative distribution is $F(x) = 0$ for $x < 0$, $F(x) = x$ for $0 \leqslant x \leqslant 1$, and $F(x) = 1$ for $1 < x$. Its density is $f(x) = 0$ for $x < 0$, $f(x) = 1$ for $0 \leqslant x \leqslant 1$, and $f(x) = 0$ for $1 < x$.

Suppose that $(P_k U_k^{-1/(n-1)})/(P_j U_j^{-1/(n-1)}) < 1$ for all $k$ such that $k \neq j$. Then, for $0 \leqslant x \leqslant 1$, we have $(xP_k U_k^{-1/(n-1)})/(P_j U_j^{-1/(n-1)}) < 1$, so that

$$\prod_{k \neq j} F\, [(xP_k U_k^{-1/(n-1)})/(P_j U_j^{-1/(n-1)})] = \prod_{k \neq j} [(xP_k U_k^{-1/(n-1)})/(P_j U_j^{-1/(n-1)})].$$

Consequently, from (A5) we obtain

$$s_j = (\textstyle\int_0^1 x^{n-1} dx) \prod_{k \neq j} [(P_k U_k^{-1/(n-1)})/(P_j U_j^{-1/(n-1)})] = \frac{1}{n}(P_j/\bar{P}_j)^{-(n-1)} U_j, \tag{A7}$$

Where $\bar{P}_j$ is the weighted geometric average price of the firms other than $j$, such that

$$\bar{P}_j = [\prod_{k \neq j} P_k U_k^{-1/(n-1)}]^{1/(n-1)}. \tag{A8}$$

Consequently, letting $Y$ be the aggregate level of income, the demand for the $j$th firm's products is

$$Q_j = s_j \gamma\, Y/P_j = (P_j/\bar{P}_j)^{-n} (\bar{P}_j)^{-1} (1/n) \gamma\, Y\, U_j. \tag{A9}$$

Taking the log of both sides, we obtain.

$$q_j = -n(p_j - \bar{p}_j) + (g - \bar{p}_j) + u_j, \tag{A10}$$

where $\bar{p}_j = [1/(n-1)] \sum_{k \neq j} p_k - [1/(n-1)]^2 \sum_{k \neq j} u_k$ and $g = \log[(\gamma\, Y)/n]$, in which $u_k = \log U_k$. We thus obtain the desired outcome.

In the case where $P_k U_k^{-1/(n-1)}/(P_j U_j^{-1/(n-1)}) \geq 1$ for some $k \neq j$, the expression of $s_j$ does not have an exact log-linear representation. However, if we use the log-linear approximation, we obtain (A1).

The remarkable feature of the above demand function is that the own-price elasticity is constant and equal to the number of firms. Thus, if the number of firms increases, competition is intensified.

# Notes

1. Auction market goods include agricultural products, cotton, lumber, rubber, and some primary metals. The market for these products is well organized and employs auction and/or similar methods. For more about auction markets, see Okun (1981).
2. See Tobin (1972) for the consensus of these studies about the USA in the 1970s. See also Coutts *et al.* (1978) for empirical studies in the UK in the 1970s. For recent studies, see Ch. 1 above.
3. However, the argument of this chapter is different from Okun's. Okun argued that cost-oriented pricing is considered 'fair', and that firms having a customer–supplier relationship with their customers use this pricing practice in order to keep up a good relationship with their customers. The argument of this chapter, which is an informational one, does not depend on this assumption of fairness.
4. Thus, the firm is assumed to be either perfectly competitive or monopsonistic in input markets, although it is monopolistically competitive in the product market. This assumption is made because monopsonistically competitive markets are not as prevalent in industrialized economies as monopolistically competitive markets.

   Nishimura and Ueda (1986) analyse an industry where firms are monopolistically competitive in product markets and monopsonistically competitive in labour markets. They show that real wages are pro-cyclical in such an industry.
5. Thus, I assume that the firm knows the objective demand and cost functions. If the firm has only imperfect information about the parameters in the functions, a learning-by-doing-type model may be more appropriate.
6. I assume the firm can observe the state of demand and cost, $\alpha$ and $\beta$, before it actually sells its products. Continuing market research of various types may provide the firm with the necessary information to infer $\alpha$ and $\beta$.

   If the firm cannot observe $\alpha$ and $\beta$ independently, it is obliged to estimate them using their past values. This usually implies a slow adjustment of expectations, rather than the instantaneous adjustment postulated in the text. The past values of $\alpha$ and $\beta$ are at best noisy imperfect information about the current $\alpha$ and $\beta$. In the next chapter, in a slightly different context, it will be shown that, if the firm has only noisy imperfect information about demand and cost conditions, then its decision is more conservative than in the perfect-information case. This implies more rigid prices in the case of imperfect information about $\alpha$ and $\beta$.

7. Several interpretations are possible for $\alpha$, $\beta$, *d, s, u,* and *w*. First, they can be short-run disturbances. In this case, the industry is subject to short-lived disturbances *d, s, u,* and *w*; and *Ed, Es, Eu,* and *Ew* are their averages over time. Second, *d, s, u,* and *w* may be permanent changes whose probabilities are represented by normal distributions having parameters *Ed*, etc. Third, *d* and *s* may be permanent changes, while *u* and *s* are short-run disturbances. In the following analysis, I adopt the first interpretation.
8. The firm is risk-neutral.

# 6
# Competition and the Volatility of Investment

## 1. INTRODUCTION

One of the major features of macroeconomic time series in the United States and other industrialized countries is that there are large fluctuations in investment compared with relatively stable consumption expenditures. Investment depends on changes in technology and the state of future demand, as well as on the cost of capital and other market constraints. Previous macroeconomic studies of investment[1] mostly analyse perfectly competitive firms under certainty and examine the determinants of their investment behaviour.[2] Large fluctuations in investment are attributed to fluctuations in these determinants. Some researchers introduce uncertainty about future demand explicitly into this framework, but the results are qualitatively similar to their certainty counterparts.[3]

The analysis in Chapters 1–5, however, shows the importance of monopolistic competition and imperfect information for understanding such macroeconomic features as nominal price rigidity, monetary non-neutrality, and cost-based prices. This suggests that monopolistic competition and imperfect information may also affect macroeconomic fluctuations by influencing investment. The main purpose of this chapter is to explore this possibility.[4]

In the sections that follow I shall investigate the investment behaviour of monopolistically competitive firms under the assumption of imperfect information about the average investment. A fundamental assumption in this chapter is that a typical firm does not have perfect information about its competitors' investments; hence the average investment, which affects the firm's profit, is not known with certainty when the firm determines its own investment. The firm forms rational expectations about the unknown average investment on the basis of available information. I address two questions in this environment: (1) Does imperfect information destabilize investment? (2) Is increased competition stabilizing under imperfect information?

The answer to the first question depends on what kind of information is available about individual demand and productivity conditions. If a firm can observe its own productivity and demand conditions when determining its investment, imperfect information about the average investment increases the sensitivity of investment to industry-wide shocks, and thus destabilizes investment. This result is related to that of Lucas (1975). However, if the firm has only imperfect information about its own productivity and demand conditions, the result depends on the accuracy of its forecast of these conditions. If the forecast is accurate, imperfect information increases the sensitivity of investment and destabilizes it. If, however, the forecast contains a large error, imperfect information reduces the sensitivity of investment and stabilizes it.

By contrast, the answer to the second question is unambiguous. Increased competition always increases the sensitivity of investment to industry-wide shocks, and thus destabilizes investment, regardless of whether or not the firm's own demand and cost conditions are observed.

The destabilizing effect of competition stems from two ingredients in our monopolistically competitive investment model under imperfect information. One is the rigidity of rational expectations; the other is the negative effect of the average investment on the firm's optimal investment level.

On the one hand, under the simple informational structure in this chapter the firm forms rational expectations about the average investment based on local conditions. Because of the possibility of local–global confusion, these rational expectations about average investment are less sensitive to industry-wide shocks than the actual average investment. On the other hand, in our log-linear monopolistically competitive framework, the firm's optimal investment depends negatively on its expectations about the average investment.[5]

For example, suppose there is an unexpected industry-wide increase in productivity. If the other firms do not change their investments, then a given firm increases its investment by a large amount. By contrast, if the other firms increase their investment, the increase in the given firm's investment is rather small because of the investment-reducing effect of the average investment. However, under imperfect information, the given firm's expectations about the other firms' investments (and thus about the average investment) do not increase as much as the actual investments of the other firms. This is because of the rigidity of rational expectations. Consequently, the investment-reducing effect of the average investment is reduced under imperfect information. Thus, a given firm increases its own investment more under imperfect information than under perfect information. Since increased competition implies that the firm's investment becomes more dependent on rigid expectations, it further reduces the investment-reducing effect of the average investment and increases the firm's investment. In this way, increased competition increases the volatility of investment. A similar argument holds true for an industry-wide demand increase.

The plan of this chapter is as follows. In Section 2 the model is laid out. In order to concentrate the analysis on the effect of imperfect average-investment information, I assume perfect information in the product market. The case of productivity shocks is investigated in this section. The firm does not have perfect information about the industry-wide productivity shock when determining its investment. Two cases are considered. In the first, the firm observes its own productivity condition in determining its investment, while in the second, the firm has only imperfect information about this condition. In Section 3 the case of demand shocks is analysed. The future demand condition is not observable when the firm determines its investment, but the firm has a noisy information about it. The main findings of this chapter are presented in these two sections. In Section 4, the analysis is extended to the cases of increasing unit variable costs, risk aversion, and free entry. I show that the main results of Section 2 and 3 still hold true in a general setting; in addition, the sensitivity of investment may be different between the peak and the trough of demand fluctuations if we allow free entry. Section 5 concludes the chapter.

## 2. PRODUCTIVITY SHOCKS AND INDUSTRY INVESTMENT

In this chapter, we consider the investment decisions of firms in a monopolistically competitive industry. The model is the same as that in Chapter 5, except that capital stocks are explicitly analysed.

In order to make the analysis clear, I assume the simplest investment technology. That is, capital goods in this industry are assumed to be depreciated fully in one period: they are used up in one period, like seeds in agriculture. The characteristic of investment analysed in this chapter is that the investment decision takes place before actual market conditions are known to firms. (It is also possible to interpret the model so as to analyse the demand for variable inputs of production, as long as decisions about such variable inputs must be made before actual market conditions are known to firms. In this interpretation, 'investment' in the following analysis is replaced by 'demand for variable inputs'.)

In this setting, the firm's problem is reduced to the following two-period problem. In the first period the firm determines its capital stock for the next period. In the second period the firm determines the price of its products, taking into account its own capital stock and the average price in the market. At the end of the second period, the firm produces the products and sells them to consumers. The product market in the second period is assumed to be monopolistically competitive, while for simplicity the labour market in the second period, the financial market in the first period, and the capital goods market in the first period are all assumed to be perfectly competitive.

In Sections 2 and 3 I assume constant unit variable costs,[6] risk-neutral firms, and an exogenously determined number of firms. The effects of increasing unit variable costs, risk aversion, and free entry will be discussed in Section 4. In this section I analyse the case of productivity shocks. There is no shock in demand. Demand shocks will be investigated in Section 3.

Let us consider the information available to the firm in each period. In the first period (investment period), productivity shocks are realized. There are two kinds of productivity shocks: industry-wide and firm-specific. The individual productivity shock at the firm level consists of these two shocks. The firm is assumed to observe its own productivity shock, but it does not observe the two components separately.[7] (The case in which the own-productivity condition is not observable will be discussed later in this section.) The firm is also assumed to have no information about the other firms' productivity and investment levels. It must determine its investment before knowing the average investment and the industry-wide productivity condition.

In the second period (production period), the firm is assumed to have all information. It knows the average capital stock, the average productivity, and the average price in the market. Thus, there is no uncertainty in the second period. This assumption is made in order to concentrate on the effect of competition[8] in the investment process.[9]

The following analysis depends crucially on our assumption of imperfect information and induced strategic uncertainty in the first (investment) period. This seems a realistic assumption about industries in which many relatively small firms compete with one another. In such industries, information-sharing is not practical because of large administrative costs, as well as anti-trust considerations.[10] The model in this chapter is intended to describe these industries.[11]

It is helpful to consider the firm's decision backwards, from the second period to the first.[12] Throughout this chapter, all variables are in logarithm, if not otherwise noted. Investment goods are taken as a numeraire, so that all prices in this chapter are relative ones.

### 2.1. *The Second Period*

The demand for the firm's products in the second period is

$$q^d = -\,m(p - \bar{p}) + \bar{q}^d, \tag{1}$$

where

$$\bar{q}^d = -\,b\bar{p}. \tag{2}$$

Here $p$ is the firm's price, $\bar{p}$ is the average price, $q^d$ is the individual demand, and $\bar{q}^d$ is the average demand. The parameter $m$ is the price elasticity of the individual demand, and $b$ is that of the average demand. We assume $m > b \geqslant 1$; that is, the slope of the individual demand curve is flatter than that of the market demand curve.[13]

In the case of productivity shocks, the production function is

$$q = l + \gamma k + \beta \tag{3}$$

where

$$\beta = g + x.$$

Here $q$ is output, $l$ is labour, and $k$ is capital. I assume that the parameter $\gamma$ in (3) satisfies $1/(m-1) > \gamma > 0$. This condition is necessary for profit maximization. The term $\beta$ represents the productivity shock, which consists of the industry-wide component $g$ and the firm-specific component $x$. The random variables $g$ and $x$ satisfy $Eg = Ex = Egx = 0$, $Eg^2 = \sigma^2_g$, and $Ex^2 = \sigma^2_x$.

Note that the capital stock, $k$, is determined in the first period, and thus is given in the second period. It differs from firm to firm. The firm is identified by a pair $(k, x)$ in the second period. Because of perfect information, the firm $(k, x)$'s problem is to maximize its real profits $\exp(\pi) = \exp(p)\exp(q^d) - \exp(w)\exp(l)$ with respect to $p$. The number of firms is sufficiently large that the average of $x$ is approximated by its mathematical expectation, $Ex$ $(= 0)$, and that firms ignore the dependence of the average price on their own price in determining their price. Then, the individual optimal price is

$$p = \log[m/(m-1)] + w - \gamma k - \beta. \tag{4}$$

The average price is $\bar{p} = \log[m/(m-1)] + w - \gamma\bar{k} - g$, where $\bar{k}$ is the average of $k$.

Using (4) we have the second-period equilibrium profit function

$$\pi(k, \bar{k}, \beta, g) = \phi_0 + \phi_v(k - \bar{k}) + \phi_{\bar{k}}\bar{k} + (m-1)\beta - (m-b)g, \tag{5}$$

where

$$\begin{aligned} \phi_0 &= -b\log m + (b-1)\log(m-1) - (b-1)w, \\ \phi_v &= (m-1)\gamma, \quad \text{and} \quad \phi_{\bar{k}} = (b-1)\gamma. \end{aligned} \tag{6}$$

Because $m > b \geqslant 1$ and $1/(m-1) > \gamma > 0$, we have $1 > \phi_v > \phi_{\bar{k}} \geqslant 0$.

The second-period profit function has the following properties. First, if, *ceteris paribus*, the firm's productivity ($\beta$) increases, its profit increases ($m - 1 > 0$); whereas if the other firms' productivity ($g$) increases, its profit decreases ($-(m-b) < 0$). Second, if, *ceteris paribus*, the firm's capital stock ($k$) increases, its profit increases ($\phi_v > 0$); whereas if the other firms' capital stock ($\bar{k}$) increases, its profit decreases ($-\phi_v + \phi_{\bar{k}} < 0$). If the firm's investment is not accompanied by investments by the other firms, it has a cost advantage relative to them in the second period. The firm can then lower its price relative to the other firm's prices, attract more customers, and thus make more profits. By contrast, if the other firms' investment increases, the firm suffers from a cost disadvantage, so that its profit decreases. This is the way competition among firms operates in the investment process.

### 2.2. *The First Period*

In the first period, the firm knows the functional form of the profit function and the cost of investment:

$$c = c_0 + k. \tag{7}$$

Here $c_0$ is a constant. Thus, we assume a constant marginal cost of investment.[14]

Information available to the firm is imperfect. First, the average investment $\bar{k}$ is not observable in determining its own investment. Second, although $\beta$ is observable, $g$ and $x$ in $\beta$ are not independently observable. All other parameters in (3)–(7) are known to the firm. The discount rate $r$ is also known to the firm.

The firm forms expectations about $\bar{k}$ and $g$ rationally, based on available information, including $\beta$. Specifically, $\bar{k}$ and $g$ are assumed to be jointly normally distributed with mean $(e(\bar{k}|\Omega), e(g|\Omega))$ and variance–covariance matrix $V(\bar{k}, g|\Omega)$ where $e(\bar{k}|\Omega)$ and $e(g|\Omega)$ are respectively, the linear least-squares regressions of $\bar{k}$ and $g$ on $\Omega$, and where $V(\bar{k}, g|\Omega)$ is their error variance–covariance matrix.

Note that the firm is identified in the first period by the firm-specific productivity disturbance $x$. Then, firm $x$'s problem in the first period is to maximize $\hat{E}\{(1+r)^{-1} \exp[\pi(k, \bar{k}, \beta, g)] - \exp(c)\}$ with respect to $k$, subject to (5) and (7). Here $\hat{E}$ is the expectation operator with respect to the firm's subjective distribution of $\bar{k}$ and $g$.

The following optimal investment formula is derived from the first-order condition of optimality:

$$\begin{aligned} k = (1-\phi_v)^{-1} [z_g + (m-1)\beta - (m-b)\, e(g|\Omega) \\ - (\phi_v - \phi_{\bar{k}})\, e(\bar{k}|\Omega)]. \end{aligned} \tag{8}$$

where

$$z_g = z^* + \frac{1}{2} f_g^t V(\bar{k}, g|\Omega) f_g \quad \text{and} \quad z^* = \log \phi_v + \phi_0 - c_0 - \log(1+r),$$

in which $f_g^t = [-(\phi_v - \phi_{\bar{k}}), -(m-b)]$. Here $t$ denotes the transpose.[15]

Note that $e(\bar{k}|\Omega)$ and $e(g|\Omega)$ are based on information $\beta$. Consequently, (8) implies that the average investment $\bar{k}$ is solely dependent on the average of $\beta$, that is, $g$. Thus, $\bar{k}$ and $g$ are perfectly correlated. Uncertainty in (8) is reduced to uncertainty about only one variable, $\bar{k}$ (or $g$). Using this fact and the undetermined coefficient method (see Appendix *A* at the end of this chapter), we obtain

$$e(g|\Omega) = \lambda\,\beta$$

$$e(\bar{k}|\Omega) = \frac{1}{1-\phi_{\bar{k}}}\,z_g + \frac{m-1-(m-b)\,\lambda}{1-\phi_v + (\phi_v - \phi_{\bar{k}})\,\lambda}\,\lambda\,\beta, \tag{9}$$

where

$$\lambda = \frac{\sigma_g^2}{\sigma_g^2 + \sigma_x^2}$$

and

$$z_g = z^* + \frac{1}{2}\left[(\phi_v - \phi_{\bar{k}})\,\frac{m-1-(m-b)\,\lambda}{1-\phi_v+(\phi_v-\phi_{\bar{k}})\,\lambda} + (m-b)\right]^2 \lambda\,\sigma_x^2 .$$

Consequently, taking (9) into account, we get

$$\bar{k} = \frac{1}{1-\gamma\,(b-1)}\,z_g + \frac{m-1-(m-b)\,\lambda}{1-\gamma\,[m-1-(m-b)\,\lambda]}\,g. \tag{10}$$

The formula in (10) completely characterizes the average investment under imperfect information.

Let us now compare the imperfect-information case with the perfect-information case. Perfect information about $\bar{k}$ implies $e(\bar{k}|\Omega) = \bar{k}$ and $V(\bar{k}|\Omega) = 0$. From (8), it is straightforward to show that the average investment under perfect information is given by

$$\bar{k} = \frac{1}{1-\gamma\,(b-1)}\,z^* + \frac{b-1}{1-\gamma\,(b-1)}\,g. \tag{11}$$

From the above two average-investment equations, we immediately obtain two characteristics of the sensitivity of the average investment to the industry-wide productivity shock $g$. First, imperfect information makes the average investment more sensitive to the industry-wide productivity shock than perfect information, because

$$\frac{m-1-(m-b)\,\lambda}{1-\gamma\,[m-1-(m-b)\,\lambda]} > \frac{b-1}{1-\gamma\,(b-1)}\,.$$

Second, competition makes the average investment more sensitive to the industry-wide productivity shock under imperfect information ($\partial[\partial\bar{k}/\partial g$ in (10)$]/\partial m > 0$), although it has no effect on its sensitivity under perfect information ($\partial[\partial\bar{k}/\partial g$ in (11)$]/\partial m = 0$).

### 2.3. *The Reaction Curve*

The above results can be explained in the 'reaction function' framework. Suppose that $g = 1$. Let $\Delta\bar{k}$ denote the response of the average investment such that $\Delta\bar{k} = \bar{k} - \bar{\bar{k}}$, where $\bar{\bar{k}}$ is the unconditional mean of $\bar{k}$. Under imperfect information, $\bar{\bar{k}} = [1 - \gamma(b-1)]^{-1}z_g$, while under perfect information, $\bar{\bar{k}} = [1 - \gamma(b-1)]^{-1}z^*$. Next, let the average expectation about the average investment, $\bar{e}(\bar{k}|\Omega)$, be the average of $e(\bar{k}|\Omega)$ over all firms. Then I define the response of the average expectation, $\Delta\, \bar{e}(\bar{k}|\Omega)$, such that $\Delta\, \bar{e}(\bar{k}|\Omega) = \bar{e}(\bar{k}|\Omega) - \bar{k}$. Similarly, the average expectation about $g$ is defined as the average of $e(g|\Omega)$ over all firms. The response of the average expectation about $g$, $\Delta\, \bar{e}(g|\Omega)$, is defined analogously, but we have $\Delta\, \bar{e}(\bar{g}|\Omega) = \bar{e}(g|\Omega)$, because the unconditional mean of $g$ is zero.

Using these definitions, (9), and the assumption that $g = 1$, the individual investment formula (8) can be transformed into the following 'reaction function':

$$\Delta \bar{k} = \frac{1}{1-\gamma\,(m-1)}\,[(m-1) - (m-b)\,\Delta\bar{e}\,(g|\Omega)] - \frac{(m-b)\,\gamma}{1-\gamma\,(m-1)}\,\Delta\bar{e}\,(\bar{k}|\Omega). \tag{12}$$

This equation characterizes the firm's response as a reaction to the expected response of the average investment. The average is taken here in order to cancel out the effect of the firm-specific disturbance $x$.

On the one hand, under perfect information, we have $\Delta\, \bar{e}(g|\Omega) = g = 1$ by definition, so that the perfect-information reaction function is

$$\Delta \bar{k} = \frac{b-1}{1-\gamma\,(m-1)} - \frac{(m-b)\,\gamma}{1-\gamma\,(m-1)}\,\Delta\bar{e}\,(\bar{k}|\Omega). \tag{13}$$

This reaction function is represented by $AA$ in Fig. 6.1. In this figure, the vertical axis is $\Delta\, \bar{k}$, and the horizontal axis is $\Delta\, \bar{e}(\bar{k}|\Omega)$. The equilibrium is the intersection of this reaction curve and the 'expectation curve', which relates the average expectation to the average investment. The expectation curve under perfect information is $OC$, the 45° line, because by definition we have $\Delta\, \bar{k} = \Delta\, \bar{e}(\bar{k}|\Omega)$. Thus, the perfect information equilibrium is $E$.

On the other hand, under imperfect information, we have

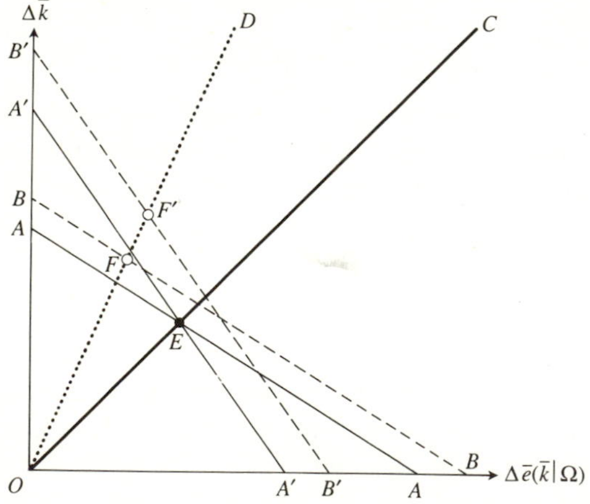


FIG. 6.1. Productivity shocks

$\bar{e}(g|\Omega) = \lambda g = \lambda$. Consequently, the imperfect-information reaction function is

$$\Delta \bar{k} = \frac{m-1-(m-b)\,\lambda}{1-\gamma\,(m-1)} - \frac{(m-b)\,\gamma}{1-\gamma\,(m-1)}\,\Delta \bar{e}\,(\bar{k}\,|\,\Omega). \qquad (14)$$

This is represented by *BB* in Fig. 6.1. *BB* is above *AA* by $[(m - b)\ (1 - \lambda)]/[1 - \gamma\ (m - 1)] > 0$. Next, the expectation curve under imperfect information is no longer the 45° line. Under imperfect information, we obtain $\Delta \bar{k} = (1/\lambda)\ \Delta \bar{e}(\bar{k}|\Omega)$ (see (9) and (10)), which is represented by *OD*. Because $\lambda$ is less than unity (the average expectation is stickier than the actual average investment), *OD* is steeper than *OC*. The imperfect-information equilibrium is the intersection at *F* of *BB* and *OD*. It is evident from this figure that, as long as $\lambda < 1$, imperfect information makes investment more responsive to *g*, and thus more volatile.

The effect of imperfect information can be conveniently decomposed into two parts: the impact effect and the repercussion effect. The impact effect is the effect of imperfect information when expectations about $\bar{k}$ are held constant. This is the effect of uncertainty about the average productivity *g*. Note that, for a given $\beta$, an increase in *g* implies that the firm will suffer from a cost disadvantage. This reduces the profitability of production (see (5)), and thus reduces the incentive for investment. However, because of the signal-extraction problem, the estimate of *g* is less sensitive to the signal $\beta$. This is because part of the signal could be local. Since the firm underestimates the average productivity increase (and the cost disadvantage in the next period) when $g = 1$, it believes that it has room to expand its own investment, even if its expectations about the average investment do not change. Thus, the impact effect is positive. It is measured by the vertical distance between *BB* and *AA*.

The repercussion effect is the effect of imperfect information through expectations about $\bar{k}$, taking the impact effect as given. Because of the signal-extraction problem with respect to $\bar{k}$, $\lambda$ is less than unity, which implies that the estimate of the average investment is less sensitive to the signal $\beta$. Since the firm underestimates the average investment when $g = 1$, it again believes that it has room to expand its own investment. Thus, the repercussion effect is also positive. This effect is measured by $(1/\lambda)$, the degree of rotation of *OD* from *OC*.[16]

These two effects of imperfect information affect investment in the same direction, and thus investment is unambiguously more sensitive to the industry-wide productivity shock under imperfect information.

Next, consider the effect of increased competition. An increase in *m* rotates *AA* clockwise around *E*. Thus, the perfect-information equilibrium does not change. However, *BB* shifts to *B'B'*, and the new imperfect-information equilibrium is *F'*, which is above *F* as long as $\lambda < 1$. Increased competition unambiguously increases the sensitivity of investment.

This result can also be explained by local–global confusion in the signal-extraction problem. Again, take the case of $g = 1$. Increased competition implies that the firm expects larger returns from an increase in its capital stock (an increase in $\phi_v$ in the equilibrium profit function), provided such an increase is not accompanied by an increase in the other firms' capital stock. If the firm's investment is matched by the other firms, the profit opportunity arising from increased competition dissipates. ($\phi_{\bar{k}}$ in the profit function is independent of $m$.) Under imperfect information, the average investment must be estimated relying on $\beta$. Because the estimate of the average investment is less sensitive to the signal than the actual average investment, the initial incentive to increase investment does not dissipate, even after the average investment has been rationally estimated. Thus, the average investment becomes more sensitive to $g$, and its volatility increases.

## 2.4. *Additional Uncertainty about the Individual-Productivity Condition*

So far, we have assumed that the individual-productivity shock is observed in the first (investment) period. Thus, there has been no uncertainty about the firm's own productivity condition. This is the case, for example, if firms purchase machines and observe their productivity in the first period. In this setting, we have investigated imperfect information about the average investment (imperfect-investment information). Uncertainty caused by this imperfect information can be called 'strategic uncertainty', because it is uncertainty about the other firms' strategies (levels of investment).

In some cases, however, the firm's own productivity condition may not be observable in the first period. For example, the firm may have to determine its investment well before it knows its actual productivity. In such cases, the firm faces another kind of imperfect information, namely, imperfect information about its own productivity condition (imperfect own-productivity information). Uncertainty caused by imperfect own-productivity information can be called non-strategic uncertainty, because it does not involve uncertainty about the strategic interaction among firms.

The effect of non-strategic uncertainty is the opposite of the effect of strategic uncertainty. Non-strategic uncertainty *reduces* the sensitivity of investment.

Suppose that $\beta$ is now not observable in the first period, and that a productivity signal,

$$\hat{\beta} = \beta + y, \tag{15}$$

is assumed to be observed,[17] where $y$ is an observational error. The random variable $y$ is independent of $g$ and $x$ and satisfies $Ey = 0$ and $Ey^2 = \sigma_y^2$. Using the same procedure employed earlier, we obtain

$$\bar{k} = \frac{1}{1-\gamma\,(b-1)}\;\hat{z}_g + \frac{(m-1)\,\hat{\nu} - (m-b)\,\hat{\lambda}}{1-\gamma\,\{m-1-(m-b)\,\hat{\lambda}\}}\;g \tag{16}$$

where

$$\hat{\lambda} = \frac{\sigma_g^2}{\sigma_g^2+\sigma_x^2+\sigma_y^2},\quad \hat{\nu} = \frac{\sigma_g^2+\sigma_x^2}{\sigma_g^2+\sigma_x^2+\sigma_y^2},\ \text{and}\ \hat{z}_g = z^* + \frac{1}{2}\hat{f}_g^t V(\bar{k}, g, \beta\,|\,\Omega)\hat{f}_g$$

in which $\hat{f}_g^t = [-(\phi_v - \phi_{\bar{k}}),\ -\ (m-b),\ m-1]$. From this relation, it can be shown that competition increases the sensitivity of the average investment even in this framework. However, because $\hat{\lambda} < \lambda$ and $\hat{\nu} < 1$, (16) and (10) show that imperfect information about the firm's own productivity condition reduces the sensitivity of the average investment to the industry-wide productivity shock.

The intuition behind this result is simple. Suppose that the firm observes an increase in the signal $\hat{\beta}$. Every firm knows that there is a chance that the change in the signal is only an observational error, so it increases investment by less than it would if there were no uncertainty about the productivity condition. Thus, the average investment is less responsive to the industry-wide productivity shock if the firm's own productivity condition is not observable.

## 3. DEMAND SHOCKS AND INDUSTRY INVESTMENT

Let us turn to the case of demand shocks. In the following, I show that qualitatively the same results are obtained in the demand-shock case as in the productivity-shock case.

### 3.1. *The Second Period*

The average demand and the individual demand are, respectively,

$$\bar{q}^d = -\ b\bar{p} + d, \tag{17}$$

and

$$q^d = -\ m\,(p-\bar{p}) + \bar{q}^d + u = -\ m(p-\bar{p}) - b\bar{p} + \alpha, \tag{18}$$

where

$$\alpha = d + u.$$

Here, the random variables $d$ and $u$ are normally distributed, satisfying $Ed = Eu = Edu = 0$, $Ed^2 = \sigma_d^2$, and $Eu^2 = \sigma_u^2$. The term $\alpha$ is the individual demand disturbance, which consists of $d$, the disturbance common to all firms, and $u$, the idiosyncratic one. Because information is perfect in the second period, the firm's optimal price is $p = \log\ [m/$

$(m - 1)] + w - \gamma k$. Consequently, the second-period profit function is

$$\pi (k, \bar{k}, \alpha) = \phi_0 + \phi_v (k - \bar{k}) + \phi_{\bar{k}} \bar{k} + \alpha. \tag{19}$$

### 3.2. *The First Period*

Note that $\alpha$ is the demand condition of the next period, so, in general, it is not observable. However, in order to make the analysis clear, we first assume that $\alpha$ is observable. This case corresponds to that of the observable own-productivity shock in the previous section. A more realistic case, in which $\alpha$ is not observable, is considered later in this section.

When $\alpha$ is observable, the firm is identified by $u$ in the second period. The firm $u$ maximizes $\hat{E}\ (1 + r)^{-1} \exp [\pi (k, \bar{k}, \alpha)] - \exp (c_0 + k)$.

The second-period profit function (19) is simplier in the demand-shock case than is the function (5) in the productivity-shock case, because the average demand $d$ does not independently enter the profit function. Otherwise, the two profit functions are quite similar. The constant term and the coefficients of $k - \bar{k}$ and $\bar{k}$ are the same. The coefficient of $\alpha$ in (19) is positive as is the coefficient of $\beta$ in (5). Thus, one can expect the demand-shock case to be qualitatively similar to the productivity-shock case.

Using the same procedure as that employed in the previous section, we obtain

$$\bar{k} = \frac{1}{1 - \gamma (b - 1)} z_d + \frac{1}{1 - \gamma [(m - 1) - (m - b) \xi]} d, \tag{20}$$

where $z_d = z^* + \frac{1}{2} (\phi_v - \phi_{\bar{k}})^2\ V (\bar{k} | \Omega)$, and $\xi = \sigma_d^2 / (\sigma_d^2 + \sigma_u^2)$.[18] By contrast, the average investment under perfect information is

$$\bar{k} = \frac{1}{1 - \gamma (b - 1)} z^* + \frac{1}{1 - \gamma (b - 1)} d. \tag{21}$$

Comparing these two expressions, we can see that the same conclusion is obtained in the demand-shock case as in the productivity case. Imperfect investment information increases the sensitivity of the average investment to the industry-wide demand shock. An increase in competition also increases its sensitivity.

### 3.3. *The Effect of Imperfect Own-Demand Information*

Next, let us consider a more realistic case, in which the firm has only imperfect information about $\alpha$. Suppose that the firm can obtain the following noisy signal $\hat{\alpha}$:[19]

$$\hat{\alpha} = \alpha + v, \tag{22}$$

where $v$ is a normally distributed forecast error, which is independent of $d$ and $u$ and satisfies $Ev=0$ and $Ev^2=\sigma_v^2$. This case corresponds to the case in the previous section, where the firm's own productivity is not observable.

The determination of the average investment in this case can be explained by Fig. 6.2, which is similar to Fig. 6.1. In this figure, we assume that $d = 1$; $\Delta\bar{k}$ and $\Delta\bar{e}(\bar{k}|\Omega)$ are defined in the same way as in Fig. 6.1. Note that the optimal investment formula in the case of imperfect information about $\alpha$ is

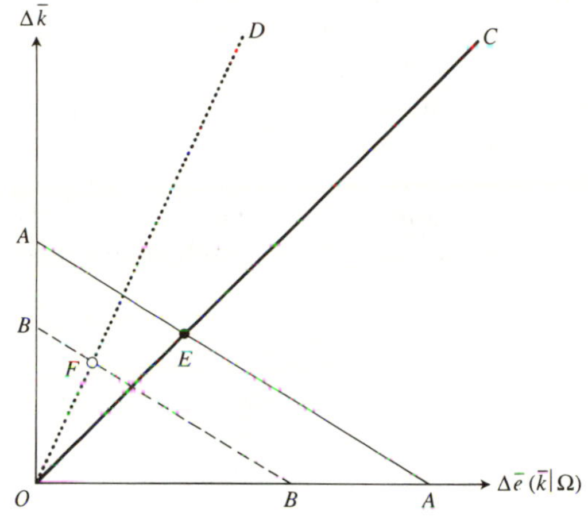


FIG. 6.2. Demand shocks

$$k = (1-\phi_v)^{-1}\,(\hat{z}_d + e\,(\alpha|\Omega) - (\phi_v - \phi_{\bar{k}})\,e\,(\bar{k}|\Omega)], \tag{23}$$

where

$$\hat{z}_d = z^* + \frac{1}{2} f_d^t\, V\,(\bar{k},\ \alpha|\Omega)\, f_d$$

in which $f_d^t = [-(\phi_v - \phi_{\bar{k}}),\ 1]$. Thus, from (23), the reaction function is

$$\Delta\,\bar{k} = \frac{1}{1-\gamma\,(m-1)}\,\Delta\bar{e}\,(\alpha|\Omega) - \frac{(m-b)\,\gamma}{1-\gamma\,(m-1)}\,\Delta\bar{e}\,(\bar{k}|\Omega). \tag{24}$$

Under perfect information, we have $\Delta\bar{e}(\alpha|\Omega) = d = 1$. $AA$ represents this perfect-information reaction curve. $OC$ is the 45° line representing the expectation curve. Thus, the perfect-information equilibrium is the intersection at $E$ of $AA$ and $OC$.

Under imperfect information, $\Delta\bar{e}\,(\alpha|\Omega) = \hat{\tau}d = \hat{\tau}$, where

$$\hat{\tau} = \sigma_\alpha^2/(\sigma_\alpha^2 + \sigma_v^2) = (\sigma_d^2 + \sigma_u^2)/(\sigma_d^2 + \sigma_u^2 + \sigma_v^2).$$

The reaction curve in this case is $BB$. $BB$ is below $AA$ by $(1-\hat{\tau})/[1-\gamma(m-1)]$. $OD$ is the expectation curve such that $\Delta\bar{k} = (1/\hat{\xi})\,\Delta\bar{e}(\bar{k}|\Omega)$, where $\hat{\xi} = \sigma_d^2/(\sigma_d^2 + \sigma_u^2 + \sigma_v^2)$. The imperfect-information equilibrium is the intersection at $F$ of $BB$ and $OD$. From this figure, it is evident that the overall effect of imperfect information on the sensitivity of investment is ambiguous.

We obtain an ambiguous result in this case, because we have two conflicting effects of imperfect information. As explained earlier, if $\alpha$ is observable, imperfect investment information increases the sensitivity of $\bar{k}$ to $d$. This effect can be represented in Fig. 6.2 as the effect of switching from $OC$ to $OD$, where $AA$ is held unchanged. However, as can be inferred from the case of imperfect information about own productivity, imperfect information about own demand reduces the sensitivity. The possibility of confusion makes the firm underestimate $\alpha$, so that it will not increase investment as much as in the case of perfect own-demand information. Thus, $BB$ in Fig. 6.2 lies below $AA$. This effect reduces the sensitivity of the average investment to the industry-wide demand shock.

By contrast, increased competition always increases the sensitivity. The reason is the same as in the case of productivity shocks.

### 3.4 *Summary*

The results in this and the previous section can be summarized as follows. Regardless of the nature of shocks, increased competition always increases the sensitivity of the average investment to industry-wide shocks under imperfect information, while it has no effect on the sensitivity under perfect information. Thus, competition is destabilizing.

The effect of imperfect average-investment information is also destabilizing, because it increases the sensitivity of the average investment. However, imperfect information about the individual productivity shock and the individual demand shock decreases the sensitivity. Consequently, the overall effect of imperfect information depends on the relative magnitudes of these two effects.

If the productivity condition in the production stage is relatively predictable in the investment stage compared with the demand condition, the effect of imperfect information is determined by the nature of the shocks. If productivity is subject to shocks, imperfect information increases the volatility of investment. However, if demand is subject to shocks, the result is ambiguous.

## 4. EXTENSION

In this section, I show that the results obtained in the previous sections hold true, even if three changes are made in the basic assumptions of the model, namely, increasing unit variable costs, risk aversion, and free entry.

The model considered in this section is the model of demand shocks in which $\alpha$ is observable ($v = 0$). This is the simplest of the models presented in the previous sections.

## 4.1. *Increasing Unit Variable Costs*

I sketch the main result here; the detailed discussion is relegated to Appendix B. Suppose that the production function is now

$$q = \delta l + \gamma k, \tag{25}$$

where $\delta$ and $\gamma$ satisfy $1 > \delta > 0$, $1 > \gamma > 0$, and $[m/(m-1)] > \delta + \gamma$.[20] Then, the second-period profit function has the form

$$\pi(k, \bar{k}, d, u) = \phi_0^* + \phi_v^*(k - \bar{k}) + \phi_{\bar{k}}^* \bar{k} + \phi_d^* d + \phi_u^* u, \tag{26}$$

where $\phi_0^*$, $\phi_v^*$, $\phi_{\bar{k}}^*$, $\phi_d^*$, and $\phi_u^*$ are constants depending on the parameters of the model. Specifically, we obtain $\phi_d^* \neq \phi_u^*$, as long as $m > b$. This implies that, although $\alpha$ is observable, its observability is not sufficient correctly to infer $\phi_d^* d + \phi_u^* u$. Thus, increasing unit variable costs introduce additional uncertainty into the profit function. The random variables $d$ and $u$ must be estimated from $\alpha$. Because $\phi_d^* > 0$ and $\phi_u^* > 0$, the effect of local–global confusion in estimating $d$ and $u$ is similar to that in estimating $\alpha$, in the case where $\alpha$ is unobservable. Increasing unit variable costs reduce the sensitivity of investment under imperfect information. Whether this sensitivity-reducing effect dominates the sensitivity-increasing effect of imperfect average-investment information depends on the parameters of the model. In Appendix B I show that in this particular example the overall effect of imperfect information is to increase volatility if and only if $\gamma + \delta > 1$. Thus, the results obtained in the previous sections still hold, even though unit variable costs of production are increasing, as long as the technology exhibits increasing returns to scale.

## 4.2. *Risk Aversion*

Next, consider the effect of risk aversion. Suppose that the firm is owned by one investor having a constant relative risk aversion. The investor receives income $Y$ in the current period but no income in the next period. Then, the firm maximizes $\hat{E}\,[(1 + r)^{-1} u(V') + u(V)]$, where $u(V) = V^{\zeta}/\zeta$, $V' = \exp\,[\phi_0 + \phi_v k - (\phi_v - \phi_{\bar{k}})\bar{k} + \alpha]$, and $V = Y - \exp\,(c_0 + k)$. Here $\zeta$ satisfies $\zeta \neq 0$ and $\zeta < 1$, and $r$ is the (utility) discount rate.

The optimal investment formula in this case is

$$k = [1 - \zeta\phi_v + (1 - \zeta)\, h]^{-1} \times [z_r + \zeta\alpha - \zeta(\phi_v - \phi_{\bar{k}})\, e\,(\bar{k} \mid \Omega)], \tag{27}$$

where

$$z_r = z_r^* + \frac{1}{2}\zeta^2 (\phi_v - \phi_{\bar{k}})^2 V(\bar{k}|\Omega), \text{ and}$$

$$z_r^* = z^* + (1-\zeta)(g-\phi_0).$$

Here, $h = \exp(c_0 + \bar{\bar{k}}) / [Y - \exp(c_0 + \bar{\bar{k}})]$, and $g = \log[Y - \exp(c_0 + \bar{\bar{k}})] + h\bar{\bar{k}}$.[21] Using a procedure similar to the one in the previous section,[22] we obtain the following average-investment equation:

$$\bar{k} = \frac{z_r}{1 - \zeta\gamma(b-1) + (1-\zeta)h} + \frac{\zeta}{1 - \zeta\gamma(m-1) + \zeta\gamma(m-b)\xi + (1-\zeta)h} d. \tag{28}$$

The qualitative results of the previous sections still hold under risk aversion. From (28), it is easy to see that imperfect information increases the sensitivity of the average investment, and that increased competition increases the sensitivity under imperfect information. However, the magnitude of these effects is now dependent on the parameter of risk aversion, $\xi$.

### 4.3. *Free Entry*

In the preceding analysis, the number of firms is fixed. However, in many industries new firms enter the market if there is a profit opportunity, and old firms exit if their operation is unprofitable. Thus, the number of firms is endogenously, rather than exogenously, determined. In the remainder of this section, I investigate the effect of free entry on the sensitivity of investment to industry-wide shocks.

The effect of free entry can be decomposed into two parts. First, free entry may affect the average demand but may leave the own-price elasticity $m$ of the individual demand unchanged. Second, free entry may change $m$, which is the degree of competitiveness in the industry (see the appendix to Chapter 5).

Let us consider the first effect. The average demand is

$$\bar{q}^d = (-b\bar{p} + d) - t, \tag{29}$$

where $t = \log T$. Here, $T$ is the number of firms. If the number of firms increases, then the average demand (total demand divided by the number of firms) decreases. The individual demand is now $q^d = -m(p - \bar{p}) - b\bar{p} + \alpha - t$, which also decreases when $t$ increases. However, under the constant unit variable cost, the second-period price is independent of $t$. Using this fact, we can show that the second-period profit function is given by

$$\pi(k, \bar{k}, \alpha, t) = (\phi_0 - t) + \phi_v(k - \bar{k}) + \phi_{\bar{k}}\bar{k} + \alpha. \tag{30}$$

Thus, if we replace $\phi_0$ with $\phi_0 - t$, the analysis in the previous two sections holds true without any change, as long as $t$ is known with certainty.

Consider the determination of the number of firms. There is a fixed cost of production. (Until now we have ignored this fixed cost, because it does not affect the short-run behaviour of firms.) A new firm enters the market (and an old firm stays in the market) if the unconditional mean of its profit is non-negative. The number of firms is determined by the zero-expected-profit condition. Using the perfect information about the structure of the economy, including the distributional characteristics of the disturbances, the firm can calculate this unconditional mean of the profit. It then correctly predicts the number of firms in the market. Thus, there is no uncertainty about $t$. Consequently, the sensitivity of the average investment to industry-wide productivity and demand shocks does not depend on the number of firms, $t$. Free entry does not affect the result obtained in the fixed-number model at all.

Next, let us turn to the case in which the number of firms affects the own-price elasticity $m$. If an increase in the number of firms (t) increases the competitiveness of the industry ($m$), then free entry produces an asymmetric response of investment to industry-wide shocks between peaks and troughs in demand fluctuations.

In order to incorporate the effect of demand fluctuations, let us assume $\bar{q}^d = g - b\bar{p} + d$, where $g$ represents the observable general economic condition. The number of firms is larger under strong average demand (a large $g$) than under weak average demand (a small $g$), because the number of firms is determined by the zero-expected-profit condition. The results of Sections 2 and 3 imply that an increase in $m$ increases the sensitivity of investment to industry-wide shocks. Consequently, the sensitivity is larger when $g$ is large than when $g$ is small. Therefore the average investment is more sensitive to industry-wide shocks, and thus more volatile, at the peak of demand fluctuations than in the trough.

## 5. CONCLUDING REMARKS

The major finding of this chapter is that increased competition unambiguously increases the volatility of investment under imperfect information about the average investment, regardless of whether the shocks are on the demand side or the supply side, and regardless of whether they are observed with noise or without it. This is in a sharp contrast to the effect of competition on the volatility of prices under imperfect information about the average price. In Chapter 5 we showed that increased competition unambiguously reduces the volatility of prices or, equivalently, increases their rigidity.

The model developed here has many shortcomings as a model of investment. The most serious may be the characterization of capital as an input used up in one period. This assumption reduces the firm's investment problem to a static two-period problem, and thus simplifies the expectation formation of firms. To generalize the monopolistically competitive investment model in an explicit dynamic rational expectations framework is a challenging task and an important topic for future research.

# Appendix A: Derivation of Rational Expectations

## A1. *Productivity Shocks*

We first consider the case in which $\beta$ is observable. Recall the firm's optimal investment formula (8). Note that because $\beta = g + x$, we have $e(g|\Omega) = \lambda\beta$ and $V(g|\Omega) = \lambda\sigma_x^2$, where $\lambda = \sigma_g^2/(\sigma_g^2 + \sigma_x^2)$. Let us assume that

$$\bar{k} = L + Mg. \qquad (A_1)$$

We then obtain $g = (1/M)(\bar{k} - L)$, so that the second-period profit function is

$$\pi = \phi_0 + \phi_v k - \left(\phi_v - \phi_{\bar{k}} + \frac{m-b}{M}\right)\bar{k} + (m-1)\beta + (m-b)\frac{L}{M}.$$

(A1) also implies that $e(\bar{k}|\Omega) = L + M\lambda\beta$ and $V(\bar{k}|\Omega) = M^2\lambda\sigma_x^2$.

Using these expectations, we can transform the first-order condition (8) into

$$(1-\phi_v)k = z_g + (m-1)\beta + (m-b)\frac{L}{M} - \left(\phi_v - \phi_{\bar{k}} + \frac{m-b}{M}\right)e(\bar{k}|\Omega) \qquad (A_2)$$

$$= z_g + (m-1)\beta + (m-b)\frac{L}{M} - \left(\phi_v - \phi_{\bar{k}} + \frac{m-b}{M}\right)(L + M\lambda\beta),$$

where

$$z_g = z^* + \frac{1}{2}\left(\phi_v - \phi_{\bar{k}} + \frac{m-b}{M}\right)^2 V(\bar{k}|\Omega)$$

$$= z^* + \frac{1}{2}\left[(\phi_v - \phi_{\bar{k}})M + (m-b)\right]^2 \lambda\sigma_x^2.$$

From the above transformed condition, rational expectations can be obtained by the following steps. First, average (A2) over all firms to get the expression of $\bar{k}$ in terms of $g$. Then, apply $e(\cdot|\Omega)$ on both sides of the resulting expression. Collecting terms in the resulting expression, we obtain

$$L = (1-\phi_{\bar{k}})^{-1} z_g \text{ and } M = \frac{m-1-(m-b)\lambda}{1-\phi_v+(\phi_v-\phi_{\bar{k}})\lambda}.$$

Consequently we get

$$e(\bar{k}|\Omega) = (1-\phi_{\bar{k}})^{-1} z_g + [1-\phi_v + (\phi_v - \phi_{\bar{k}})\lambda]^{-1} [m-1-(m-b)\lambda]\lambda\beta.$$

Second, let us consider the case in which only $\hat{\beta} = \beta + y$ is observable. The first-order condition is

$$(1-\phi_v)k = [\hat{z}_g + (m-1)e(\beta|\Omega) - (m-b)e(g|\Omega) - (\phi_v - \phi_{\bar{k}})e(\bar{k}|\Omega)]. \quad (A_3)$$

Note that, because $\hat{\beta} = \beta + y = g + x + y$, we have $e(g|\Omega) = \hat{\lambda}\hat{\beta}$ and $e(\beta|\Omega) = \hat{\nu}\beta$, where $\hat{\lambda} = \sigma_g^2/(\sigma_g^2 + \sigma_x^2 + \sigma_y^2)$ and $\hat{\nu} = (\sigma_g^2 + \sigma_x^2)/(\sigma_g^2 + \sigma_x^2 + \sigma_y^2)$. Let us assume that

$$\bar{k} = \hat{L} + \hat{M}g. \quad (A_4)$$

We continue the same procedure as in the case of observable $\beta$. Then, we have

$$\hat{L} = \frac{\hat{z}_g}{1-\phi_{\bar{k}}}, \quad \hat{M} = \frac{(m-1)\hat{\nu} - (m-b)\hat{\lambda}}{1-\phi_v + (\phi_v - \phi_{\bar{k}})\hat{\lambda}}, \text{ and}$$

$$e(\bar{k}|\Omega) = \frac{\hat{z}_g}{1-\phi_{\bar{k}}} + \frac{(m-1)\hat{\nu} - (m-b)\hat{\lambda}}{1-\phi_v + (\phi_v - \phi_{\bar{k}})\hat{\lambda}}\hat{\lambda}\hat{\beta}.$$

## A2. *Demand Shocks*

We consider the case in which only $\hat{\alpha} = \alpha + v$ is observable. The case in which $\alpha$ is observable can be obtained by setting $v = 0$. The firm's optimal investment formula is

$$k = (1-\phi_v)^{-1}[\hat{z}_d + e(\alpha|\Omega) - (\phi_v - \phi_{\bar{k}})e(\bar{k}|\Omega)]. \quad (A_5)$$

Note first that, from $\hat{\alpha} = \alpha + v = d + u + v$, we have $e(\alpha|\Omega) = \hat{\tau}\hat{\alpha}$ and $e(d|\Omega) = \hat{\xi}\hat{\alpha}$, where $\hat{\tau} = \sigma_\alpha^2/(\sigma_\alpha^2 + \sigma_v^2) = (\sigma_d^2 + \sigma_u^2)/(\sigma_d^2 + \sigma_u^2 + \sigma_v^2)$ and $\hat{\xi} = \sigma_d^2/(\sigma_d^2 + \sigma_u^2 + \sigma_v^2)$. Let $k = L + Kd$. Insert these expressions into the optimal investment formula (A5) and average over all firms. We then obtain $\bar{k}$ as a function of $d$. Apply $e(\cdot|\Omega)$ to the both sides of the resulting expression and collect terms. Then we have

$$L = \frac{\hat{z}_d}{1-\phi_{\bar{k}}}, \quad K = \frac{\hat{\tau}}{1-\phi_v + (\phi_v - \phi\bar{k})\hat{\xi}}, \text{ and}$$

$$e(\bar{k}|\Omega) = \frac{\hat{z}_d}{1-\phi_{\bar{k}}} + \frac{\hat{\tau}}{1-\phi_v + (\phi_v - \phi_{\bar{k}})\hat{\xi}}\hat{\xi}\hat{\alpha}.$$

## A3. *Risk Aversion*

The firm's optimal investment formula is

$$k = [1-\zeta\phi_v + (1-\zeta)h]^{-1}[z_r + \zeta\alpha - \zeta(\phi_v - \phi_{\bar{k}})e(\bar{k}|\Omega)].$$

Note that $e(d|\Omega) = \xi\alpha$, where $\xi = \sigma_d^2/(\sigma_d^2 + \sigma_u^2)$. Let $e(\bar{k}|\Omega) = J + K\alpha$. Then, using the same procedure as in the demand-shock case, we obtain from the above investment formula

$$e\,(\bar{k}\,|\,\Omega) = [1-\zeta\phi_{\bar{k}} + (1-\zeta)\,h]^{-1}\,z_r +$$
$$[1-\zeta\phi_v + \zeta\,(\phi_v-\phi_{\bar{k}})\,\xi + (1-\zeta)\,h]^{-1}\,\zeta\,\xi\,\alpha.$$

Using this, we obtain the average-investment equation in the text.

# Appendix B: The Case of Increasing Unit Variable Costs

## B1. *The Second Period*

The firm's problem is

$$\underset{p}{\text{Max}}\,[\exp\,(p)\,\exp\,(q^d) - \exp\,(w)\,\exp\,(l)],$$

subject to the demand function $q^d = -\,m(p-\bar{p}) - b\bar{p} + \alpha$ and the production function $q = \delta_l + \gamma k$. The optimal price is

$$p = (1+c_1 m)^{-1}\,[a^* + h\,(k) + c_1\alpha + c_1\,(m-b)\,\bar{p}], \qquad (A_6)$$

where

$$a^* = \log\,[m/(m-1)],\ h\,(k) =$$
$$w - \delta^{-1}\,\gamma\,k - \log\delta,\ \text{and}\ \ c_1 = \delta^{-1} - 1. \qquad (A_7)$$

The average price is then

$$\bar{p} = (1+c_1 b)^{-1}\,[a^* + h\,(\bar{k}) + c_1 d]. \qquad (A_8)$$

Using the above results, we have the following second-period profit function:

$$\pi\,(k,\,\bar{k},\,d,\,u) = \phi_0^* + \phi_v^*\,(k-\bar{k}) + \phi^*_{\bar{k}}\,\bar{k} + \phi_d^*\,d + \phi_u^*\,u, \qquad (A_9)$$

where

$$\phi_0^* = \log\left\{1 - \frac{\delta\,(m-1)}{m}\right\} - \frac{b-1}{1+c_1 b}\,a^* - \frac{b-1}{1+c_1 b}\,(w-\log\delta);$$

$$1 > \phi_v^* = \frac{(m-1)\,\gamma}{(1+c_1 m)\,\delta} > 0;\quad 1 > \phi_{\bar{k}}^* = \frac{(b-1)\,\gamma}{(1+c_1 b)\,\delta} > 0;$$

$$\phi_d^* = \frac{1+c_1}{1+c_1 b} > 0;\qquad \phi_u^* = \frac{1+c_1}{1+c_1 m} > 0.$$

## B2. *The First Period*

The firm's problem in the first period is now

$$\underset{k}{Max}\,\hat{E}\left\{(1+r)^{-1}\,\exp\,[\pi\,(k,\,\bar{k},\,u,\,d) - \exp\,[c]\right\},$$

Where $\hat{E}$ is taken with respect to the subjective distribution of $\bar{k}$, $d$, and $u$. The optimal investment formula is

$$k = (1-\phi_v)^{-1}\left[z_i - (\phi_v^* - \phi_{\bar{k}}^*)\, e\,(\bar{K}|\Omega) + \phi_d^*\, e\,(d|\Omega) + \phi_v^*\, e\,(u|\Omega)\right], \qquad (A_{10})$$

where

$$z_i = z_i^* + \frac{1}{2} f_i^t V(\bar{k},\ u,\ d|\Omega)\, f_i$$
$$z_i^* = \log \phi_v^* + \phi_0^* - c_0 - \log(1+r), \qquad (A_{11})$$

in which $f_i^t = [-(\phi_v^* - \phi_{\bar{k}}^*),\ \phi_u^*,\ \phi_d^*]$. By the method of undetermined coefficients, the following forecasts are obtained from (A10):

$$e\,(u|\Omega) = (1-\xi)\,\alpha,\ e\,(d|\Omega) = \xi\alpha, \text{ and } e\,(\bar{k}|\Omega) = \psi_0 + \psi_d\,\xi\alpha, \qquad (A_{12})$$

where

$$\psi_0 = (1-\phi_{\bar{k}}^*)^{-1}\, z_i$$
$$\psi_d = [1 - \xi\phi_{\bar{k}}^* - (1-\xi)\,\phi_v^*]^{-1}\,[\phi_u^*\,(1-\xi) + \phi_d^*\xi]. \qquad (A_{13})$$

Here $\xi = \sigma_d^2/(\sigma_d^2 + \sigma_u^2)$. Using the above results, we obtain the following average-investment equation under imperfect information:

$$\bar{k} = \psi_0 + \psi_d d. \qquad (A_{14})$$

Next, consider the case of perfect information. It is straightforward to show that the corresponding average-investment equation under perfect information is

$$\bar{k}^* = \psi_0^* + \psi_d^* d, \qquad (A_{15})$$

where

$\psi_0^* = (1-\phi_{\bar{k}})^{-1} z_i^*$, and $\psi_d^* = (1-\phi_{\bar{k}})^{-1}\,\phi_d^*$.

The effect of imperfect information is summarized in the ration $\psi_d/\psi_d^*$. From (A13) – (A15), we obtain

$$\frac{\psi_d}{\psi_d^*} = \left[\frac{1-\phi_{\bar{k}}^*}{1-\xi\phi_{\bar{k}}^* - (1-\xi)\,\phi_v^*}\right]\left[\frac{\phi_u^*(1-\xi) + \phi_d^*\xi}{\phi_d^*}\right]. \qquad (A_{16})$$

The term in the first bracket is the effect of imperfect information about $\bar{k}$ (the repercussion effect). This is larger than unity. The term in the second bracket is the effect of imperfect information about $d$ and $u$ (the impact effect). This term is less than unity. The overall effect depends on whether technology exhibits long-run increasing returns to scale ($\gamma + \delta > 1$) or decreasing returns to scale ($\gamma + \delta + < 1$), as shown below.

Note that

$$\frac{\psi_d}{\psi_d^*} - 1 = \frac{\Delta\,(1-\xi)\,(\gamma+\delta-1)}{\phi_d^*\,[\delta(1-\phi_{\bar{k}}) - \Delta\gamma\,(1-\xi)]}, \qquad (A_{17})$$

where

$$\Delta = (\phi_v^* - \phi_{\bar{k}}^*)\,\frac{\delta}{\gamma} = (\phi_d^* - \phi_u^*)\,\frac{1}{c_1} = \frac{(1-c_1)\,(m-b)}{(1+c_1 m)\,(1+c_1 b)} > 0. \qquad (A_{18})$$

It is straightforward to show that the denominator in (A17) is positive under our assumptions. Consequently, if $\delta+\gamma>1$, we obtain $(\psi_d/\psi^*_d)>1$.

Next, consider the effect of competition. As in the effect of imperfect information *per se*, the sign of $\partial(\psi_d/\psi^*_d)/\partial m$ is dependent on the degree of long-run returns to scale. Recall (A16). As explained in the previous subsection, the first term on the right-hand side of (A16) is the repercussion effect, while the second term is the impact effect. The derivative of the first term with respect to $m$ is shown to be positive. However, because $\partial\phi_u/\partial m < 0$, the derivative of the second term is negative. Since we have $\partial\Delta/\partial m > 0$, it can be shown from (A17) that $\partial(\psi_d/\psi^*_d)/\partial m > 0$ if and only if $\gamma+\delta>1$.

# Notes

1. See e.g. Jorgenson (1963) for the neoclassical investment theory, Eisner and Strotz (1963) and Gould (1968) for the investment theory based on adjustment costs, and Tobin (1969) and Tobin and Brainard (1977) for the $q$ theory of investment. Yoshikawa (1980) and Hayashi (1982) unify these approaches from the neoclassical viewpoint. Nishimura (1983) shows that such individual optimal investment behaviour leads to the 'accelerator' model of aggregate investment. The argument is quite simple, and is presented here. (Actually, the result obtained in Nishimura 1983 is somewhat more complicated. However, this is because of a mistake in equation transformation.) Suppose, for simplicity, that there is no depreciation. Let $k$ be the capital stock, and $y$ the output. $y = f(k)$ is the production function. The first fundamental assumption here is that there are perfect rental markets for the capital stock. Then, the equilibrium condition in rental markets is $r = f'(k)$, where $r$ is the real rate of interest, and $f' = \mathrm{d}f/\mathrm{d}k$. The second fundamental assumption is that all economic agents have perfect foresight. Then, actual movements in prices and quantities coincide with expected ones. Differentiating the production function with respect to time, we obtain $\dot{y} = f'(k)\dot{k}$, where $\dot{x} = \mathrm{d}x/\mathrm{d}t$. Substituting the rental market equilibrium condition into this relation, we get $\dot{y} = r(\dot{k})$. Note that $\dot{k} = I$, where $I$ is investment, under the assumption of no depreciation. Consequently, we obtain $I = (1/r)\dot{y}$. This is the familiar accelerator relationship, where the accelerator parameter is equal to the reciprocal of the real rate of interest.
2. These models can easily be extended to the case of monopoly firms, as long as there is no strategic interdependence among them.
3. For studies of individual firms, see e.g. Hartman (1972), Pindyck (1982), Abel (1983), and Ueda and Yoshikawa (1986). For studies of industry equilibrium, see Lucas and Prescott (1971).
4. There is a sizeable microeconomic literature on investment in duopolistic/oligopolistic industries: see e.g. Brander and Spencer (1983) and Okuno-Fujiwara and Suzumura (1987). However, little in the way of analysing investment behaviour in the monopolistically competitive macroeconomic framework has been attempted.

5. In the terminology of Bulow *et al.* (1985), investment is a strategic substitute in this monopolistically competitive market.
6. Weitzman (1985), among others, argues that this is a reasonable assumption for short-run analysis.
7. A possible example is as follows: in the first period machines have already been bought and are found to be good, but the firm does not know whether this is a general phenomenon or is attributable to its own luck.
8. In Chs. 2 and 5, I have shown that competition increases the elasticity of output to aggregate shocks under imperfect second-period price information, although competition does not influence the elasticity under perfect information. A more volatile output may induce more volatile investment. Thus, competition is likely to destabilize investment under imperfect price information. However, by assuming perfect information in the second period, this possibility can be ruled out. Consequently, the effect of competition found in this chapter is mainly that from the investment process.
9. What I am concerned with in the following analysis is the sensitivity (or, more precisely, elasticity) of investment to aggregate shocks. It should be noted here that competition affects the average level of investment, for an obvious reason. An increase in competition increases the average level of output; in order to increase output, investment must be increased; thus, competition increases the average level of investment.
10. Partial information-sharing involving only a subset of firms is also possible, but it does not fully eliminate imperfect information about the average investment.
11. Information-sharing may not be practical even if the number of firms is relatively small. Explicit information-sharing through trade associations and the like may not be feasible because of anti-trust law considerations. The authorities may be suspicious of such activities because they may lead to tacit collusion. Moreover, even if we ignore such considerations, non-co-operative firms may not find it profitable to agree on a binding information-sharing agreement. (See the literature of information-sharing in oligopolistic markets, such as Clarke 1983; Vives1985; and Gal-Or 1986.) Although collusion coupled with information-sharing always yields the maximum profit (monopoly profit), a binding information-sharing agreement under non-cooperative behaviour is not always profit-increasing. In addition, there are some doubts about the practicality of information-sharing if a binding agreement is not possible. In order to have true information-sharing, it is necessary for firms to announce their information truthfully. However if the agreement is not binding, there may be the possibility of strategic misrepresentation (see Okuno-Fujiwara *et al.* 1990). Information-sharing and the accompanying possibility of strategic misrepresentation are confounding issues, which are beyond the scope of this chapter.
12. In this chapter I analyse the subgame-perfect Bayesian Nash investment equilibrium in this industry.
13. It is possible to derive the demand function from a log-linear log-normal model of the representative consumer having CES utility (see Sect. 2 of Ch. 2). In this interpretation, *m* is a parameter in the utility function. Sattinger (1984), using the framework of Houthakker (1974), also provides an alternative derivation of the demand function based on the heterogeneity of consumer preferences

(see the app. to Ch. 5). In this alternative interpretation, $m$ is equal to the number of firms.

14. The increasing cost of investment does not change the results obtained in this chapter; see n. 15.
15. In the case of increasing marginal costs of investment (that is, $c = c_0 + (1 + c_1)k$, where $c_1 > 0$), the optimal investment formula is

$$k = (1+c_1-\phi_v)^{-1}\,[\tilde{z}_g+(m-1)\,\beta-(m-b)\,e\,(g|\Omega) - (\phi_v - 1 - \phi_{\bar{k}})\,e\,(\bar{k}|\Omega)],$$

where $\tilde{z}_g$ is appropriately defined. Thus, the investment formula under increasing marginal costs differs from the one in the text in that $1 - \phi_{\bar{k}}$ and $\bar{z}_g$ are replaced by $1+c_1-\phi k$ and $\tilde{z}_g$, respectively. Because such changes do not significantly affect the following analysis, the increasing marginal cost of investment does not affect the results of this chapter.
16. The smaller $\lambda$ is, the larger $(1/\lambda)$ is, and thus the more volatile investment is. Thus, an increase in the volatility of the firm-specific productivity shock (an increase in $\sigma_x$) increases the volatility of investment.
17. For example, consider the motor car industry. There are several product types, such as four-door sedans, within which there are firms producing differentiated products. The disturbance $x$ is 'type-specific' and is uniform over all products within the same type. However, firms producing the same type have different information about their productivity conditions and estimate them differently. Thus, the firm is characterized by its own forecast error, $y$, and the type of products it produces, $x$.
18. The optimal investment formula is $k=(1-\phi_v)^{-1}\,[z_d+\alpha-(\phi_v-\phi\bar{k})\,e(\bar{k}|\Omega)]$. Using the undetermined coefficient method similar to the one employed in the case of productivity shocks (see App. A to this chapter), we obtain $e(d|\Omega)=\xi\alpha$ and $e(\bar{k}|\Omega)=(1-\phi\bar{k})^{-1}z_d+[1-\phi_v+(\phi_v-\phi\bar{k})\,\xi]^{-1}\,\xi\alpha$. Consequently, taking (6) into account, we obtain the average investment in the text.
19. A more desirable procedure is to assume explicit dynamic stochastic processes about $d$, $u$, and $v$, and to analyse the optimal forecast. The model in the text can be considered an approximation of such a dynamic model.
20. The last assumption is necessary for profit maximization.
21. $g$ and $h$ are the coefficients of the linear approximation of log $[Y-\exp\,(c_0+k)]$ around $\bar{\bar{k}}$, where $\bar{\bar{k}}$ is the unconditional mean of $\bar{k}$. That is, $\log\,[Y - \exp\,(c_0 + k)] \approx g - hk$.
22. The derivation of rational expectations is presented in App. A.

# 7

# The Stochastic Expectational Equilibrium and Co-ordination Failure in Expectation Formation

## 1. INTRODUCTION

Imperfect competition is characterized by strategic interdependence. Under imperfect competition, one firm's optimal price depends on the optimal prices of the other firms. If one firm's optimal price depends positively on the other firms' prices, concerted price cuts may be desirable for all firms, but an individual price cut may not be to the advantage of any single given firm. This type of co-ordination failure under imperfect competition has been analysed under the perfect-information assumption (see Chapter 1).

Co-ordination failure may produce not only a suboptimal equilibrium, but also a multiple of such equilibria, some of which are Pareto-inferior to the others (see Cooper and John 1988).[1] Firms in the industry may be 'trapped' in one of the inferior equilibria, although they may obtain higher profits if they act co-operatively.

The purpose of this chapter is to show that a similar co-ordination failure and multiple equilibria may also be present in the expectation-formation process in an imperfectly competitive industry under imperfect information. I shall also investigate the effect of competition on the possibility of multiple expectational equilibria. Thus, I shall examine the relationship between competition and co-ordination failure in expectation formation.[2]

The Industry I have chosen to investigate is the monopolistically competitive one of Chapter 5. There are many firms competing with one another. A strong form of imperfect information is assumed, in which firms are obliged to announce their prices without having any direct information about those of other firms (or, more precisely, about the average price). In Chapter 5, this strong imperfect-information assumption and the assumed log-linear framework are sufficient to produce a unique rational expectations equilibrium.

However, in the model of Chapter 5 imperfect information may reduce the expected profit of the firm. (This is the case if the firm's marginal cost increases rapidly with production.) Thus, there may be an incentive for the firm to eliminate such imperfect information. Although information-sharing among all firms in the industry may not be practical, it may be possible for the firm to get a sample of some other firms' actual prices before it determines its own price. This chapter shows that such behaviour may cause multiple expectational equilibria and thus lead to co-ordination failure in expectation formation among firms.[3] The results obtained in this chapter also suggest that there is a strong possibility of multiple expectational equilibria if competition among firms is weak.

The plan of this chapter is as follows. In Section 2 the concept of the stochastic expectational equilibrium used in the chapter is explained, and the possibility of multiple expectational equilibria is discussed in non-technical terms. The similarity between co-ordination failure under perfect information and co-ordination failure in expectation formation is also investigated. The formal model is presented and discussed in Section 3. Here, the stochastic expectational equilibrium is defined and analysed, although its derivation is relegated to the Appendix of this chapter. In Section 4 the effect of competition on the possibility of multiple expectational equilibria is discussed. We obtain multiple expectational equilibria when competition is minimal, while we are likely to get a unique equilibrium if competition is intense. This section also provides an example of multiple expectational equilibria. The final section discusses the policy implication of co-ordination failure in expectation formation.

## 2. THE STOCHASTIC EXPECTATIONAL EQUILIBRIUM

Let us consider a monopolistically competitive industry, in which the demand for one firm's products depends on its own price and the average price. Firms are symmetric, in the sense that they are homogeneous except for firm-specific demand disturbances. Suppose that industry-wide demand conditions are altered, so that all firms have to adjust their prices. Firms know the local demand condition, which consists of the industry-wide and firm-specific disturbances, but they do not distinguish the industry-wide demand disturbance from the firm-specific one. The firm cannot observe the average price; however, it can obtain a random sample of some of the other firms' prices and infer the average price from this contemporaneous price information.

The availability of partial contemporaneous information about other firms' prices introduces an externality into expectation formation. Such information reveals, though only partially, the other firms' expectations about the average price. These expectations reflect the other firms' own information, which is unknown to the given firms. The firm changes its expectations using this new information and ultimately changes its price. Thus, one firm's price influences the other firms' prices by changing their expectations.

Suppose, for example, that, as the result of its sampling, firm B observes the price of firm A. If firm B knew exactly how firm A forms its expectations about the average price, firm A's price would reveal its condition, which is unobservable to firm B. Firm B could then improve its forecast of the average price using this information. However, because, in general, firm B does not know firm A's exact expectation-formation process, the observation of firm A's price does not completely reveal its condition. However, firm B usually has some prior information about firm A's environment and can form reasonable prior expectations about firm A's expectation-formation process. In this case, firm B utilizes the observation of firm A's price to update its expectations about firm A's expectation-formation process and condition. It then forecasts the average price using these updated expectations, in addition to its own information.

In this situation, all firms generally have an incentive to quote their prices after observing those of the other firms and updating their expectations. One possible approach to analysing this situation, which is often used in game theory, is to specify a particular sequence of moves (for example, (1) firm A first determines its price; then (2) firm B observes firm A's price and determines its own price; then (3) firm C observes firm B's price; . . .), and then to analyse the Nash equilibrium of the game.[4] However, such an analysis is generally very complicated in imperfect-information models and depends on the specific description of the sequence. Such a description is rather arbitrary, or situation-specific.

In order to avoid the complexity and arbitrariness of such sequential analysis and to obtain a tractable result, let us consider the following price-offer process among firms and analyse the 'rational-expectations equilibrium' in this price-offer process. In one round of the price-offer process, all firms simultaneously offer prices and are then allowed to obtain a random sample of some other firms' prices. They may update their expectations about the other firms' expectation-formation processes and the condition of the industry depending on the result of the sampling. In the next round, they may alter their prices. The rational expectations equilibrium is defined as the stationary state in this price-offer process, in which, first, the price distribution among firms does not change and, second, firms' expectations about the other firms' expectation-formation processes coincide with the actual expectation-formation processes.

The rational expectations equilibrium of the price-offer process can be described as a *stochastic expectational equilibrium*. It is stochastic because individual prices are stochastic, as they depend on the result of the sampling; although the price distribution is unchanged, individual prices keep changing. It is an expectational equilibrium because no firm has an incentive to change its expectations about the other firms' expectation-formation processes even after observing their prices through a random sampling. In the equilibrium, its expectations are fulfilled. If firms are endowed with rational expectations, this stochastic expectational equilibrium is reached instantaneously.

This approach corresponds to the 'equilibrium' analysis used in many macroeconomic theories. (See e.g. Kohn (1986) for a discussion of 'equilibrium analysis' and 'sequence analysis' in macroeconomics.) In this approach, one is concerned not with the dynamic adjustment process, as in sequential analysis, but only with the stationary state of the process.

The rational expectations equilibrium in the price-offer process may be explained by assuming a hypothetical informational *tâtonnement* process with an information agency. The information agency surveys and announces the expectation-formation processes of firms in each round of the price-offer process. Its role is similar to the hypothetical Walrasian auctioneer in the price *tâtonnement* process of perfectly competitive markets.

Let us consider a symmetric model where firms are homogeneous except for firm-specific demand disturbances; therefore, firms use the same expectation-formation process about the average price. This we call the expectation function. Its actual values (actual expectations) differ from firm to firm because of differences in local conditions and sampling results.

Consider the $t$th round in the hypothetical informational *tâtonnement* process. Suppose that in the $(t-1)$th round of the process we have a certain price distribution among firms determined by their past decisions. Also, at the end of this round the expectation function is announced by the information agency, which it obtains from its survey of firms made in the past. At the beginning of $t$th round, the firm uses this information (believing that the other firms in fact use such an expectation function), along with random samples from the actual price distribution in the $(t-1)$th round to form optimal expectations about the average price. This determines the firm's optimal price in the $t$th round, and consequently the new price distribution among firms in the $t$th round is also determined. After all firms have announced their prices, the agency surveys the expectation-formation process (expectation function) of all firms and makes it public at the end of the $t$th round. Because the number of firms is very large, no firm has an incentive to misrepresent its expectation function. Firms again take a sample of the other firms' prices at the end of the $t$th round. The process then repeats itself. In the stationary state of this hypothetical informational *tâtonnement* process, the expectation function does not change, and thus firms' expectations about other firms are unchanged and fulfilled. Consequently, the price distribution does not change, although individual prices may change intertemporally, because the result of the random sampling differs from time to time. This is the rational expectations equilibrium defined above.

Once the concept of the price-offer process and its stochastic expectational equilibrium is accepted, the subsequent analysis is rather straightforward. The availability of contemporaneous price information introduces an externality into the expectation-formation process which is not present in the model of Chapter 5. In that model, firms form their expectations independently, based on local conditions. However, when firms can obtain contemporaneous information about price distribution, their expectation formations are interrelated. Such interdependence in expectation formation may produce multiple expectational equilibria, as interdependence of optimal strategies leads to multiple equilibria in some cases, according to the co-ordination failure literature.

The possibility of multiple equilibria arises in an imperfectly competitive model only if the model generates nonlinear reaction functions, as well as strategic complementarity (see Cooper and John 1988). This is easily understood in the case of a duopoly, because the (symmetric) equilibrium is unique if the reaction functions are linear. The reason we may obtain multiple expectational equilibria in our imperfect-information monopolistically competitive model is similar to the above argument. The externality stemming from the availability of contemporaneous price-distribution information makes the 'expectational reaction function' nonlinear, and this nonlinearity produces multiple (symmetric) expectational equilibria in some cases. (The expectational reaction function is the optimal expectation function conditional on the other firms' expectation functions in the hypothetical informational *tâtonnement* process.)

Note that this non-uniqueness of the expectational equilibria (or, in the terminology of macroeconomics, the non-uniqueness of rational expectations) is completely different from the non-uniqueness considered in the previous macroeconomic rational expectations literature. (See Evans and Honkapohja (1986) for a brief summary of the literature.) In this literature, non-uniqueness is due to a peculiar structure of stochastic linear difference equations generated by the model, namely, insufficient restrictions imposed on the solution process. In this chapter, however, the model does not generate stochastic difference equations, so such a problem does not exist. The culprits causing our non-uniqueness problem are the externality arising from the availability of contemporaneous imperfect information about price distribution and the induced nonlinearity in the expectation-formation process.

## 3. EXTERNALITY IN EXPECTATION FORMATION IN MONOPOLISTIC COMPETITION UNDER IMPERFECT INFORMATION

### 3.1. *The Model*

Our starting-point is the static log-linear model of monopolistic competition under imperfect information presented in Chapter 5. The model is designed to facilitate the analysis of the effects of imperfect information and competition among price-making, quantity-taking firms on the sensitivity of their prices to demand and cost changes.

In this chapter, for the sake of analytic simplicity, I analyse the case in which there are only demand disturbances. However, the model can be easily extended to the case of cost disturbances. Firms are homogeneous except for firm-specific disturbances. The model is log-linear in order to get explicit values for the rational expectations of firms. As will become clear later, the basic results of this chapter are not dependent on the particular structure of the model. The choice of this model is made only for analytic tractability. All variables are in logarithm.

The demand for a particular firm's products is given by

$$q = -\, m(p - \bar{p}) + (g - b\bar{p}) + d + u. \tag{1}$$

Here, $g$ is a constant; $m$ and $b$ are the own-price and average-price elasticities, respectively, that satisfy $m > b \geqslant 1$; $q$ is the firm's output; $p$ is the firm's price; $\bar{p}$ is the average price; $d$ is the industry-wide disturbance; and $u$ is the firm-specific disturbance. Here, $m$ can be considered the degree of competition among the firms in the industry, whereas $b$ is that among the industries in the economy.

The average price $\bar{p}$ is not observable when the firm determines its price $p$. The disturbances $d$ and $u$ are not directly observable either. However,

$$\alpha = d + u \tag{2}$$

is assumed to be observable. The random variables d and $u$ are normally distributed and satisfy $Ed = Eu = Edu = 0$, $Ed^2 = \sigma_d^2$, and $Eu^2 = \sigma_u^2$. The individual cost is

$$c = c_0 - \log(c_1 + 1) + (c_1 + 1)q, \tag{3}$$

where $c_0 > 0$ and $c_1 > 0$. The latter assumption implies increasing marginal costs.

The firm's problem in this industry is as follows. Given its expectations about $\bar{p}$, which are summarized in its subjective probability distribution of $\bar{p}$, it maximizes its expected profits $\hat{E}\,[\exp(p)\exp(q) - \exp(c)]$, where $\hat{E}$ is the expectation operator with respect to the firm's subjective distribution of $\bar{p}$.

The firm forms rational expectations about $\bar{p}$. It expects that $\bar{p}$ is normally distributed with mean $e(\bar{p}|\Omega)$ and variance $V(\bar{p}|\Omega)$, where $e(\bar{p}|\Omega)$ is the linear least squares regression of $\bar{p}$ based on all available information, and $V(\bar{p}|\Omega)$ is its error variance. $\Omega$ includes $\alpha$, as well as information about the distribution characteristics and the values of the parameters in the demand and cost functions.

Under these assumptions, the optimal pricing formula is

$$p = (1 + c_1 m)^{-1}\,[a + c_0 + c_1(g + \alpha) + c_1(m - b)\,e(\bar{p}|\Omega)] \tag{4}$$

where

$$a = \log\,[m/(m-1)] + \tfrac{1}{2}\,c_1\,(c_1 + 2)\,(m-b)^2\,V\,(\bar{p}\,|\,\Omega). \tag{5}$$

Through some calculation based on the results obtained in Chapter 5, we arrive at the following unique rational expectations about the expectation function $e(\bar{p}|\Omega)$, such that

$$e(\bar{p}\,|\,\Omega) = e(\bar{p}\,|\,\alpha) = \frac{a + c_0 + c_1 g}{1 + c_1 b} + \frac{c_1 \gamma}{(1 + c_1 m)(1-\gamma) + (1 + c_1 b)\gamma}\,\alpha, \tag{6}$$

where

$$\gamma = \sigma_d^2/(\sigma_d^2 + \sigma_d^2). \tag{7}$$

### 3.2. *A New Feature: Private Information about the Average Price*

The new feature introduced in this chapter is private information about the average price, although such information contains noise and differs from one firm to another. Specifically, I assume that

$$z = \bar{p} + \eta \tag{8}$$

is observable, where $\eta$ is the firm-specific observational error.

One possible candidate as the source of such information is the result of the random sampling taken from the other firms in the industry. Let $n$ be the number of samples one firm has. Then $z$ is simply

$$z = (1/n)\,\sum_i^n p_i, \tag{9}$$

where $p_i$ is $i$th sample from the distribution of $p$. It is well known that $Ez = \bar{p}$ and $V(z) = (1/n)V(p)$, where $V(p)$ is the variance of $p$. Let $\eta$ be such that $\eta = z - \bar{p}$. We then have the information in the form of (8). In the following, this interpretation of $z$ is adopted. Here I assume that the first $n$ samples are obtained at no cost, but that to sample more than $n$ firms is prohibitively expensive. This assumption is made for the sake of analytic simplicity, rather than for its roots in reality. (See Cukierman (1979) for the determination of $n$.)

Note that in this case we have $E\eta = 0$ and $\sigma_\eta^2 = V(\eta) = (1/n)V(p)$. Obviously, $Ed\eta = Eu\eta = 0$. However, $\sigma_\eta^2$ is related to $\sigma_u^2$ (the variance of $u$, which generates the non-degenerate distribution of $p$ around $\bar{p}$). This will be discussed later.

Note that firms are identical except for the disturbances $(\eta, u)$. Thus, a firm is identified by a pair $(\eta, u)$. Then, the average price $p$ is defined as $\bar{p} = \int_{\eta,u} pf\,(\eta,\, u)\; d\eta du$, where $f$ is the density function of $(\eta,\, u)$.

### 3.3. *The Stochastic Expectational Equilibrium*

I use the undetermined coefficient method to obtain the stochastic expectational equilibrium. The derivation is relegated to the Appendix, but I will sketch it here.

In the stochastic expectational equilibrium, the price distribution is unchanged, and the expectation-formation process used in determining firms' prices is the same as the actual expectation-formation process. This process can be described as the expectation function where $e(\bar{p}|z, \alpha) = J + Kz + L\alpha$ for the firm having $(z, \alpha)$. The firm can then form rational expectations about the expectation function in a way similar to that in previous chapters. One complication is the existence of $z$, the result of the sampling. In the following, I investigate how $z$ affects rational expectations.

A given firm calculates the other firms' optimal price policies given the present price distribution; these are determined by

$$(1+c_1 m)\, p = [a + c_0 + c_1\,(g+\alpha) + c_1\,(m-b)\,(J + Kz + L\alpha)]. \tag{10}$$

The formula in (10) determines the price distribution around the average price $\bar{p}$.

First, consider the dependence of the sampling error variance $\sigma_\eta^2$ on the demand variance $\sigma_u^2$. Under the assumption of the expectational equilibrium, this distribution is the same as the one from which the firm takes its sample. Thus, (10) also determines the nature of the sampling error $\eta$, especially the dependence of $\sigma_\eta^2$ on $\sigma_u^2$. Let us take the variance on both sides of (10), treating $\bar{p}$ and $d$ as given. We then obtain

$$(1+c_1 m)^2\, V(p) = c_1^2 \sigma_u^2 + [c_1\,(m-b)\,K]^2\, \sigma_\eta^2 + [c_1\,(m-b)\,L]^2\, \sigma_u^2. \tag{11}$$

Note that $\sigma_\eta^2 = (1/n)\, V(p)$. Thus, we have

$$\sigma_\eta^2 \left\{(1 + c_1 m)^2 n - [c_1\,(m-b)K]^2\right\} = \left\{c_1^2 + [c_1\,(m-b)\,L]^2\right\}\sigma_u^2, \tag{12}$$

which implies that $\sigma_\eta^2$ is proportional to $\sigma_u^2$. It should be noted here that because $\sigma_\eta^2 > 0$, $\sigma_u^2 > 0$, and $c_1 > 0$, $K$ should satisfy

$$n > \left[\frac{c_1\,(m-b)\,K}{1+c_1 m}\right]^2. \tag{13}$$

Next, consider the information contained in the sampling result $z$. Averaging the individual prices in (10), we obtain

$$\bar{p} = \frac{[a + c_0 + c_1 g + c_1\,(m-b)J] + c_1\,[1 + (m-b)\,L]\,d}{1 + c_1 m - c_1\,(m-b)\,K}. \tag{14}$$

Because of the definition $(z = \bar{p} + \eta)$, we get

$$z = \frac{[a + c_0 + c_1 g + c_1\,(m-b)\,J] + c_1[1 + (m-b)\,L)d}{1 + c_1 m - c_1\,(m-b)\,K} + \eta.$$

From this, it is evident that $z$ conveys information about $d$.

In addition to $z$, the individual demand condition $\alpha$ also reveals information about $d$ (equation (2)). Using these two kinds of information, the firm forms the linear least-squares regression of $d$ on $z$ and $\alpha$. The result depends on $J$, $K$, and $L$, because $z$ is dependent on them. The linear least-squares regression of $\bar{p}$ on $z$ and $\alpha$ is then derived by substituting the obtained regression of $d$ on $z$ and $\alpha$ into the average price formula (14). Here the dependence of $\sigma_\eta^2$ on $\sigma_u^2$ is explicitly taken into account.

In order to get the expectational equilibrium, the original expression of the expectation function $e(\bar{p}|\alpha, z)$ must be equal to the derived expression. (The derived expression of the expectation function is the 'expectational reaction function' mentioned in Section 2.) Thus, equating coefficients, we obtain three nonlinear equations of $J$, $K$, and $L$, which characterize the expectational equilibrium. Let

$$A = c_1 [1 + (m - b) L], \tag{15}$$

$$B = 1 + c_1 m - c_1 (m - b) K, \tag{16}$$

$$D = c_0 + c_1 g + a + c_1 (m - b) J, \tag{17}$$

$$F = (1 + c_1 m)^2 n - [c_1 (m - b) K]^2, \tag{18}$$

and

$$G = c_1^2 + [c_1 (m - b) L]^2. \tag{19}$$

The rational expectations value of $J$, $K$, and $L$ satisfy

$$BJ = \frac{B^2 [(\sigma_u^2)^{-1} + (\sigma_d^2)^{-1}]}{[A^2 (F/G) + B^2] (\sigma_u^2)^{-1} + B^2 (\sigma_d^2)^{-1}} D, \tag{20}$$

$$BK = \frac{A^2 (F/G) (\sigma_u^2)^{-1}}{[A^2 (F/G) + B^2] (\sigma_u^2)^{-1} + B^2 (\sigma_d^2)^{-1}} B, \tag{21}$$

and

$$BL = \frac{AB^2 (\sigma_u^2)^{-1}}{[A^2 (F/G) + B^2] (\sigma_u^2)^{-1} + B^2 (\sigma_d^2)^{-1}}. \tag{22}$$

Because $A$ and $B$ are solely dependent on $K$ and $L$ and independent of $J$, (21) and (22) determine $K$ and $L$. $J$ is then determined by (20). It should be noted here that, in addition to (20)–(22), we have the constraint (13) described earlier.

This system of equations is nonlinear, and in general it is impossible to obtain explicit solutions. There may be multiple equilibria. Even the existence of an equilibrium is not necessarily apparent. This nonlinearity is the salient feature of an industry with private contemporaneous average-price information. Note that the system is still linear, so the nonlinearity is not due to some additional nonlinearity outside the expectation-formation process. The fact is that the expectation-formation process itself generates the nonlinearity.

In this expectational equilibrium, no firm cha ges its expectations, so the firm's optimal price policy remains the same. Consequently, the price distribution does not change. However, the firm's *price* may change from one round to the next, depending on the particular realization of $\eta$.

### 3.4. *Noisy Public Information*

It should be noted here that the qualitative result is the same when noisy public average-price information is available, instead of noisy private average-price information. For example, the government's announcement of the current average price produces a similar nonlinearity, if such an announcement involves a substantial error. Now, suppose that $z$ is not available, but that a different kind of information, $x$, such that

$$x = \bar{p} + \xi \tag{23}$$

is announced by the government. The government gets $x$ by taking a sample of firms in the industry as private firms, although the number of sample firms may be greater than the number of private firms.

The basic difference between private and public information is that the latter is common knowledge, while the former is not. The information $x$ is known to all firms and is common to them. This implies that the firm is identified only by $u$. Consequently, letting $e(\bar{p}|\Omega) = e(\bar{p}|x, \alpha) = J + Kx + L\alpha$, (11) is now replaced by,

$$(1 + c_1 m)^2 V(p) = c_1^2 \sigma_u^2 + [c_1 (m - b) L]^2 \sigma_u^2, \tag{24}$$

implying that

$$\sigma_\xi^2 [(1 + c_1 m)^2 n] = \{c_1^2 + [c_1 (m - b) L]^2\} \sigma_u^2 \tag{25}$$

By the same token, instead of (14), we obtain

$$(1 + c_1 m)\bar{p} = [c_0 + c_1 g + a + c_1 (m - b) J] + c_1 [1 + (m - b) L] d + c_1 (m - b) Kx. \tag{26}$$

In spite of these differences, however, public information also causes a nonlinearity in expectation formation. This can be easily understood if one traces the expectation-formation process once more, using the above results. Thus, the nonlinearity in the expectation-formation process is due to the availability of noisy contemporaneous average-price information, and whether such information is public or private is of no consequence.

## 4. COMPETITION AND THE POSSIBILITY OF MULTIPLE EXPECTATIONAL EQUILIBRIA

In this section I examine the effect of competition on the possibility of multiple expectational equilibria. Two polar cases will be investigated. In one case, competition is very weak ($m = b + \varepsilon$, where $\varepsilon \approx 0$, while in the other, competition is very intense ($m \to \infty$). It should be noted that $m$ is the degree of competition among the firms in this industry, while $b$ is that among industries. Profit maximization requires $m > b$.

In the remainder of this section I am concerned with the approximate expectational equilibrium in which the second order of smallness is ignored. This strategy is proved to be effective, because it enables us to reduce the dimension of the nonlinearity, and to get more definitive results in this highly nonlinear model.

I assume that B in (21) is not zero. If B *were* zero, we would obtain $A = C = 0$, implying $p = z$. However, under this strategy the price distribution would be indeterminate. I ignore this possibility, because in this case the expectational equilibrium is not well defined.

### 4.1. *Very Weak Competition*

In the case of very weak competition ($m = b + \varepsilon$, where $\varepsilon \approx 0$), ignoring the second order of smallness ($\varepsilon^2$) and taking account of $L = (B/A)(G/F)K$ from (21) and (22), we obtain

$$K = \left\{1 + \left[\frac{\phi - \gamma K}{c_1^2\,(1 + 2\varepsilon L)}\right]\left(\frac{c_1^2}{n\phi}\right)\left(1 + \frac{\sigma_u^2}{\sigma_d^2}\right)\right\}^{-1} \tag{27}$$

and

$$L = \frac{1 + c_1 b + c_1\varepsilon - c_1\varepsilon K}{c_1 + c_1\varepsilon L}\left(\frac{c_1^2}{n\phi}\right)K = \frac{(1 + c_1 b + c_1\varepsilon - c_1\varepsilon K)\,c_1}{(1 + \varepsilon L)\,n\phi}K. \tag{28}$$

where $\phi = (1 + c_1 b)(1 + c_1 b + 2c_1\varepsilon)$, and $\gamma = (1 + c_1 b)2c_1\varepsilon$. Consequently, (27) and (28) can be transformed into

$$L = \left[\gamma\left(1 + \frac{\sigma_u^2}{\sigma_d^2}\right)K^2 - \phi\left(n + 1 + \frac{\sigma_u^2}{\sigma_d^2}\right)K + n\phi\right]\left[n\phi 2\varepsilon\,(K - 1)\right]^{-1} \tag{29}$$

and

$$n\phi\left(L + \frac{1}{2\varepsilon}\right)^2 + c_1^2\left(K - \frac{1 + c_1 b + c_1\varepsilon}{2c_1\varepsilon}\right)^2 = \frac{n\phi + (1 + c_1 b + c_1\varepsilon)^2}{4\varepsilon^2}. \tag{30}$$

Figure 7.1 illustrates the loci of (29) and (30) in the $(K, L)$ plane. On the one hand, $L$ and $K$ satisfying (30) are found on the ellipse around $(K_0, L_0)$, where $K_0 = (1 + c_1 b + 2c_1\varepsilon)/(2c_1\varepsilon)$ and $L_0 = -1/(2\varepsilon)$, as shown in this figure. On the other hand, (29) determines $L$ as a function of $K$. Let $f(K)$ be the right-hand side of (29). Then, we obtain $f(-\infty) = -\infty$, $f(1-0) = +\infty$, $f(1+0) = -\infty$, $f(+\infty) = +\infty$, and $f'(K) > 0$ for all $K$ except $K = 1$. Consequently, the locus of (29) has two parts, as depicted in the figure. Both are monotonically increasing with $K$.

Next, consider $(K_1, L_1) = (0, -1/(2\varepsilon))$. It is easy to show that $(K_1, L_1)$

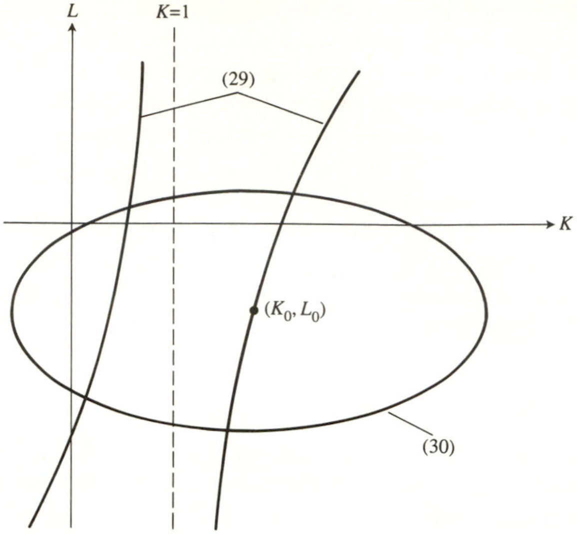


FIG. 7.1. Multiple expectational equilibria

is inside the ellipse (30) and that $(K_1, L_1)$ satisfies (29). Thus, the locus of (29) traverses the ellipse determined by (30) from below, in the region where $K \leqslant 1$. Consequently, there exist two pairs of $K$ and $L$ in this region that satisfy both (29) and (30). Moreover, because $(K_0, L_0)$ is obviously inside the ellipse and at the same time satisfies (29), there also exist two pairs of $K$ and $L$ in the region where $K \geqslant 1$ which satisfy (29) and (30). Note that $L$ and $J$ are determined by $K$ through (29) and (20), respectively. Therefore, we have four expectational equilibria in this example.

Let us compare the above result with the benchmark case of no average price information. Letting $m$ converge to $b$ in (6), we obtain $L = c_1/(1 + c_1 b)$, and of course, $K = 0$. Thus, the equilibrium in an industry with noisy average-price information is very different from that in an industry without such information. Moreover, even if we rule out the 'counterintuitive cases' of negative $L$, we still have two equilibria in the former case.

### 4.2. *Very Strong Competition*

Next, consider the case of a very competitive industry ($m \to \infty$). Dividing both sides of (21) by $c_1 m$, and letting $m$ go to infinity, we obtain

$$(1-K)\,K = \frac{(n-K^2)\,(\sigma_u^2)^{-1}}{(n-K^2)\,(\sigma_u^2)^{-1} + (1-K)^2\left[(\sigma_u^2)^{-1} + (\sigma_d^2)^{-1}\right]}\,(1-K). \quad (31)$$

Consequently, if

$$n > \frac{[1 + (\sigma_u^2/\sigma_d^2)]^2}{4\,(\sigma_u^2/\sigma_d^2)}, \tag{32}$$

then the equilibrium is unique, having $K = 1$, $L = 0$, and $J = 0$. Otherwise, there are multiple equilibria.

Figure 7.2 shows the range of the unique equilibrium in the $(n, [\sigma_u^2/\sigma_d^2])$ plane. This figure depicts the upper and lower bound of the uniqueness range. It shows that, for $n \geqslant 2$, the range is sufficiently large that the equilibrium is unique for realistic values of $\sigma_u^2$ and $\sigma_d^2$. For example, in order to get multiple equilibria for $n = 2$, either $\sigma_u^2$ must be at least six times as large as $\sigma_d^2$, or it must be less than one-fifth of $\sigma_d^2$. Moreover, as $n$ increases, the range widens up further. Thus, in practice, the possibility of multiple expectational equilibria can be ignored. This is in sharp contrast to the case of very weak competition, in which we always obtain multiple equilibria.

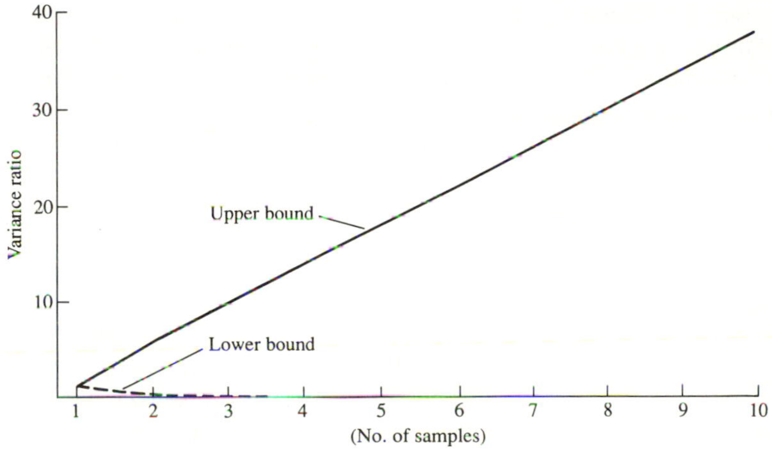


FIG. 7.2. The region of unique equilibrium

Finally, comparing the case of noisy average-price information with the benchmark case of no average-price information, we can conclude that intense competition has the same effect on rational expectations, regardless of whether average-price information is available or not. In the case of noisy average-price information in this section, we obtain $L = 0$, as in the benchmark case in the previous section (see (6)).

## 5. CONCLUDING REMARKS

In this chapter I have shown that the availability of contemporaneous information about price distribution induces a multiplicity of expectational equilibria in a monopolistically competitive industry under imperfect information, which otherwise generates a unique equilibrium. The contemporaneous information about price distribution generates an expectational externality, which causes the nonlinearity in expectation formation. Such a nonlinearity is capable of producing multiple expectational equilibria if competition among firms is weak. By contrast, when the industry is very competitive, the equilibrium is likely to be unique. Thus, the degree of competition plays a crucial role in the industry, as it determines whether or not the expectational equilibrium is unique.

The existence of multiple expectational equilibria implies the possibility that these equilibria are Pareto-ranked.[5] Thus, it is possible that the industry is 'trapped' in a Pareto-inferior expectational equilibrium. In such a case, some form of government intervention facilitating an exchange of information among firms may be beneficial.

Although a policy analysis is beyond the scope of this chapter, I can sketch a possible policy for restoring a Pareto-superior equilibrium. Suppose, for example, that the government announces the 'desirable' expectation formation formula $e(\bar{p}|z, \alpha)$, corresponding to the best expectational equilibrium, and asks firms to use this formula. Note that such $J$, $K$, and $L$ can be computed without knowing the actual $\alpha$ and $z$. Firms are likely to adopt such a formula, because the resulting equilibrium is clearly desirable to them. If all firms adopt the formula, then the desired equilibrium will be reached. The crucial question here, of course, is under what conditions the government can persuade firms to adopt the formula. We need a careful analysis of this aspect before actually recommending particular policies.

Another problem, which aggravates the persuasion problem, arises when the ranking of equilibria according to the government's objective (social welfare based on consumer utility) is different from the ranking according to the firms' objective (profits). Because the industry is imperfectly competitive, this is a real possibility. In this case, some form of penalty for non-compliance may be additionally needed to convince a given firm that the other firms are employing the announced formula. When firms are convinced that their competitors are using the formula, they themselves will use it, and the desired result will be obtained.

## Appendix: The Derivation of the Expectational Equilibrium

In this appendix, the expectational equilibrium is derived. First, (10) implies that the average price is determined by

$$(1+c_1 m)\bar{p} = [a+c_0+c_1(g+d)+c_1(m-b)\ (J+K\bar{p}+Ld)]. \qquad (A_1)$$

Thus, the firm obtains (14). Substituting $z - \eta$ for $\bar{p}$, and rearranging the terms, the firm gets

$$[1+c_1 m-c_1(m-b)K]z - [c_0+c_1 g+a+c_1(m-b)J]$$
$$= c_1[1+(m-b)L]d + [1+c_1 m-c_1(m-b)K]\ \eta. \qquad (A_2)$$

Second, because $z$ is observable, the left-hand side of this equation is known to the firm. Thus, using this and $\alpha = d + u$, the firm can form the linear least-squares prediction (the optimal expectation) of $d$ based on $z$ and $\alpha$. Let

$$z' = Bz - D.$$

Using this and the definitions of $A$–$G$ in the text, we can reformulate the problem of forming the optimal forecast of $d$ based on $z$ and $\alpha$ as follows.

From (10), the definitions of $A$ and $B$, and the initial assumption (2), we have

$$z' = Ad + B\eta. \qquad (A_3)$$

Note also that

$$F\sigma_\eta^2 = G\sigma_u^2. \qquad (A_4)$$

Then, the problem is to form the linear least-squares regression of $d$ on $z$ and $\alpha$ from (2) and (A3). The result is $e(d|z,\ \alpha) = \theta_1\ (Bz - D) + \theta_2\alpha$, where

$$\theta_1 = \frac{A\ (\sigma_\eta^2)^{-1}}{A^2\ (\sigma_\eta^2)^{-1} + B^2\ [(\sigma_u^2)^{-1} + (\sigma_d^2)^{-1}]}$$
$$= \frac{A(F/G)\ (\sigma_u^2)^{-1}}{[A^2(F/G) + B^2]\ (\sigma_u^2)^{-1} + B^2(\sigma_d^2)^{-1}} \qquad (A_5)$$

and

$$\theta_2 = \frac{B^2\ (\sigma_u^2)^{-1}}{A^2(\sigma_\eta^2)^{-1} + B^2\left[(\sigma_u^2)^{-1} + (\sigma_d^2)^{-1}\right]}$$
$$= \frac{B^2\ (\sigma_u^2)^{-1}}{[A^2(F/G) + B^2]\ (\sigma_u^2)^{-1} + B^2(\sigma_d^2)^{-1}}. \qquad (A_6)$$

Applying $e(\cdot|z,\ \alpha)$ on both sides of (A2), and using the above results, the firm gets

$$[1+c_1 m-c_1(m-b)K]\ e\ (\bar{p}|z,\ \alpha) = [a+c_0+c_1 g+c_1(m-b)J]$$
$$+\ c_1[1+(m-b)L]\ e\ (d|z,\alpha). \qquad (A_7)$$

From (A7), we then have

$$B(J + Kz + L\alpha) = D + A\ [\theta_1(Bz - D) + \theta_2\alpha], \qquad (A_8)$$

which implies $BJ = (1 - A\theta_1)D$, $BK = A\theta_1 B$, and $BL = A\theta_2$. Thus, we get the relations in the text.

# Notes

1. In the models surveyed in Chapter 1, the equilibrium is unique. However, this is not a general characteristic of these models, but the result of the particular log-linear specification. If the model is not linear, there may be multiple equilibria.
2. An informational externality is also present in perfectly competitive markets under imperfect information, and a similar co-ordination failure occurs in such markets. In fact, King (1983) shows the possibility of multiple, Pareto-ranked equilibria in the model of Lucas (1973), if the interest rate in the economy-side bond market is observable. In this case, the interest rate is noisy contemporaneous information about the current price level.
3. The other type of co-ordination failure, which is based on the implicit cost of price adjustment, was analysed in Chapters 2 and 3.
4. Or, more precisely, the Bayesian subgame-perfect Nash equilibrium of this game.
5. It should be noted that the model in this chapter can be considered as a reduced form of the model with homogeneous consumers having Dixit–Stiglitz-type CES utility (see Sect. 2 of Ch. 2). For an alternative derivation based on consumers' preferences, see appendix to Ch. 5.

# PART III

# RELATIVE PRICE RIGIDITY: CONSEQUENCES OF BUYER IMPERFECT INFORMATION

# 8
# Customer Markets and Relative-Price Sensitivity

## 1. INTRODUCTION

In a seminal paper on the microfoundation of macroeconomics, Phelps and Winter (1970) introduced the notion of a non-Walrasian product market, in which perfectly informed, price-setting, quantity-taking firms compete for imperfectly informed, repetitive consumers, called 'customers'. The assumption that firms have perfect information about the market makes customer-market models different from the models analysed in the previous chapters, in which imperfect information on the side of firms plays a crucial role. Okun (1981) argued the importance of such customer-supplier relationships for understanding price rigidity. He contended that in such 'customer markets' prices are insensitive with respect to short-run demand changes but responsive to permanent cost changes.

This chapter analyses the short-run price behaviour in these customer markets. I adopt the customer-flow dynamics model of Phelps and Winter as a model of customer markets.[1] In their model, price information diffuses only gradually. In the short run customers are immobile, although they may change suppliers in the long run, as other firms' policies eventually become known to them. Into this model I introduce a new element: short-run disturbances in economic conditions. Firms may adjust their prices to changes in conditions that consumers cannot observe. Thus, the criterion for a customer in choosing a particular supplier is not the current price but the current policy (price distribution). I investigate the optimal price policy of the firms and explore its implications for short-run price movement. The model is presented and discussed in Section 2.

One example of the customer market described in this chapter is that for rented accommodation. The high cost of moving from one flat to another causes short-run immobility. Information about other flats' rents and quality (and, consequently, their quality-adjusted rents) becomes known to consumers only gradually, through contact with the residents of those flats. In such a market, a consumer does not search actively in every period unless he is a new entrant: he stays in his present flat as long as it is satisfactory, and moves only if he becomes dissatisfied.

Section 3 contains the main results of this chapter. It is shown that the sensitivity of the customer-market price to demand and cost fluctuations depends crucially on the shape of the customers' indirect utility functions. Because the firm has only a short-run monopoly on its customers, it must take into consideration the long-run consequence of its price policy on the customers' utility. Thus, the customers' attitude towards the price risk, summarized in the curvature of their indirect utility functions, influences the short-run optimal price policy of the firm. If the customers dislike price fluctuations (their indirect utility functions are concave in the firm's price), then the customer-market price (or, more precisely, the relative price) is inflexible with respect to short-run changes in demand and cost, as argued by Okun. Competition makes the customer-market price less flexible in this case, because a higher reservation utility of the customers implies that the firm should respect their preference more than before. However, in the case of convex indirect utility functions the price is flexible, which is contrary to Okun's assertion. Competition implies more flexible customer-market prices in this case.

If consumers are consumption-risk-averse (that is, if their direct utility functions are concave), and if there is no adjustment cost in the consumption process, then their indirect utility functions are convex in the customer-market price in most cases if products are divisible, while they are concave if the products are indivisible as long as the consumers continue to buy the same quantity.[2] This suggests that customer-market prices are likely to be flexible in markets of divisible goods, such as petrol, while they are inflexible in markets of indivisible goods.

Section 4 argues that the scope of rigid prices is much wider than the above discussion suggests if the adjustment cost in the consumption process (or, in a slightly different framework, the near-rational behaviour of consumers) is taken into consideration. Because of the well-known envelope relationship, the adjustment of the consumption pattern to small temporary changes in price produces only a second-order improvement of utility. Consequently, a small adjustment cost in the consumption process is enough to prevent consumers from changing their quantity of consumption. Since the fixed quantity of consumption makes the indirect utility function concave, customer-market prices become rigid. A numerical example in Section 4 illustrates the practical importance of this argument. Section 4 also shows that rigid customer-market prices are more sustainable than flexible ones, when consumers have current price information. Flexible customer-market prices produce a large variance in prices among firms, and thus make it attractive to depart from the present supplier and buy from the firm with the lowest price. This tends to destroy the customer–supplier relationship. Rigid customer-market prices do not have such tendency.

Section 5 concludes the chapter with some remarks on the macroeconomic implications of the results obtained.

## 2. A MODEL OF CUSTOMER MARKETS

Consider an industry with identical firms. In the following I shall concentrate on a representative firm. I shall analyse this firm and its customers in the customer-flow dynamics model of Phelps and Winter (1970). Information diffusion is sufficiently sluggish that customers do not have current information; thus, their information is intertemporally imperfect. The customers are attached to firms in the short run, and firms have a short-term monopoly on their customers.[3]

There is uncertainty in economic conditions. The criterion for a customer in choosing a particular supplier is his expected utility from being a customer of that supplier. I assume that the customer considers the firm's price as a random variable, and that he learns its probability distribution from his past experience with the firm. If the expected utility of being a customer of the current supplier based on this learned probability distribution is less than that of patronizing another supplier he happens to know through contact with its customers, he will change his supplier.

Because I am concerned with the short-run behaviour of the firm's optimal price, I assume that the industry is in a steady state, in the sense that (1) no new consumers enter the market, and existing consumers are all the customers of some firm; (2) the firm has the optimal set of customers; and (3) the customers know the probability distribution of the current supplier's price, as well as the distribution of expected utility offered elsewhere in the industry. I rule out the possibility that the firm could renege, because such behaviour may antagonize its customers and create a bad reputation. A firm planning to stay in the industry for a long time is not likely to choose such a policy.

Let $p$ be the firm's product price, $c$ the cost parameter (increasing $c$ implies a higher marginal cost), $Y$ the demand parameter representing the condition of the total demand at the firm, and $y$ the income of the marginal customer whom the firm wishes to retain in the long run. All variables in this chapter are in real terms. There is uncertainty about the values of $c$, $Y$, and $y$—the firm-specific as well as the industry-wide uncertainty. Let $w = (c, Y, y)$. The triplet $w$ is assumed to be a set of continuous random variables having $f(w)$ as their density function. In the following, we concentrate our analysis on an open convex set of $w$ in which $f(w) > 0$.

The firm's indirect utility function $u(p, Y, c)$ is given by

$$u(p, Y, c) = \phi\{pd(p, Y) - C[d(\mathrm{p}, Y), c]\}, \tag{1}$$

where $d(p, Y)$ is the total demand for the firm's products, $C(d, c)$ is its cost, and $\phi$ is the firm's utility function.[4] In (1) I assume, first, that the firm satisfies all demand[5] and, second, that the volume of the marginal customer's demand is negligible compared with that of other customers. Thus, the dependence of $d$ on $y$ is ignored.

I assume that $u$ is twice differentiable with respect to $p$ and $w$. In the following analysis, I employ a quadratic approximation to $u$; that is, I assume that all the second partial derivatives of $u$ can be treated as parameters in the range of $p$, $Y$, and $y$ relevant to our analysis. Define

$$a(x, z) = \partial^2 u/\partial x \partial z, \qquad \text{for } x,\ z = p,\ Y, \text{ and } y.$$

The firm's utility function $u$ is assumed to satisfy $a(p, p) < 0$ and $a(p, c) > 0$. Under these assumptions, we have $dp^*(w)/dc > 0$, where $p^*(w)$ is the monopoly price satisfying the first order optimality condition,[6]

$$u_p[p^*(w),\ Y,\ c] = 0, \tag{2}$$

of the following unconstrained expected utility maximization problem:

$$\underset{p\,(w)}{\text{Max}} \int_w u[p(w), Y, c]\, f(w)\, dw. \tag{3}$$

Thus, the monopoly price behaves in a non-perverse way.

Let $v(p, y)$ be the indirect utility function of the marginal customer, and let $V$ be his steady-state reservation expected utility.[7] I assume only one type of marginal customer, who buys a positive amount of products in every state, although the extension to the case of heterogeneous marginal customers whose demand is zero in some states is relatively straightforward. If the firm's price policy is $p(w)$, the marginal customer's expected utility is $\int_w v[p(w),\ y]\ f(w)dw$. Thus, the firm should employ a price policy making this no less than $V$, in order to retain the marginal customer. Note that the assumption that the customer cannot observe $c$ and $Y$ is essential in this formulation; otherwise, $V$ would be contingent on $c$ and $Y$.

The firm's short–run problem in the customer market is to maximize its expected utility subject to the constraint of retaining the marginal customer:

$$\underset{p\,(w)}{\text{Max}} \int_w u[p(w), Y, c]\, \mathrm{f}\,(w)\, dw \tag{4}$$

subject to

$$\int_w v[p(w), y]\, f\,(w)\, dw \geqq V. \tag{5}$$

I assume that

$$\int_w v\, [p^*(w), y]\, f\,(w)\, dw < V. \tag{6}$$

Otherwise problem (4) is reduced to a simple monopoly pricing problem.

Let us now consider the marginal customer's indirect utility function, $v\ (p, y)$. The function $v$ is assumed to be twice differentiable with respect to $p$ and $y$ in the range of $p$ and $y$ relevant to our analysis and satisfies $v_p < 0$ and $v_y > 0$. As in the case of $u$, I employ a quadratic approximation to $v$. Define

$$b(x,\ z) = \partial^2 v / \partial x\, \partial z, \text{ for } x,\ z = p, \text{ and } y.$$

As to $b(p, p)$, however, we cannot a priori determine its sign. A consumer having $v$ such that $b(p, p) < 0$ can be called price-risk-averse, while a consumer with $b(p,p) > 0$ can be described as price-risk-loving. In this chapter both such cases are analysed.

Let $p^c(w)$ be the optimal customer-market pricing policy. Under the above assumptions, the Kuhn–Tucker condition (which is necessary for the optimum under regularity conditions) of the firm's constrained maximization is reduced to

$$u_p\,[p^c(w),\ Y,\ c] + \lambda v_p\,[p^c(w),\ y] = 0 \tag{7}$$

and

$$\int_w v\,[p^c(w),\ y]\, f(w)\,dw = V, \tag{8}$$

where $\lambda$ is the positive Lagrangean multiplier of the constraint (5). Equations (7) and (8) completely characterize the optimal pricing policy $p^c(w)$.

Let $q(w, \lambda; u, v)$ be a price satisfying (7). Then, substituting this into (8), we obtain

$$\int_w v\,[q(w,\ \lambda;\ u,\ v),\ y]\, f(w)\,dw = V, \tag{9}$$

so that we have $\lambda = \lambda(V; f, u, v)$. Consequently, the optimal policy is $p^c(w) = q\,[w, \lambda(V; f, u, v); u, v]$.

The customer-market optimal price $p^c(w)$, is always lower than the monopoly price $p^*(w)$, as long as $v_p$ is negative. As in the case of the monopoly price, I assume that the customer-market price behaves normally with respect to cost changes; that is, I assume that cost increases, *ceteris paribus*, raise the customer-market price. In the next section, the behaviour of the customer-market price $p^c(w)$ described in (7) and (8) is analysed and compared with the monopoly price $p^*(w)$ in (2).

## 3. THE SENSITIVITY OF THE CUSTOMER-MARKET PRICE TO DEMAND AND COST FLUCTUATIONS

In this section I analyse, first, the sensitivity of the optimal price to differences in demand and cost conditions and, second, the effects of competition on price sensitivity. The competition examined here is that which increases the steady-state reservation utility of the marginal customer.

Let us first consider the sensitivity of the optimal price to cost differences. Because $u$, $v$, and $f$ are held unchanged, $\lambda(V; f, u, v)$ can be treated as a constant if $V$, the marginal customer's reservation expected utility, does not change. In the following, the difference in the optimal price $dp^c$ is derived for the difference in the cost parameter $dc$ in the optimal pricing policy $p^c(w)$.

Differentiating (7) with respect to $c$, while keeping $\lambda$ constant, we have

$$[a(p, p)+\lambda b(p, p)] \frac{dp^c}{dc} + a(p, c) = 0 \tag{10}$$

Consequently, we get

$$\frac{dp^c}{dc} = \frac{-a(p, c)}{a(p, p)+\lambda \mathrm{b}(p, p)}. \tag{11}$$

The normal-price-behaviour assumption implies that $a(p, p) + \lambda b(p, p) > 0$.

In the case of price risk aversion ($b(p, p) > 0$), from (11) we obtain

$$0 < \frac{dp^c}{dc} < \frac{-a(p, c)}{a(p, p)} = \frac{dp^*}{dc}. \tag{12}$$

This means that the customer-market price is less flexible than the monopoly price.

The customer-market firm shuns price changes, because they adversely affect the marginal customer's expected utility if he is price-risk-averse, while the monopoly firm does not have to worry about such effects. Thus, the customer-market price becomes less flexible than the monopoly price. This conclusion holds regardless of the degree of the firm's own risk aversion.

Consider, then, the influence of competition on the flexibility of the customer-market price in this price-risk-averse case. Competition increases the marginal customer's reservation expected utility, $V$. Equation (11) implies that a higher $\lambda$ leads to a stickier optimal price. (Recall the assumption that all the second partial derivatives are constant.) Note that $\lambda$ is the Lagrangean multiplier to constraint (5), which is determined in (9). This is the 'cost' of retaining the marginal customer. Thus, if competition increases this retaining cost, it decreases the flexibility of the price.

Differentiating (9) with respect to $V$, we have

$$\frac{d\lambda}{dV} \int_w v_p q_\lambda f(w)\, dw = 1. \tag{13}$$

If $b(p, p) < 0$, then under our assumptions we have $q_\lambda < 0$, because, from (7),

$$[a(p, p)+\lambda b(p, p)]\, q_\lambda + v_p = 0. \tag{14}$$

Consequently, we have $v_p\, q_\lambda > 0$, which means

$$\int_w v_p q_\lambda f(w)\, dw > 0 \tag{15}$$

Thus, from (13) we obtain $d\lambda/dV > 0$. The higher the marginal customer's reservation utility, the higher the cost of retaining him. Consequently, we can conclude that competition makes the customer-market price less flexible.

In the case of a price-risk-loving marginal customer ($b(p, p) > 0$), we obtain just the opposite conclusion. In this case,

$$\frac{dp^c}{dc} = \frac{-a\,(p,\ c)}{a(p,\ p) + \lambda b\,(p,\ p)} > \frac{-a(p,\ c)}{a(p,\ p)} = \frac{dp^*}{dc} \tag{16}$$

Thus, the customer-market price in the case of the price-risk-loving marginal customer is more flexible than the monopoly price, with respect to cost changes. Moreover, (13) and (14) imply that an increase in $V$ makes $dp^c/dc$ increase. Thus, competition increases the flexibility.

Next, consider the sensitivity of $p^c$ to demand changes. The effect of changes in the demand parameter $Y$ can be analysed in the same way as the effect of cost changes. Because $v$ does not depend on $Y$, we have

$$\frac{dp^c}{dY} = \frac{-a\,(p,\ Y)}{a(p,\ p) + \lambda b\,(p,\ p)} \tag{17}$$

Note that I do not make any assumption about the sign of $a(p, Y)$. Both a negative $a(p, Y)$ (giving $dp^*/dY > 0$ and $dp^c/dY > 0$ and a positive $a(p, Y)$ (giving $dp^*/dY < 0$ and $dp^c/dY < 0$) are possible. However, the absolute value of $dp^c/dY$ is smaller than that of $dp^*/dY$ in the case of price risk aversion, because the absolute value of the denominator in (17) is larger than that of $dp^*/dY$ by $|\lambda b\,(p,\ p)|$. Thus the customer-market price is less flexible than the monopoly price. Moreover, an increase in $\lambda$ increases the absolute value of the denominator in (17) and thus decreases the absolute value of $dp^c/dY$. Because increased competition raises $\lambda$, this implies that competition makes the customer-market price less flexible. On the other hand, in the case of the price-risk-loving marginal customer, the absolute value of the denominator in (17) decreases from that of $dp^*/dY$ by $|\lambda b\,(p,\ p)|$, although it is still positive under our assumption of normal price behaviour. From this and the foregoing discussion, the following proposition is obtained.

> PROPOSITION. If the marginal customer is price-risk-averse (price-risk-loving), then the customer-market price is less flexible (more flexible) than the monopoly price with respect to temporary changes in demand and cost. Under this condition, competition makes the customer-market price more rigid (flexible).

Finally, let us consider the case in which $Y$ is highly correlated with $y$. Then, the indirect dependence of $v$ on $Y$ should be explicitly taken into consideration. In this case the marginal customer's price risk aversion is not sufficient to make the customer-market price less flexible than the monopoly price. Unlike cost changes in the firm's production, $Y$ affects the marginal customer's utility function, as well as the total demand for the firm's products. The change in the marginal customer's income may offset his price risk aversion. The consumer may not be as hostile to price fluctuations if such fluctuation are at least partly compensated by accompanying changes in his real income. If this offsetting effect is sufficiently large, it may dominate the influence of price risk aversion. In such a case, the customer-market price may become more flexible than the monopoly price even in the case of price risk aversion.

Suppose, for analytic simplicity, that $y = Y$. We then have $\partial v/\partial Y = v_y$. Consequently, in this case we obtain

$$\frac{dp^c}{dY} = \frac{-[a(p,\ Y)+\lambda b(p,\ y)]}{a(p,\ p)+\lambda b(p,\ p)},$$

which implies

$$\frac{dp^c}{dY} - \frac{dp^*}{dY} = \frac{\lambda[b(p,p)\ a(p,Y)-b(p,y)\ a(p,p)]}{a(p,p)\ [a(p,p)+\lambda b(p,p)]}. \tag{18}$$

Consequently, if

$$|b(p,p)|\left|\frac{a(p,Y)}{a(p,p)}\right| > |b(p,y)|$$

is satisfied, in addition to $b\ (p,\ p) < 0$, then the customer-market price is less flexible than the monopoly price. Here $b\ (p,\ y)$ represents the effect of real income on the customer's attitude towards the price risk. Thus, the above condition implies that, if this effect is sufficiently small, then the customer-market price is inflexible even in the case of perfectly correlated $Y$ and $y$. Moreover, we obtain

$$\frac{d}{d\lambda}\left(\frac{dp^c}{dY}\right) = [a(p,p)+\lambda b(p,p)]^{-2}\ [b(p,p)a(p,Y)-b(p,y)a(p,p)]. \tag{19}$$

Consequently, under the conditions that produce rigid prices, competition that raises the reservation expected utility of the marginal customer leads to a less flexible customer-market price.

## 4. THE SCOPE OF RIGID CUSTOMER-MARKET PRICES

### 4.1. *Habit-Forming and Near-Rational Behaviour*

The proposition in the previous section shows that the flexibility of the customer-market price depends crucially on whether the marginal customer is price-risk-averse or price-risk-loving. In other words, it depends on the curvature of his indirect utility function. Although the standard restriction imposed on the utility function (quasi-concavity) does not necessarily imply the convexity or concavity of $v$ in $p$, we are able to get more definitive results when we restrict our attention to strongly concave utility functions (consumption-risk-averse customer).

Suppose, as in standard consumer theory, that there is no adjustment cost in the consumption process, so that the customer chooses his consumption freely. Then, if the products are divisible, and if the concavity of the utility function is not too strong, $b(p,\ p)$ is positive. (Turnovsky *et al.*

(1980) derive the conditions under which $b\ (p, p)$ is positive. See also Nishimura (1985).) On the other hand, if the firm's products are indivisible, then $b\ (p, p)$ is negative, as long as the customer buys the same quantity. If the marginal customer buys $n$ units of the firm's products, his indirect utility function is $v(p, y) = \Psi\ (n, y - pn)$, where $\Psi$ is a strongly concave direct utility function, and $y - pn$ is the expenditure on commodities other than the firm's products. We then have $b\ (p, p) < 0$ in the range of prices at which the marginal customer continues to buy $n$ units.[8] Thus, if the customer is consumption-risk-averse, the degree of the flexibility of the customer-market price under the assumption of no adjustment cost depends mainly on whether or not the firm's products are divisible. Because the number of economically significant indivisible goods is not likely to be large, the above discussion seems to limit the scope of rigid customer-market prices.

The scope, however, expands greatly if we take into account the adjustment cost in the consumption process as household production. Consumption is a process of forming habits, although this is generally ignored in standard microeconomic consumption theory.[9] One consequence of this habit-forming characteristic is that it is generally costly (in utility terms) for consumers to change their consumption pattern. This can best be interpreted using the existence of the adjustment cost in the consumption process. Like a firm facing the adjustment cost in the investment process, the customer does not adjust his consumption pattern instantaneously when market conditions are altered. The adjustment is at best gradual and thus produces a serial correlation of various consumption variables. If a non-negligible adjustment cost of changing the consumption pattern exists, a small temporary change in the price may not alter the quantity purchased by the marginal customer. If the marginal customer is constrained to purchase a fixed quantity, his indirect utility becomes concave. Because the concavity of the utility function leads to rigid customer-market prices, the adjustment cost renders even the prices of divisible goods rigid.

A similar conclusion is obtained in the slightly different framework of near-rational behaviour of consumers. According to this literature (see Akerlof and Yellen 1985), the marginal customer is not likely to change his consumption basket in the face of a small change in prices. This is because such an adjustment would produce only a second-order improvement of his utility, provided that the consumption basket is initially optimal. Thus, customer-market prices also become sticky in this case.[10]

The magnitude of the adjustment cost and/or the near-rational behaviour necessary to produce rigid customer-market prices is illustrated in Table 8.1. Here the marginal customer is assumed to have a Cobb–Douglas utility function

$$u\ (x,\ z\ ) = x^{\alpha} z^{1-\alpha},$$

TABLE 8.1. The Cost of Non-Adjustment: A Cobb–Douglas Case

| Price | First-best[a] | Second-best[b] | Cost of non-adjustment[c] | $b(p, p)$[d] |
|---|---|---|---|---|
| *Case 1*: $\alpha = 0.01$ | | | | |
| 0.7 | 94.8916 | 94.8374 | 0.0571 | −0.0001 |
| 0.8 | 94.7650 | 94.7429 | 0.0233 | −0.0001 |
| 0.9 | 94.6534 | 94.6483 | 0.0054 | −0.0001 |
| 1 | 94.5538 | 94.5538 | 0.0000 | −0.0001 |
| 1.1 | 94.4637 | 94.4592 | 0.0047 | −0.0001 |
| 1.2 | 94.3815 | 94.3647 | 0.0179 | −0.0001 |
| 1.3 | 94.3060 | 94.2701 | 0.0381 | −0.0001 |
| *Case 2*: $\alpha = 0.2$ | | | | |
| 0.7 | 65.1116 | 64.2399 | 1.3388 | −0.5559 |
| 0.8 | 63.3957 | 63.0419 | 0.5581 | −0.5718 |
| 0.9 | 61.9198 | 61.8382 | 0.1317 | −0.5886 |
| 1 | 60.6287 | 60.6287 | 0.0000 | −0.6063 |
| 1.1 | 59.4839 | 59.4130 | 0.1192 | −0.6250 |
| 1.2 | 58.4577 | 58.1911 | 0.4560 | −0.6448 |
| 1.3 | 57.5293 | 56.9628 | 0.9848 | −0.6657 |
| *Case 3*: $\alpha = 0.4$ | | | | |
| 0.7 | 58.8404 | 56.9146 | 3.2729 | −4.2159 |
| 0.8 | 55.7800 | 54.9958 | 1.4060 | −4.5671 |
| 0.9 | 53.2130 | 53.0313 | 0.3415 | −4.9717 |
| 1 | 51.0170 | 51.0170 | 0.0000 | −5.4418 |
| 1.1 | 49.1086 | 48.9482 | 0.3266 | −5.9937 |
| 1.2 | 47.4288 | 46.8194 | 1.2849 | −6.6489 |
| 1.3 | 45.9343 | 44.6240 | 2.8526 | −7.4373 |

*Notes*: The utility function is $u(x, z) = x^{\alpha}z^{1-\alpha}$; the budget is $px + z = y$; income satisfies $y = 100$; and the initial price is $p = 1$.

[a] The level of utility if the consumer adjusts his consumption to the price change.

[b] The level of utility if the consumer continues to consume the quantity $g$ which is optimal for $p = 1$. The quantity $g$ is equal to 1 for $\alpha = 0.01$, 20 for $\alpha = 0.2$, and 40 for $\alpha = 0.4$.

[c] The utility loss measured as a percentage of initial income.

[d] The value of $\partial^2 v/\partial p^2$ in the case of non-adjustment. Here $v(p, y) = g^{\alpha}(y - pg)^{1-\alpha}$.

where $x$ is the level of consumption of a given firm's products, and $z$ is the real expenditure on other products. The customer maximizes this utility subject to the budget constraint $px + z = y$. The parameter $\alpha$ represents the expenditure share of $x$. The price of $x$, $p$, is assumed to fluctuate around $p = 1$. The income is set equal to 100. Table 8.1 shows the following for each value of $p$: (*a*) The first-best utility, in which the consumer chooses $x$ freely; (*b*) the second-best utility, in which the customer's purchase is fixed at $g$, which is set equal to the optimal $x$ under the initial price ($p = 1$); (*c*) the cost of non-adjustment as a percentage of initial income, which is the difference between the first-best and the second-best utilities divided by the marginal utility of income (recall that initial income is 100); and (*d*) the value of the second partial derivative of

$$v(p, y) = g^{\alpha} (y - pg)^{1-\alpha}$$

with respect to $p$.

This table suggests that the scope of rigid customer-market prices may be large (see case 2). The expenditure on this firm's products is one-fifth of the total budget. The table shows that the 10 per cent fluctuation in price produces a loss of only 0.1 per cent of the total budget, when the customer does not adjust $x$. Thus, the adjustment cost, whose size is a mere 0.1 per cent of the total budget, prevents the customer from adjusting $x$. Moreover, in this case the value of $b(p, p)$ is clearly non-negligible. Thus, this firm's price is likely to be more rigid than the monopoly price. Even in case 3, in which the expenditure share is four-tenths of the total budget, the 10 per cent fluctuation in price causes a loss of only 0.3 per cent of the total budget, and in this case we have a very large absolute value of $b(p, p)$. The firm's price becomes very sticky, as long as the customer does not adjust his quantity, which is likely under a 10 per cent price fluctuation. On the other hand, if the expenditure share is very small, we have an almost negligible $b(p, p)$, although the loss is also very small (case 1). In this case, rigidity loses its practical importance.

### 4.2. *The Possibility that Consumers Get Current Price Information*

The foregoing analysis predicts that many customer markets have rigid prices. There is another explanation of the observation that customer-market prices are rigid. It is related to the possibility that consumers get current price information, so that they can change suppliers after they know other firms' prices.

Until now it has been assumed that the information diffusion process is quite sluggish, so that customers cannot observe the current prices of firms. I now relax this assumption. Note that I have implicitly assumed the existence of a large cost in changing suppliers: this underlies the assumption of the short-run immobility of customers. Thus, it is not always profitable to buy products from the supplier with the lowest price, even if current price information is available.

Customers calculate the gains and losses from changing suppliers and determine whether or not to stick to their current supplier. The gains from changing suppliers depend on the variance in prices among firms. A large variance implies that many customers will find their current supplier's price high relative to the firm with the lowest price. Consequently, more customers will prefer to change suppliers in the large-variance than in the small-variance case. Thus, in the former case the stable customer–supplier relationship is more difficult to sustain. As has been already noted, flexible customer-market prices imply a large variance in prices among firms. Consequently, customer markets with flexible prices will be unsustainable in many cases, if we allow the possibility that at least some customers have current price information. Thus, observed customer-market prices are likely to be rigid, because customer markets with rigid prices are more sustainable.

## 5. CONCLUDING REMARKS

This chapter predicts that customer-market prices are rigid to temporary demand and cost changes. However, all prices in the chapter are real prices, so what is explained is the rigidity of relative prices (the firm's price relative to those of its competitors), rather than that of nominal prices. It is the latter that is critical in explaining business cycles, not the former. As a consequence, one may be uncertain that this chapter, as it stands, has much relevance for business-cycle theory.

Relative price rigidity, however, may cause nominal price rigidity if it is supplemented by a cost of changing nominal prices (a menu cost). If the benefit from changing nominal prices is smaller than the menu cost, the firm does not adjust its nominal price to nominal demand shocks.

Consider an economy with many identical customer markets, as described above. Suppose that the money supply is increased. Further, suppose that other firms do not adjust their prices to the change in the money supply. Then, if the firm adjusts its price, this implies a change in the relative price. The customer–supplier relationship implies only a small change in the firm's optimal price in this case. Consequently, the benefit from adjusting the price is rather small. Thus, a small menu cost may be sufficient to prevent the firm from adjusting its price to the change in the money supply. If the menu cost is larger than the benefit, then no adjustment is a Nash equilibrium, and money becomes non-neutral. The larger the degree of relative price rigidity, the smaller the menu cost capable of causing monetary non-neutrality. (Ball and Romer (1990) present several examples of the interaction between relative price rigidity and the menu cost.)

Finally, the market for rented accommodation can serve as an example of customer markets. The habit-forming nature of consumption is generally found in this market. Thus, there is large adjustment cost involved in changing flats, in addition to the cost of moving. Moreover, the share of rents in the consumer's expenditure is large. This chapter implies that the consumer is very price-risk-averse under these conditions. Consequently, rents are rigid to temporary changes in demand and cost conditions. Because rents change only if large permanent changes occur, moderately long-term leases with fixed terms of trade are often found in this market.[11]

Long-term leases are also found in contracts between private landlords and large corporations, the latter of which are presumably fairly risk-neutral. This may seem inconsistent with the rigid-price argument based on the price risk aversion of buyers. However, in this case it seems that buyers (large corporation) effectively set the terms of trade and offer them to sellers (private landlords). Although large corporations are risk-neutral, they must consider the price risk aversion of private landlords in setting rents. Thus, rents are sticky, and long-term leases become attractive because they save on negotiation costs.

# Notes

1. There are various models of customer markets, other than the Phelps–Winter customer-flow model, having the rigid-price property. They include the customer-market kinked-demand-curve models of Negishi (1979), Stiglitz (1979), Okun (1981), and Woglom (1982). Nishimura (1982) presents a microeconomic foundation model of these customer-market kinked-demand-curve models. See also Bils (1989) and Gottfries (1990) for different explanations of price rigidity in customer markets.
2. The welfare consequence of price variability has been extensively discussed in the literature in many different contexts. See Waugh (1944), Samuelson (1972), Oi (1961), and Turnovsky *et al.* (1980).
3. The short-run immobility of customers may be caused by a large search cost, which makes frequent search unattractive, or by a large adjustment cost of changing suppliers. The former may be important in consumer-product markets, while the latter is emphasized in industrial markets. For various examples of buyers' short-run immobility in industrial markets, see Corey (1976). For a theoretical analysis of the various long-run consequences of the mobility cost, see Phelps and Winter (1970) and Weizsacker (1984).

   Note that the number of customers is assumed to be so large that (implicit as well as explicit) individual contract negotiation is prohibitively expensive in this market. Moreover, it is also assumed that quantity-contingent prices (such as nonlinear price schedules) are impractical in this market, because a large administrative cost is involved in such a price system if the number of buyers is very large. Thus, the firm is obliged to offer a unique price to all of its customers, regardless of the quantitites they purchase.

4. Although $d$ is an integer if the product is indivisible, it is treated as a real number.
5. If the price elasticity of demand is greater than the marginal customer's cost–benefit ratio of consuming the firm's products, then the firm satisfies all demand that its price induces. See Nishimura (1985) for details.
6. Throughout this chapter, $p(w)$ is assumed to be differentiable with respect to $w$.
7. $V$ is determined in a long-run industry equilibrium similar to the one analysed in Phelps and Winter (1970). In such an equilibrium, competition among firms plays an important role. However, I assume that $V$ is given, because I am concerned with the short run.
8. Note that, if the quantity of purchases changes at some price, then $v$ is no longer differentiable with respect to $p$ at that price. Thus, in the case of indivisible products, we shall restrict our attention to the range of $p$ and $y$ where the quantity remains unchanged.
9. This characteristic of consumption has been emphasized mostly in a macroeconomic framework. See Duesenberry (1949) and the literature of economic growth with habit-forming consumption.
10. The near-rational-behaviour argument (or the consumption-adjustment-cost argument) does not in general hold for a customer (who is not the marginal customer) whose optimal consumption of the firm's products is currently zero. Because his consumption level is the corner solution of the optimization problem, the adjustment may produce a first-order improvement for such a customer in this case. He may change his consumption plan and buy a positive amount of the products, even if the price change is small. Thus, the total demand for the firm's products is sensitive to a small change in the firm's price because of the existence of customers whose consumption is zero in some states and positive in others.
11. I do not argue that rigid customer prices are solely responsible for making long-term leases popular in the rented accommodation market. Preventing opportunistic behaviour is also an important incentive for signing a long-term lease.

# 9

# Consumer Search and Price Pledges

## 1. INTRODUCTION

In Chapter 8, we examined customer markets in which customers do not actively search within a given period. Information in customer markets diffuses through random encounters among the customers. The effect of consumers' imperfect information and of gradual information diffusion on the pricing behaviour of firms was analysed within this framework.

In some consumer-goods markets, however, consumers do actively search for the lowest price. In the last two decades, considerable attention has been focused on the effects of consumers' imperfect information on the pricing behaviour of firms. Its macroeconomic consequences are emphasized by Alchian (1970) and Okun (1975) in the context of the microeconomic foundations of macroeconomics. They argue that costly search makes customers willing to pay a premium to do business with suppliers who pledge a constant price despite demand fluctuations. In addition, they conjecture that this tendency is strong enough to make equilibrium prices rigid with respect to changes in demand, at least in the short run.

This chapter investigates the validity of these claims, using a model that is a variant of Salop and Stiglitz (1977). The model assumes that buyers face imperfect information about current prices and their location, and that they must incur search costs in order to obtain necessary information. Into this model I introduce the possibility of price pledges. Such a pledge reduces consumers' search costs and uncertainty. Consequently, consumers are willing to pay a higher price for a pledged firm's product. However, a pledge excludes the possibility of adjusting prices to current economic conditions, because the pledge must be made before the realization of a particular state. This means that the firm loses flexibility, which may cause losses on its side. Whether or not the firm adopts a pledge policy depends on the relative magnitude of the benefits and costs of the pledge. Moreover, these benefits and costs are generally influenced by the actions of other firms. An explicit analysis of this mutual dependence is therefore required, in order to investigate the validity of the conjecture of Alchian and Okun in an equilibrium setting.

Although the model presented in this chapter is a simplistic market-equilibrium model in which many strong assumptions are made (homogeneity of buyers and sellers, unit-quantity purchases, only two states of nature, constant returns to scale, etc.), it nevertheless suggests that the conjecture of Alchain and Okun is correct under a wide range of conditions. Indeed, unless the search cost is very small or the cost (and also demand) variation is very large, or both, the market equilibrium is likely to be characterized by rigid prices (price pledges) in the case of a positive correlation between demand and cost. The possibility of a rigid price equilibrium is even higher in the case of a negative correlation.

## 2. SLUGGISH INFORMATION DIFFUSION, COSTLY SEARCH, AND PRICE PLEDGES

Consider a market for perishable goods with homogeneous firms and homogeneous consumers. Firms are endowed with constant-returns-to-scale technology. Consumers buy one unit of the goods. Their indirect utility function is $u(p)$, with $u' < 0$, $u(0) = +\infty$, and $u(+\infty) = 0$, where $p$ is the price of the goods.[1] I assume that the size of individual firms and consumers is negligible compared with the size of the market. Specifically, I assume a continuum of firms and consumers. A firm is identified by a point in the interval $[0, M]$, while a consumer is identified by a point in $[0, N]$, where $M$ and $N$ are positive real numbers.

There is uncertainty in this market. First, the set of consumers entering the market differs from one state of nature to another. For simplicity, I assume that there are only two states. Let $\pi_i$ be the occurrence probability of state $i$, satisfying $\pi_1 + \pi_2 = 1$ and $\pi_i > 0$. In state 1 consumers in $[0, N_1]$ enter the market, while in state 2 those in $[0, N_2]$ enter the market. Here, $N_1$ and $N_2$ are positive real numbers satisfying $N_i \leq N$. Second, the marginal cost also depends on the state of nature. The term $c_1$ is the marginal cost in state 1, and $c_2$ is the marginal cost in state 2, where $c_1 > c_2$. However, the set of firms is state-independent. Firms can observe the state in each period.

Consumers, on the other hand, cannot observe the state of nature, although they are assumed to know the price distribution in each state of nature through, say, past experience in the market. In order to obtain information about the price and location of a particular price offer in the current period, consumers must incur search costs. Following Salop and Stiglitz (1977), I assume that, if consumers incur a search cost $b$ (in terms of utility), they get perfect information about current prices and their location in the market. For example, this assumption is satisfied if a government agency posts a list of all prices with the names of offering firms and their location. Consumers then get necessary price information if they make a trip to the agency. However, such a trip takes time, which reduces utility.

The main feature introduced into this imperfect-information model with exogenous uncertainty is the possibility of price pledges by firms. Firms can pledge constant (non-contingent) prices over states of nature *before* a particular state of nature is realized, and the individual pledge information is assumed to be conveyed to all consumers at no cost. Suppose that firms can mail price adverts to all consumers at no cost, but that it takes time to reach them. Firms are not allowed to change their prices after they send the adverts, and they are obliged to satisfy all demand that their pledge creates.[2] Pledged firms must thus determine non-contingent prices before the actual state is known to them. By contrast, unpledged firms are free to determine their prices after observing the current state, and have no obligation to satisfy all demand. Consumers have perfect information about the place and the price of pledged firms; they do not have such information about unpledged firms. In order to get information about unpledged firms, consumers must incur the search cost $b$.

Under the foregoing assumptions, consumers have two options. First, they can choose their supplier from among pledged firms, about which they have perfect information. Second, they can incur the search cost to get complete information about the rest of the firms (the unpledged firms), so as to choose their supplier from among all firms in the market.[3] They make the choice that yields the most utility. (In the case that they are indifferent about incurring or not incurring the search cost, they are assumed to choose randomly between the two. Thus, if the utility of incurring and of not incurring the search cost is the same, one-half of the consumers incur the cost, and the other half do not.)

Note that consumers who incur the search cost know about both pledged and unpledged firms, while consumers who do not pay the cost have information only about pledged ones. Thus, the potential customers of the unpledged firms are consumers who incur the search cost $b$ and thus have perfect information about the market, while all consumers are potential customers of pledged firms.[4] Consumers shop randomly among firms when their offers are the same. Because of the assumption of random shopping and homogeneous firms, a pledged firm obtains the same number of customers as other pledged firms if their offers are the same. The same is true for an unpledged firm.[5]

Finally, following Salop and Stiglitz (1977), we assume 'Nash' behaviour on the part of consumers. On the part of firms, we assume 'Stackelberg' behaviour with respect to consumers and 'Nash' behaviour with respect to other firms. Thus, consumers take firms' prices and other consumers' decisions as given, while firms take consumers' behaviour, not their decisions, as given, although they take other firms' prices as given. In our model, in which consumers have perfect pledge information and perfect information about the price distribution in each state of nature, this implies that a firm can influence a consumers' choice between incurring and not incurring the search cost (i.e. between being partially and completely informed) through its price policy, although it cannot change the policies of other firms.

Assuming that consumers purchase goods in each state and that firms produce output in at least one state of nature, and given the assumptions made above, the equilibrium is defined as follows. Consumers maximize their expected utility by making an appropriate choice about incurring the search cost and choosing their supplier. Firms maximize their expected profits, first, by appropriately determining whether to pledge non-contingent prices or not; second, if they decide to pledge non-contingent prices, by determining what price to offer; third, if they decide not to make the pledge, by determining what price to charge in each state. Finally, firms obtain zero expected profit by competing with each other because of constant-returns-to-scale technology.

The following definitions are used throughout this chapter: $p_i^e$ is the unpledged firms' equilibrium (contingent) price in state $i$, and $\hat{p}^e$ is the pledged firms' equilibrium (non-contingent) price. The term $\bar{c}$ is the long-run unit cost, defined as

$$\bar{c} = \frac{c_1 \pi_1 N_1 + c_2 \pi_2 N_2}{\pi_1 N_1 + \pi_2 N_2}. \tag{1}$$

The long-run unit cost $\bar{c}$ satisfies $c_1 > \bar{c} > c_2$.

## 3. RIGID-PRICE EQUILIBRIUM VERSUS FLEXIBLE-PRICE EQUILIBRIUM

The following two theorems are the main results of this chapter. Proofs of these theorems are found in the next section.

THEOREM 1. *The Rigid-Price Equilibrium.* If

$$b > \pi_2\,[u(c_2) - u(\bar{c})], \tag{2}$$

then a unique equilibrium exists in which all firms pledge $\hat{p}^e = \bar{c}$.

THEOREM 2. *The Flexible-Price Equilibrium.* If

$$\pi_2\,[u(c_2) - u(\bar{c})] > b, \tag{3}$$

then a unique equilibrium exists in which all firms do not make the pledge but offer $p_1^e = c_1$ and $P_2^e = c_2$.

Let us consider the implications of these theorems. If expenditure on these particular goods is small compared with the total budget, the marginal utility of composite goods consisting of other goods is approximately constant. In this case, the indirect utility function can be approximated by a linear function under the unit-quantity purchase assumption. Then, we have

$$\pi_2\,[u(c_2) - u(\bar{c})] \propto \pi_1 \pi_2 \frac{N_1}{\pi_1 N_1 + \pi_2 N_2} (c_1 - c_2). \tag{4}$$

If there is positive correlation between demand and cost ($N_1 > N_2$), then an increase in the ratio of the demand in state 1 to the long-run average demand ($\pi_1 N_1 + \pi_2 N_2$) implies an increase in the difference between $N_1$ and $N_2$. Consequently, theorems 1 and 2 mean that, the smaller (larger) the fluctuations in demand and cost are, the smaller (larger) $\pi_2$ $[u(c_2) - u(\bar{c})]$ is, which makes a rigid (flexible) price equilibrium more likely.

In the case of a negative correlation between demand and cost ($N_1 < N_2$), (4) implies that a rigid price equilibrium is likely if demand fluctuations are large, which is the opposite of the conclusion in the positive-correlation case. Suppose that $N_2$ is fixed and $N_1$ is decreased, so that demand variation is increased. Because in this case an increase in demand variation means weaker demand than before when cost is high, the loss arising from the rigid pledge is relatively small. Thus, a rigid-price equilibrium becomes more likely. A similar argument holds if $N_1$ is fixed and $N_2$ is increased.

Next, consider the term $\pi_1 \pi_2$ in (4). This term can be considered as a factor representing the skewness of the probability distribution of states. If the distribution is skewed to one state, $\pi_1 \pi_2$ becomes small. If, on the other hand, the distribution is symmetric, i.e. if $\pi_i = 0.5$, then $\pi_1 \pi_2$ attains its maximum. Thus, (4) implies that the market equilibrium is likely to be characterized by rigid prices if the probability distribution is skewed to one state. If the probability of the occurrence of one state of nature is much larger than the other, then the condition of this state becomes a dominant factor in the firm's expected profits. Then, the loss arising from the inflexibility of the pledge is negligible, so that we have a rigid price equilibrium.

Table 9.1 shows numerical examples with plausible values of $N_2/N_1$ and $\pi_2$. Here $\phi\,[\pi_2, (N_2/N_1)]$ is given by

$$\phi\left(\pi_2, \frac{N_2}{N_1}\right) = \pi_2 \frac{(1-\pi_2)}{(1-\pi_2)+\pi_2\,(N_2/N_1)},$$

so that we have

$$\pi_2\,[u(c_2)-u(\bar{c})] \propto \phi\left(\pi_2, \frac{N_2}{N_1}\right)(c_1-c_2). \tag{5}$$

The function $\phi$ is depicted in Fig. 9.1. Table 9.1 reveals that, if the parameters take on realistic values, then $\phi$ is at most 2/5, and generally is much lower. Thus, the market is likely to have a rigid price equilibrium except for the cases in which cost fluctuations are very large or the search cost is negligibly small. The table also shows that $\phi$ is small in the case of a negative correlation between cost and demand. Thus, an industry is more likely to have a rigid price equilibrium if its factor markets exhibit increasing returns to scale than otherwise.

Finally, if the direct utility functions are concave, then their indirect

TABLE 9.1. Pledging Stable Prices: Numerical Examples

| Positive correlation between demand and cost ($N_1 > N_2$) | | | Negative correlation between demand and cost ($N_1 < N_2$) | | |
|---|---|---|---|---|---|
| $N_1/N_1$ | $\pi_2$ | $\phi$ | $N_2/N_1$ | $\pi_2$ | $\phi$ |
| 1/1.5 | 0.9 | 0.13 | 1.5/1 | 0.9 | 0.06 |
| 1/1.5 | 0.8 | 0.22 | 1.5/1 | 0.8 | 0.11 |
| 1/1.5 | 0.7 | 0.27 | 1.5/1 | 0.7 | 0.16 |
| 1/1.5 | 0.6 | 0.30 | 1.5/1 | 0.6 | 0.18 |
| 1/1.5 | 0.5 | 0.30 | 1.5/1 | 0.5 | 0.20 |
| 1/1.5 | 0.4 | 0.28 | 1.5/1 | 0.4 | 0.20 |
| 1/1.5 | 0.3 | 0.23 | 1.5/1 | 0.3 | 0.18 |
| 1/1.5 | 0.2 | 0.17 | 1.5/1 | 0.2 | 0.15 |
| 1/1.5 | 0.1 | 0.09 | 1.5/1 | 0.1 | 0.09 |
| 1/2 | 0.9 | 0.16 | 2/1 | 0.9 | 0.05 |
| 1/2 | 0.8 | 0.27 | 2/1 | 0.8 | 0.09 |
| 1/2 | 0.7 | 0.32 | 2/1 | 0.7 | 0.12 |
| 1/2 | 0.6 | 0.34 | 2/1 | 0.6 | 0.15 |
| 1/2 | 0.5 | 0.33 | 2/1 | 0.5 | 0.17 |
| 1/2 | 0.4 | 0.30 | 2/1 | 0.4 | 0.17 |
| 1/2 | 0.3 | 0.25 | 2/1 | 0.3 | 0.16 |
| 1/2 | 0.2 | 0.18 | 2/1 | 0.2 | 0.13 |
| 1/2 | 0.1 | 0.09 | 2/1 | 0.1 | 0.08 |
| 1/3 | 0.9 | 0.22 | 3/1 | 0.9 | 0.03 |
| 1/3 | 0.8 | 0.34 | 3/1 | 0.8 | 0.06 |
| 1/3 | 0.7 | 0.39 | 3/1 | 0.7 | 0.09 |
| 1/3 | 0.6 | 0.40 | 3/1 | 0.6 | 0.11 |
| 1/3 | 0.5 | 0.38 | 3/1 | 0.5 | 0.13 |
| 1/3 | 0.4 | 0.33 | 3/1 | 0.4 | 0.13 |
| 1/3 | 0.3 | 0.26 | 3/1 | 0.3 | 0.13 |
| 1/3 | 0.2 | 0.18 | 3/1 | 0.2 | 0.11 |
| 1/3 | 0.1 | 0.10 | 3/1 | 0.1 | 0.07 |

utility functions are concave in the price of the goods under unit-quantity purchases. Moreover, if consumers' expenditures on the goods are sufficiently large compared with the total budget, their indirect utility function is significantly concave. In this case consumers are strongly price-risk-averse. The results described in the preceding paragraphs are then strengthened. This is because price risk aversion makes the price pledge more attractive from the viewpoint of consumers, resulting in larger benefits of the pledge for the firm.[6]

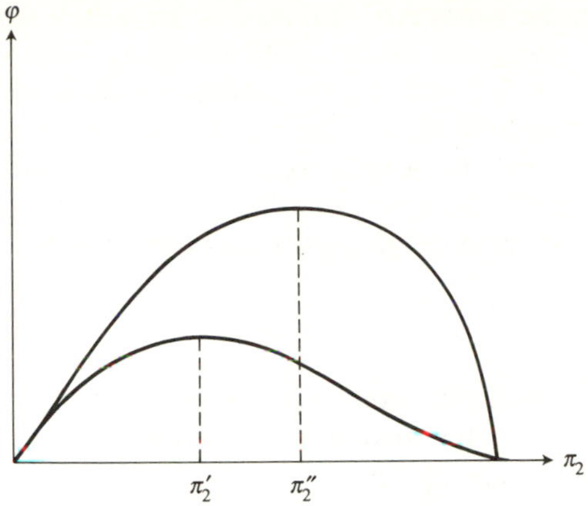


FIG. 9.1. The curvature of $\phi$. $\pi'_2 = 1/[1 + (N'_1/N'_2)^{1/2}]$; $\pi''_2 = 1/[1 + (N_1/N_2)^{1/2}]$, $N_1/N_2 > N'_1/N'_2$.

## 4. PROOFS OF THE THEOREMS

In the following, $\alpha$ is defined as the proportion of unpledged firms.

LEMMA. There is no mixed equilibrium in which some firms make the pledge but others do not.

*Proof*. Suppose there is a mixed equilibrium; that is, $1 > \alpha > 0$ in equilibrium. I first show that in this case unpledged firms produce output only in state 2. Then I derive a necessary condition for consumers' utility maximization and firms' zero expected profits. Finally, I prove that this condition is inconsistent with firms' expected profit maximization.

Note first that, because of the zero-expected-profit condition of the equilibrium under constant returns to scale, $p_i^e$ and $\hat{p}^e$ must satisfy (i) $p_i^e = c_i$ for $i$ in which unpledged firms produce output, and (ii) $c_2 \leqslant \hat{p}^e \leqslant c_1$. Second, unpledged firms produce output only in state 2. Suppose the contrary. Then there must be a positive demand at unpledged firms in state 1. Because $1 > \alpha > 0$, we have $c_1 \geqslant \hat{p}^e$ from (ii) above, and $p_1^e = c_1$ from (i). Moreover, because customers of unpledged firms are perfectly informed, $p_1^e$ must satisfy $\hat{p}^e \geqslant p_1^e$. Consequently, we have $c_1 \geqslant \hat{p}^e \geqslant p_1^e = c_1$, which implies $\hat{p}^e = c_1$. However, because $c_1 > c_2$, the condition $\hat{p}^e = c_1$ means that pledged firms have positive expected profits in equilibrium, which contradicts the zero-expected-profit condition of the equilibrium. Consequently, unpledged firms do not produce output in state 1 in a mixed equilibrium. Because unpledged firms produce output in at least one state in a mixed equilibrium, they do so in state 2. Thus, we have $p_2^e = c_2$ from (i), and consequently $\hat{p}^e \geqslant p_2^e$ from (ii).

Next, consider the consumer's utility maximization. On the one hand, the consumer's expected utility of incurring the search cost is $\pi_1 u(\hat{p}^e) + \pi_2 u(c_2) - b$, because (i) unpledged firms do not produce output in state 1 and (ii) we have $\hat{p}^e \geqslant p_2^e = c_2$. On the other hand, the expected utility of not incurring the search cost, and thus of being a customer of pledged firms, is $u(\hat{p}^e)$. Because both pledged and unpledged firms coexist in this market, there must be customers for both types of firms. This means that

$$\pi_2 \left[u(c_2) - u(\hat{p}^e)\right] = b.$$

Because of indifference, the consumer chooses randomly between incurring and not incurring the search cost, making the ratio of consumers incurring the cost equal to ½.

Now consider the zero-expected-profit condition. Note that in state 1 only pledged firms produce output and obtain positive demand. Because $\alpha$ is the ratio of unpledged firms, each pledged firm gets $N_1/[(1-\alpha)M]$ consumers in state 1. In state 2, the pledged firm obtains only those consumers not incurring the search cost, the ratio of which is ½. Consequently, each pledged firm has ½ $N_2/[(1-\alpha)M]$ consumers in state 2. Thus, the expected profits of pledged firms are given by

$$\pi_1(\hat{p}^e - c_1)\frac{N_1}{(1-\alpha)M} + \pi_2(\hat{p}^e - c_2)\frac{N_2}{2(1-\alpha)M} = \frac{2\pi_1 N_1 + \pi_2 N_2}{2(1-\alpha)M}(\hat{p}^e - c^*).$$

where $c^*$ is defined as $c^* = (2c_1\pi_1 N_1 + c_2\pi_2 N_2)/(2\pi_1 N_1 + \pi_2 N_2)$. Thus, the zero-expected-profit condition implies $\hat{p}^e = c^*$.

Finally, I show that $\hat{p}^e$ defined above is not optimal for pledged firms. Consider $\hat{p} = \hat{p}^e - \epsilon$, where $\epsilon$ is an arbitrarily small, positive real number. Then, by pledging $\hat{p}$, the unpledged firm can attract all consumers in the market, because $\pi_1 u(\hat{p}^e) + \pi_2 u(c_2) - b < \pi_1 u(\hat{p}) + \pi_2 u(c_2) - b < u(\hat{p})$, from the definition of $\hat{p}$. The firm's expected profits are then given by $(\pi_1 N_1 + \pi_2 N_2)\ (\hat{p} - \bar{c})$, which is positive because $\hat{p} = \hat{p}^e - \epsilon = c^* - \epsilon > \bar{c}$, when $\epsilon$ is sufficiently small. (Note that we have $c^* > \bar{c}$ because $c_1 > c_2$, $N_1 > 0$, and $N_2 > 0$.) This ends the proof.

### 9.1. *Proof of Theorem 1*

Suppose that other firms pledge a non-contingent price $\hat{p} = \bar{c}$. Consider first a no-pledge policy offering $p_1$ in state 1 and $p_2$ in state 2. Note that at least one of $p_i$ in this no-pledge policy must satisfy $p_i \leqslant \bar{c}$ in order to attract consumers in at least one state.

First, suppose that $p_1 \leqslant \bar{c}$ and $p_2 > \bar{c}$. Note that $p_2 > \bar{c}$ means that the no-pledge firm's price is higher than that of the pledged firms, so that no consumer visits the no-pledge firm in state 2. Also, note that $p_1 \leqslant \bar{c}$ means

$p_1 < c_1$, implying negative expected profits in state 1. Thus, the no-pledge firm cannot obtain non-negative expected profits by this policy.

Second, suppose that $p_1 > \bar{c}$ and $p_2 \leqslant \bar{c}$. The condition $p_1 > \bar{c}$ implies that the firm cannot attract consumers in state 1. So, in order to attract consumers in state 2, $p_2$ must satisfy $\pi_1 u(\bar{c}) + \pi_2 u(p_2) - b \geqslant u(\bar{c})$, which, together with (2), implies $u(p_2) > u(c_2)$, so that we get $p_2 < c_2$. Consequently, the firm cannot obtain non-negative expected profits by this policy.

Finally, suppose that $p_i \leqslant \bar{c}$ for all $i$. By this policy, the firm can attract consumers in both states if $\pi_1 u(p_1) + \pi_2 u(p_2) - b \geqslant u(\bar{c})$. However, the no-pledge firm's expected profits are negative under this policy because of (2). In the case that $p_i < \bar{c}$ for all $i$, the firm cannot obtain non-negative expected profits, because (*a*) we have the following inequality:

$$0 = \pi_1(\bar{c} - c_1)N_1 + \pi_2(\bar{c} - c_2)N_2 > \pi_1(p_1 - c_1)N_1 + \pi_2\,(p_2 - c_2)N_2,$$

and (*b*) the no-pledge firm's expected profits are (i) $\pi_1\,(p_1 - c_1)\,N_1 + \pi_2(p_2 - c_2)\,N_2$ if $\pi_1 u(p_1) + \pi_2 u(p_2) - b > u(\bar{c})$, and (ii) $\pi_1\,(p_1 - c_1)\,(N_1/2) + \pi_2\,(p_2 - c_2)\,(N_2/2)$ if $\pi_1 u(p_1) + \pi_2 u(p_2) - b = u(\bar{c})$. A similar argument establishes that the firm cannot obtain non-negative expected profits in other cases ($p_i = \bar{c}$ and $p_j < \bar{c}$ for $i, j = 1, 2$). Consequently, the firm cannot obtain non-negative expected profits by *any* no-pledge policy, when it produces output in at least one state.

Consider, then, a pledge policy. By pledging $\bar{c}$, the firm can get zero expected profit when it produces output. Pledging a higher price fails to attract consumers, while pledging a lower price leads to negative expected profits. Consequently, the firm's optimal pledge policy is to pledge $\hat{p} = \bar{c}$.

Next, consider other possible equilibria. First, suppose that under (2) there is an equilibrium in which no firm makes the pledge. Then, the zero-expected-profit condition of unpledged firms implies $p^e_1 = c_1$ and $p^e_2 = c_2$. Let us consider a pledge policy of offering $\hat{p}^* = \bar{c} + \epsilon$, where $\epsilon$ is an arbitrarily small, positive real number. Because $c_2 < \bar{c} < c_1$, we have $c_2 < \hat{p}^* < c_1$. Moreover, because (2) is equivalent to $\pi_1 u(\bar{c}) + \pi_2 u(c_2) - b < u(\bar{c})$, we have

$$\pi_1 u(c_1) + \pi_2 u(c_2) - b < \pi_1 u(\hat{p}^*) + \pi_2 u(c_2) - b < u(\hat{p}^*),$$

if $\epsilon$ is sufficiently small. Consequently, the firm attracts all consumers by offering $\hat{p}^*$. Then, the expected profits of pledging $\hat{p}^*$ are

$$\pi_1(\hat{p}^* - c_1)\,N_1 + \pi_2\,(\hat{p}^* - c_2)\,N_2 = (\pi_1 N_1 + \pi_2 N_2)\,\epsilon > 0,$$

which contradicts the zero-expected-profits condition. Consequently, an equilibrium in which no firm makes the pledge does not exist. Moreover, the lemma reveals that there is no mixed equilibrium. Consequently, only an equilibrium in which all firms make the pledge is possible under (2).

### 9.2. *Proof of Theorem 2*

Suppose that other firms do not make the pledge, and offer $p_1 = c_1$ and $p_2 = c_2$. First, consider a pledge policy $\hat{p}$, such that $\hat{p} \geqslant c_1$. Suppose that this pledge policy attracts consumers. We then have $\pi_1 u(c_1) + \pi_2 u(c_2) - b \leqslant u(\hat{p})$. However, we also have $u(\hat{p}) \leqslant u(c_1)$. Consequently, we obtain, from (3),

$$\pi_2[u(c_2) - u(c_1)] \leqslant b < \pi_2[u(c_2) - u(\bar{c})],$$

but this contradicts $c_1 > \bar{c}$. Thus, $\hat{p}$, such that $\hat{p} \geqslant c_1$ cannot attract consumers.

Now consider a pledge policy of offering $\hat{p}$, such that $c_1 > \hat{p}$. If the firm pledges this price, all consumers buy from this firm in state 1. Because $c_1 > \hat{p}$, the firm's profits in state 1 are negative. Consequently, the loss must be compensated by profits in state 2. In order to attract consumers in state 2, $\hat{p}$ must satisfy $\pi_1 u(\hat{p}) + \pi_2 u(c_2) - b \leqslant u(\hat{p})$, which, together with (3), implies

$$\pi_2[u(c_2) - u(\hat{p})] \leqslant b < \pi_2[u(c_2) - u(\bar{c})].$$

Thus, we obtain $\hat{p} < \bar{c}$. However, the expected profits of the firm are: (i) $\pi_1 (\hat{p} - c_1) N_1 + \pi_2 (\hat{p} - c_2) N_2$ if $\pi_1 u(c_1) + \pi_2 u(c_2) - b < u(\hat{p})$; (ii*a*) $\pi_1 (\hat{p} - c_1) N_1 + \pi_2 (\hat{p} - c_2) (N_2/2)$ if $\pi_1 u(c_1) + \pi_2 u(c_2) - b = u(\hat{p})$ and $\hat{p} \geqslant c_2$; and (ii*b*) $\pi_1 (\hat{p} - c_1) N_1 + \pi_2 (\hat{p} - c_2) N_2$ if $\pi_1 u(c_1) + \pi_2 u(c_2) - b = u(\hat{p})$ and $\hat{p} < c_2$. Because $\hat{p} < \bar{c} < c^*$, the firm's expected profits are negative in all three cases. Consequently, the firm cannot obtain non-negative expected profits by offering $\hat{p}$, such that $c_1 > \hat{p}$. Thus, the firm cannot obtain non-negative expected profits by any pledge policy when it produces output.

Consider, then, a no-pledge policy such that $(p_1, p_2)$. Then, it is easy to show that to offer $p_1 = c_1$ and $p_2 = c_2$ is the optimal policy, because otherwise this policy either fails to attract consumers or yields negative expected profits. Therefore, the overall optimal policy for the firm is to offer $p_1 = c_1$ and $p_2 = c_2$.

Next, consider the other possible equilibria. First, suppose that there is an equilibrium in which all firms make the pledge. Then, the zero-expected-profit condition implies $\hat{p} = \bar{c}$. Consider a no-pledge policy in which the firm does not produce output in state 1 and offers $p_2$, such that $\pi_1 u(\bar{c}) + \pi_2 u(p_2) - b = u(\bar{c})$. Note that the $p_2$ satisfying this also satisfies $p_2 < \bar{c}$, because $b > 0$. The firm can thus attract consumers in state 2 by this policy. Moreover, the above relation and (3) imply

$$\pi_2[u(c_2) - u(\bar{c})] > b = \pi_2[u(p_2) - u(\bar{c})],$$

which means $p_2 > c_2$. Thus, this no-pledge policy yields positive expected profits, which contradicts the zero-expected-profit condition. Consequently, together with the lemma, only an equilibrium in which no firm makes a pledge is possible under (3).

# Notes

1. Throughout this chapter, I assume that consumers' income is held constant so that the dependency of *u* on income is ignored.
2. This model thus assumes sluggish price-information diffusion. Butters (1977) investigates the effects of costly price advertisement under instantaneous price-information diffusion. Note that the model is easily extended to the case in which price adverts are costly with no qualitative changes.

   Incidentally, contingent pledges are not feasible in this market because of monitoring problems. Since consumers cannot observe the current state of nature, they have no means of monitoring whether firms comply to their contingent pledges.
3. Because consumers have no information about the location of unpledged firms currently in business, they are assumed to fail to find any unpledged firm if they do not incur search costs. This assumption is different from those in the literature of imperfect information and costly search, in which random shopping among *unknown* firms is possible, though costly.
4. Thus, the equilibrium prices of this market are closer to competitive prices than those in Salop and Stiglitz (1977), which assumes costless random shopping among unknown firms.
5. In addition to the assumptions made above, one technical assumption is made throughout this chapter: I assume that firms produce output as long as they obtain non-negative expected profit, although this makes them indifferent about whether to produce output or exit from the market.
6. In the case of variable quantity purchases, the indirect utility functions are likely to be non-negligibly convex with respect to the price, if the direct utility functions are concave and expenditures on this good are large compared with the total budget. (See Nishimura (1985) for this and related topics.) In this case, consumers are price-risk-loving. Consequently, the possibility of a rigid price equilibrium is smaller than in the price-risk-neutral case of the text. Note that in this case (3) must be modified appropriately, because the long-run unit cost is now dependent on the price.

# References


Abel, A. B. (1983), 'Optimal Investment under Uncertainty'. *American Economic Review*, 73: 228–33.

—— (1985), 'A Stochastic Model of Investment, Marginal *q* and the Market Value of the Firm'. *International Economic Review*, 26: 305–22.

Aitchison, J., and Brown, J. A. C. (1957), *The Lognormal Distribution with Special Reference to Its Uses in Economics*. New York: Cambridge University Press.

Akerlof, G. A., and Yellen, J. L. (1985), 'A Near-Rational Model of the Business Cycle, with Wage and Price Inertia'. *Quarterly Journal of Economics*, 100: 823–38.

Alchian, A. A. (1970), 'Information Costs, Pricing, and Resource Unemployment'. In E. S. Phelps *et al* (eds.), *Microeconomic Foundations of Employment and Inflation Theory*. New York: W. W. Norton.

Andersen, T. M. (1985), 'Price and Output Responsiveness to Nominal Changes under Differential Information'. *European Economic Review*, 29: 63–87.

Azariadis, C. (1981), 'A Reexamination of Natural Rate Theory'. *American Economic Review*, 71: 946–60.

—— and Cooper, R. (1985), 'Nominal Wage–Price Rigidity as a Rational Expectations Equilibrium'. *American Economic Review, Papers and Proceedings*, 75: 31–5.

Ball, L. and Cecchetti, S. G. (1987), 'Imperfect Information and Staggered Price Settings'. NBER, Working Paper no. 2201.

—— and Romer, D. (1989*a*), 'Are Prices Too Sticky?' *Quarterly Journal of Economics*, 104: 507–24.

—— —— (1989*b*) 'The Equilibrium and Optimal Timing of Price Changes'. *Review of Economic Studies*, 56: 179–98.

—— —— (1990), 'Real Rigidities and the Non-neutrality of Money'. *Review of Economic Studies*, 57: 183–203.

Barro, R. J. (1972), 'A Theory of Monopolistic Price Adjustment'. *Review of Economic Studies*, 39: 17–26.

—— (1977), 'Long Term Contracting, Sticky Prices, and Monetary Policy'. *Journal of Monetary Economics*, 3: 305–16.

—— (ed.) (1989), *Modern Business Cycle Theory*. Oxford: Basil Blackwell.

—— and Grossman, H. I. (1976), *Money, Employment and Inflation.* Cambridge University Press.

—— and Hercowitz, Z. (1980), 'Money Stock Revisions and Unanticipated Money Growth'. *Journal of Monetary Economics*, 6: 257–67.

Bean, C. R. (1984), 'A Little Bit More Evidence on the Natural Rate Hypothesis from the U K'. *European Economic Review*, 25: 279–92.

Benassy, J.-P. (1976), 'The Disequilibrium Approach to Monopolistic Price Setting and General Monopolistic Equilibrium'. *Review of Economic Studies*, 43: 69–81.

—— (1978), 'A Neo-Keynesian Model of Price and Quantity Determination in Disequilibrium'. In G. Schwödiauer (ed.), *Equilibrium and Disequilibrium in Economic Theory*. Boston: Reidel.

—— (1982), *The Economics of Market Disequilibrium*. New York: Academic Press.

—— (1987), 'Imperfect Competition, Unemployment and Policy'. *European Economic Reivew*, 31: 417–26.

—— (1988), 'The Objective Demand Curve in General Equilibrium with Price Makers'. *Economic Journal,* 98 (suppl.): 37–49.

—— (1990*a*) 'Non Walrasian Equilibria, Money, and Macroeconomics'. In F. H. Hahn and B. Friedman (eds.), *Handbook of Monetary Economics*. Amsterdam: North-Holland.

—— (1990*b*) 'Microeconomic Foundations and Properties of Macroeconomic Model with Imperfect Competition'. In K. J. Arrow (ed.), *Issues in Contemporary Economics: Proceedings of the 9th IEA World Congress, i: Markets and Welfare*. London: Macmillan.

—— (1991), 'Optimal Government Policy in a Macroeconomic Model with Imperfect Competition and Rational Expectations'. In W. Barnett, B. Cornet, C. D'Aspremont, J. J. Gabszewicz, and A. Mas-Colell (eds.), *Equilibrium Theory and Applications: A Conference in Honor of Jacques Dreze*. Cambridge University Press.

—— (1992), 'Monopolistic Competition'. In W. Hildenbrand and H. Sonnenschein (eds.), *Handbook of Mathematical Economics*, iv. Amsterdam: North-Holland.

Bils, M. (1987), 'The Cyclical Behavior of Marginal Cost and Price'. *American Economic Review*, 77: 838–55.

—— (1989), 'Pricing in a Customer Market'. *Quarterly Journal of Economics*, 104: 699–718.

Binmore, K., and Dasgupta, P. (1986), 'Game Theory: A Survey'. In K. Binmore and P. Dasgupta (eds.), *Economic Organizations as Games*. Oxford: Basil Blackwell.

Blanchard, O. J. (1983), 'Price Asynchronization and Price Level Inertia'. In R. Dornbusch and M. H. Simonsen (eds.), *Inflation, Debt, and Indexation*. Cambridge, Mass.: MIT Press, pp. 3–24.

—— (1986), 'The Wage Price Spiral'. *Quarterly Journal of Economics*, 101: 543–65.

—— (1987), 'Aggregate and Individual Price Adjustment'. *Brookings Papers on Economic Activity*, 1: 57–109.

—— (1990), 'Why Does Money Affect Output? A Survey'. In B. Friedman and F. Hahn (eds.), *Handbook of Monetary Economics*. Amsterdam: North-Holland.

—— and Fischer, S. (1989), *Lectures on Macroeconomics*. Cambridge, Mass.: MIT Press.

—— and Kiyotaki, N. (1987), 'Monopolistic Competition and the Effects of Aggregate Demand'. *American Economic Review*, 77: 647–66.

Blume, L. E., Bray, M. M., and Easley, D., (1982), 'Introduction to the Stability of Rational Expectations Equilibrium'. *Journal of Economic Theory*, 26: 313–17.

Boschen, J. F., (1985), 'Employment and Output Effects of Observed and Unobserved Monetary Growth'. *Journal of Money, Credit, and Banking*, 17: 153–63.

—— and Grossman, H. I. (1982), 'Tests of Equilibrium Macroeconomics Using Contemporaneous Monetary Data'. *Journal of Monetary Economics*, 10: 309–33.

Bosworth, B. D., and Lawrence, R. Z. (1982), *Commodity Prices and the New Inflation*. Washington, DC: Brookings Institution.

Brander, J. A., and Spencer, B. J. (1983), 'Strategic Commitment with R & D: The Symmetric Case'. *Bell Journal of Economics*, 14: 225–35.

Bray, M. M., and Savin, N. E. (1986), 'Rational Expectations Equilibria, Learning, and Model Specification'. *Econometrica*, 54: 1129–60.

Brunner, K., Cukierman, A., and Meltzer, A. H. (1980), 'Stagflation, Persistent Unemployment and the Permanence of Economic Shocks'. *Journal of Monetary Economics*, 6: 467–92.

—— —— —— (1983), 'Money and Economic Activity, Inventories and Business Cycles'. *Journal of Monetary Economics*, 11: 281–319.

Bulow, J. L., Geanakoplos, J. D., and Klemperer, P. D. (1985), 'Multimarket Oligopoly: Strategic Substitutes and Complements'. *Journal of Political Economy*, 93: 488–511.

Butters, G. (1977), 'Equilibrium Distributions of Sales and Advertising Prices'. *Review of Economic Studies*, 44: 465–91.

Caplin, A. S. (1985), 'The Variability of Aggregate Demand with (*S, s*) Inventory Policies', *Eonometrica*, 53: 1395–1410.

—— and Leahy, J. (1989), 'State-Dependent Pricing and the Dynamics of Money and Output'. Discussion Paper no. 448, Columbia University, October.

—— and Spulber, D. (1987), 'Menu Costs and the Neutrality of Money'. *Quarterly Journal of Economics*, 102: 703–25.

Carlton, D. W. (1979), 'Contracts, Price Rigidity, and Market Equilibrium'. *Journal of Political Economy*, 87: 1034–62.

—— (1986), 'The Rigidity of Price'. *American Economic Review*, 76: 637–58.

—— (1989), 'The Theory and the Facts of How Markets Clear: Is Industrial Organization Valuable for Understanding Macroeconomics?' In R. Schmalensee and R. D. Willig (eds.), *Handbook of Industrial Organization*, i. Amsterdam: North-Holland.

Caskey, J. (1985), 'Modeling the Formation of Price Expectations: A Bayesian Approach'. *American Economic Review*, 75: 768–76.

Clarke, R. D. (1983), 'Collusion and the Incentives for Information Sharing'. *Bell Journal of Economics*, 14: 383–94.

Cooper, R., and John, A. (1988), 'Coordinating Coordination Failures in Keynesian Models'. *Quarterly Journal of Economics*, 103: 441–63.

Corey, E. R. (1976), *Industrial Marketing*, 2nd edn. Englewood Cliffs, NJ: Prentice-Hall.

Coutts, K., Godley, W., and Nordhaus, W. (1978). *Industrial Pricing in the United Kingdom*. Cambridge University Press.

Cukierman, A. (1979), 'Rational Expectations and the Role of Monetary Policy: A Generalization'. *Journal of Monetary Economics*, 5: 213–29.

—— (1984), *Inflation, Stagflation, Relative Price, and Imperfect Information*. New York: Cambridge University Press.

Cyert, R. M., and DeGroot, M. H. (1974), 'Rational Expectations and Bayesian Analysis'. *Journal of Political Economy*, 82: 521–36.

D'Aspremont, C., Dos Santos Ferreira, R., and Gerard-Varèt, L. A. (1989), 'Unemployment in an Extended Cournot Oligopoly Model'. *Oxford Economic Papers*, 41: 490–5.

—— —— —— (1990), 'On Monopolistic Competition and Involuntary Unemployment'. *Quarterly Journal of Economics*, 105: 895–919.

Dehez, P. (1985), 'Monopolistic Equilibrium and Involuntary Unemployment'. *Journal of Economic Theory*, 36: 160–5.

Diamond, P. (1971), 'A Model of Price Adjustment'. *Journal of Economic Theory*, 3: 156–68.

Dixit, A., and Stiglitz, J. (1977), 'Monopolistic Competition and Optimum Product Diversity'. *American Economic Review*, 67: 297–308.

Dixon, H. (1987), 'A Simple Model of Imperfect Competition with Walrasian Features'. *Oxford Economic Papers*, 39: 134–60.

—— (1989), 'Bertrand–Edgeworth Equilibria when Firms Avoid Turning Customers Away'. Mimeo, Essex University.

Domberger, S. (1979), 'Price Adjustment and the Market Structure'. *Economic Journal*, 89: 96–108.

Domowitz, I., Hubbard, R. G., and Petersen, B. C. (1986), 'Business Cycles and the Relationship between Concentration and Price–Cost Margins'. *Rand Journal of Economics*, 35: 1–22.

Dornbusch, R., and Simonsen, M. H. (eds.) (1983), *Inflation, Debt, and Indexation*. Cambridge, Mass.: MIT Press.

Duesenberry, J. S. (1949), *Income, Saving, and the Theory of Consumer Behaviour*. Cambridge, Mass.: Harvard University Press.

Eaton, B. C., and Lipsey, R. G. (1989), 'Product Differentiation'. In R. Schmalensee and R. D. Willig (eds.), *Handbook of Industrial Organization*, i. Amsterdam: North-Holland.

Eisner, R., and Strotz, R. (1963), 'Determinants of Business Investment'. In *Impacts of Monetary Policy*. Englewood Cliffs, NJ: Prentice-Hall, pp. 59–337.

Evans, G., and Honkapohja, S. (1986) 'A Complete Characterization of ARMA Solutions to Linear Rational Expectations Models'. *Review of Economic Studies*, 53: 227–39.

Feige, E. L., and Pearce, D. K. (1976), 'Economically Rational Expectations: Are Innovations in the Rate of Inflation Independent of Innovations in Measures of Monetary and Fiscal Policy?' *Journal of Political Economy*, 84: 499–522.

Figlewski, S., and Wachtel, P. (1981), 'The Formation of Inflationary Expectations'. *Review of Economics and Statistics*, 63: 1–10.

Fischer, S. (1977*a*), 'Long Term Contracts, Rational Expectations, and the Optimal Money Supply Rule'. *Journal of Political Economy*, 85: 191–205.

—— (1977*b*), 'Wage Indexation and Macroeconomic Stability'. In K. Brunner and A. Meltzer (eds.), *Stabilization of the Domestic and International Economy*, Carnegie–Rochester Conference Series in Public Policy. New York: North-Holland, pp. 107–48.

Fourgeaud, C., Gourieroux, C., and Pradel, J. (1986), 'Learning Procedures and Convergence to Rationality'. *Econometrica*, 54: 845–68.

Friedman, B. (1980), 'Survey Evidence on the "Rationality" of Interest Rate Expectations'. *Journal of Monetary Economics*, 6: 453–66.

Friedman, M. (1968), 'The Role of Monetary Policy'. *American Economic Review*, 58: 1–17.

Froyen, R. T., and Waud, R. N. (1987), 'An Examination of Aggregate Price Uncertainty in Four Countries and Some Implications for Real Output'. *International Economic Review*, 28: 353–72.

—— —— (1988), 'Real Business Cycles and the Lucas Paradigm'. *Economic Inquiry*, 26: 183–201.

Frydman, R. (1982), 'Toward an Understanding of Market Processes: Individual Expectations, Learning, and Convergence'. *American Economic Review*, 72: 652–68.

—— and Phelps, E. S. (1983), *Individual Forecasting and Aggregate Outcomes: 'Rational Expectations' Reconsidered*. Cambridge University Press.

—— and Rappoport, P. (1987), 'Is the Distinction between Anticipated and Unanticipated Money Growth Relevant in Explaining Aggregate Output?' *American Economic Review*, 77: 693–703.

Gal-Or, E. (1986), 'Information Transmission: Cournot and Bertrand Equilibria'. *Review of Economic Studies*, 53: 85–92.

Geary, P. T. and Kennan, J. (1982), 'The Employment–Real Wage Relationship: An International Study'. *Journal of Political Economy*, 90: 854–71.

Gordon, R. J. (1981), 'Output Fluctuations and Gradual Price Adjustment'. *Journal of Economic Literature*, 19: 493–530.

—— (1983), 'A Century of Evidence on Wage and Price Stickiness in the United States, the United Kingdom, and Japan'. In J. Tobin (ed.), *Macroeconomics, Prices and Quantities: Essays in Memory of Arthur M. Okun*. Washington, D.C: Brookings Institution, pp. 85–121.

—— (1990), 'What is New Keynesian Economics?' *Journal of Economic Literature*, 28: 1115–71.

Gottfries, N. (1990), 'A Model of Nominal Contracts'. Mimeo, Institute for International Economic Studies, University of Stockholm, March.

—— (1991), 'Customer Markets, Credit Market Imperfections and Real Price Rigidity'. *Economica*, 58.

Gould, J. (1968), 'Adjustment Costs in the Theory of Investment of the Firm'. *Review of Economic Studies*, 35: 47–55.

Gray, J. A. (1976), 'Wage Indexation: A Macroeconomic Approach'. *Journal of Monetary Economics*, 2: 221–35.

—— (1983), 'Wage Indexation, Incomplete Information, and Aggregate Supply Curve'. In R. Dornbusch and M. H. Simonsen (eds.), *Inflation, Debt, and Indexation*. Cambridge, Mass.: MIT Press, pp. 25–45.

Green, E. J., and Porter, R. H. (1984), 'Noncooperative Collusion under Imperfect Information'. *Econometrica*, 52: 87–100.

Greenwald, B. C., and Stiglitz, J. E. (1987*a*), 'Imperfect Information, Credit Markets and Unemployment.' *European Economic Review*, 31: 444–56.

—— —— (1987*b*), 'Keynesian, New Keynesian and New Classical Economics'. *Oxford Economic Papers*, 39: 119–32.

Grossman, S. J. (1977), 'The Existence of Future Markets, Noisy Rational Expectations and Informational Externalities'. *Review of Economic Studies*, 44: 431–49.

—— (1989), 'Rational Expectations and the Informational Role of Prices'. In R. J. Barro (ed.), *Modern Business Cycle Theory*. Cambridge, Mass.: Harvard University Press, pp. 128–51.

—— and Stiglitz, J. E. (1980), 'On the Impossibility of Informationally Efficient Markets'. *American Economic Review*, 70: 393–408.

Hall, R. E. (1980), 'Employment Fluctuations and Wage Rigidity'. *Brookings Papers on Economic Activity*, 1: 91–141.

—— (1986), 'Market Structure and Macroeconomic Fluctuations'. *Brookings Papers on Economic Activity*, 2: 285–322.

—— and Lilien, D. M. (1979), 'Efficient Wage Bargains under Rational Expectations'. *American Economic Review*, 69: 868–79.

Harsanyi, J. C. (1967–8), 'Games with Incomplete Information Played by Bayesian Players, Parts I, II, and III'. *Management Science*, 14: 159–82, 320–34, and 486–502.

Hart, O. (1982), 'A Model of Imperfect Competition with Keynesian Features'. *Quarterly Journal of Economics*, 97: 109–38.

—— (1985), 'Imperfect Competition in General Equilibrium: An Overview of Recent Work', In K. J. Arrow and S. Honkapohja (eds.), *Frontiers of Economics*. New York: Basil Blackwell, pp. 100–49.

Hartman, R. (1972), 'The Effects of Price and Cost Uncertainty on Investment'. *Journal of Economic Theory*, 5: 258–66.

Hayashi, F. (1982), 'Tobin's Marginal *q* and Average *q*: A Neoclassical Interpretation'. *Econometrica*, 50: 213–24.

Hayek, F. A. (1945), 'The Use of Knowledge in Society'. *American Economic Review*, 35: 519–30.

Houthakker, H. S. (1974), 'The Size Distribution of Labour Incomes Derived from the Distribution of Aptitudes'. In W. Sellekearts (ed.), *Econometrics and Economic Theory: Essays in Honour of Jan Tinbergen*. London: Macmillan.

Iwai, K. (1974), 'The Firm in Uncertain Markets and Its Price, Wage and Employment Dynamics'. *Review of Economic Studies*, 41: 253–76.

—— (1981), *Disequilibrium Dynamics: A Theoretical Analysis of Inflation and Unemployment*. New Haven, Conn.: Yale University Press.

Jorgenson, D. W. (1963), 'Capital Theory and Investment Behavior'. *American Economic Review*, 53: 247–59.

Katona, G., and Mueller, E. (1954), 'A Study of Purchase Decisions'. In L. H. Clark (ed.), *Consumer Behavior: The Dynamics of Consumer Reaction*. New York University Press, pp. 30–85.

Ketcham, J., Smith, V. L., and Williams, A. W. (1984), 'A Comparison of Posted-Offer and Double-Auction Pricing Institutions'. *Review of Economic Studies*, 51: 595–614.

Killingthworth, M. (1983), *Labour Supply*. Cambridge University Press.

King, R. (1981), 'Monetary Information and Monetary Neutrality'. *Journal of Monetary Economics*, 7: 195–206.

—— (1982), 'Monetary Policy and the Information Content of Prices'. *Journal of Political Economy*, 90: 247–79.

—— (1983), 'Interest Rates, Aggregate Information, and Monetary Policy'. *Journal of Monetary Economics*, 12: 199–234.

Kohn, M. (1986), 'Monetary Analysis, the Equilibrium Method, and Keynes's "General Theory"'. *Journal of Political Economy*, 94: 1191–224.
Leland, H. E. (1972), 'Theory of the Firm Facing Uncertain Demand'. *American Economic Review*, 62: 278–91.
Lovell, M. C. (1986), 'Tests of the Rational Expectations Hypothesis'. *American Economic Review*, 76: 110–24.
Lucas, R. E., Jun. (1972), 'Expectations and the Neutrality of Money'. *Journal of Economic Theory*, 4: 103–24.
—— (1973), 'Some International Evidence on Output–Inflation Tradeoffs'. *American Economic Review*, 63: 326–34.
—— (1975), 'An Equilibrium Model of the Business Cycle'. *Journal of Political Economy*, 83: 1113–44.
—— (1987), *Models of Business Cycles*. Oxford: Basil Blackwell.
—— and Prescott, E. C. (1971), 'Investment Under Uncertainty'. *Econometrica*, 39: 659–81.
Maddala, G. S. (1977), *Econometrics*. New York: McGraw-Hill.
Mankiw, N. Gregory (1985), 'Small Menu Costs and Large Business Cycles: A Macroeconomic Model of Monopoly'. *Quarterly Journal of Economics*, 100: 529–38.
Maskin, E., and Tirole, J. (1988), 'A Theory of Dynamic Oligopoly, II: Price Competition'. *Econometrica*, 56: 571–600.
McCallum, B. T. (1986), 'On "Real" and "Sticky Price" Theories of the Business Cycle'. *Journal of Money, Credit, and Banking*, 18: 397–414.
Mishkin, F. (1981), 'Are Market Forecasts Rational?' *American Economic Review*, 71: 295–306.
Negishi, T. (1978), 'Existence of Under Employment Equilibrium'. In G. Schwödiauer (ed.), *Equilibrium and Disequilibrium in Economic Theory*. Boston: Reidel.
—— (1979), *Microeconomic Foundations of Keynesian Macroeconomics*. Amsterdam: North-Holland.
Newman, J. W. (1978), 'Consumer External Search: Amount and Determinants'. In A. G. Woodside, J. N. Sheth, and P. D. Bennett (eds.), *Consumer and Industrial Buying Behaviour*. New York: North-Holland, pp. 79–94.
Nikaido. H. (1975), *Monopolistic Competition and Effective Demand*. Princeton University Press.
Nishimura, K. G. (1982), 'Customer–Supplier Relationship and the Theory of Prices and Quantities'. Unpublished Ph.D. dissertation, Yale University.
—— (1983), 'Rational Expectations and the Theory of Aggregate Investment'. *Economics Letters*, 11: 101–6.
—— (1985), 'Customer Markets and Price Sensitivity'. Discussion Paper 85-F–2, University of Tokyo.
—— (1986*a*), 'Rational Expectations and Price Rigidity in a Monopolistically Competitive Market'. *Review of Economic Studies*, 53: 283–92.
—— (1986*b*), 'A Simple Rigid-Price Macroeconomic Model under Incomplete Information and Imperfect Competition'. Mimeo, University of Tokyo, October.
—— (1988*a*), 'A Note on Price Rigidity: Pledging Stable Prices under Sluggish

Information Diffusion and Costly Search'. *Journal of Economic Behaviour and Organization*, 10: 121–31.

—— (1988*b*), 'Expectational Coordination Failure'. *Economic Studies Quarterly*, 39: 322–34.

—— (1988*c*), 'Monopolistic Compettititon, Imperfect Information, and Macroeconomics'. Discussion Paper 88-F–4, University of Tokyo.

—— (1988*d*), 'Small Information Costs, Rationally "Irrational" Expectations, and the Optimal Government Policy'. Discussion Paper 88–F–13, University of Tokyo.

—— (1989*a*), 'Customer Markets and Price Sensitivity'. *Economica*, 56: 187–98.

—— (1989*b*), 'Indexation and Monopolistic Competition in Labour Markets'. *European Economic Review*, 33: 1605–23.

—— (1991), 'Monopolistic Competition, Differential Information, and Industry Investment'. *International Economic Review*, 32: 809–21.

—— and Toda, H. (1987), 'Competition and Macroeconomic Adjustment'. Discussion Paper 87–F–8, University of Tokyo.

—— and Ueda, K. (1986), 'Imperfect Information and Rigidity of Prices and Wages in Monopolistic–Monopsonistic Competition'. Discussion Paper 85–F–19, University of Tokyo.

Nordhaus, W. D. (1972), 'Recent Developments in Price Dynamics'. In O. Eckstein (ed.), *The Econometrics of Price Determination*. Washington, DC: Board of Governors of the Federal Reserve System, pp. 16–49.

Oi, W. Y. (1961), 'The Desirability of Price Instability under Perfect Competition'. *Econometrica*, 29: 58–64.

Okun, A. M. (1975), 'Inflation: Its Mechanics and Welfare Cost'. *Brookings Papers on Economic Activity*, 2: 351–401.

—— (1981), *Prices and Quantities: A Macroeconomic Analysis*. Washington, DC: Brookings Institution.

Okuno-Fujiwara, M., and Suzumura, K. (1987), 'Capacity Commitment, Oligopoly and Welfare'. Mimeo, University of Tokyo, February.

—— Postlewaite, A., and Suzumura, K. (1990), 'Strategic Information Revelation'. *Review of Economic Studies*, 57: 25–47.

Oswald, A. J. (1985), 'The Economic Theory of Trade Unions: An Introductory Survey'. *Scandinavian Journal of Economics*, 87: 160–93.

Parkin, M. (1986), 'The Output–Inflation Trade-off When Prices Are Costly to Change'. *Journal of Political Economy*, 94: 200–24.

Persson, M. (1979), 'Rational Expectations in Log-linear Models'. *Scandinavian Journal of Economics*, 81: 378–86.

Pesando, J. E. (1975), 'A Note on the Rationality of the Livingston Price Expectations'. *Journal of Political Economy*, 83: 849–58.

Phelps, E. S., and Winter, S. G., Jun. (1970), 'Optimal Price Policy Under Atomistic Competition'. In E. S. Phelps *et al.*, *Microeconomic Foundations of Employment and Inflation Theory*. New York: W. W. Norton, pp. 309–37.

—— *et al.* (1970), *Microeconomic Foundations of Employment and Inflation Theory*. New York: W. W. Norton, pp. 309–37.

Pindyck, R. S. (1982), 'Adjustment Costs, Uncertainty, and the Behavior of the Firm'. *American Economic Review*, 72: 415–27.

Plott, C. R. (1982), 'Industrial Organization Theory and Experimental Economics'. *Journal of Economic Literature*, 20: 1485–527.
Porter, R. H. (1983), 'Optimal Cartel Trigger-Price Strategies'. *Journal of Economic Theory*, 29: 313–38.
Pratt, J. W., Wise, D. A., and Zeckhauser, R. (1979), 'Price Differences in Almost Competitive Markets'. *Quarterly Journal of Economics*, 97: 189–211.
Qualls, P. D. (1979), 'Market Structure and Cyclical Flexibility of Price–Cost Margins'. *Journal of Business*, 52: 305–25.
Rotemberg, J. J. (1982), 'Monopolistic Price Adjustment and Aggregate Output'. *Review of Economic Studies*, 49: 517–31.
—— (1987), 'The New Keynesian Microfoundations'. *NBER Macroeconomic Annual*, 2: 69–104.
—— and Saloner, G. (1986), 'A Supergame-Theoretic Model of Price Wars during Booms'. *American Economic Review*, 76: 390–407.
Sachs, J. (1979), 'Wages, Profits, and Macroeconomic Adjustment: A Comparative Study'. *Brookings Papers on Economic Activity*, 2: 269–319.
—— (1980), 'The Changing Cyclical Behavior of Wages and Prices, 1890–1976' *American Economic Review*, 70: 78–90.
Salop, S. (1976), 'Information and Monopolistic Competition'. *American Economic Review*, 66: 240–5.
—— and Stiglitz, J. E. (1977), 'Bargains and Ripoffs: A Model of Monopolistically Competitive Price Dispersion'. *Review of Economic Studies*, 44: 493–510.
Samuelson, P. A. (1972), 'The Consumer Does Benefit from Feasible Price Stability'. *Quarterly Journal of Economics*, 86: 479–93.
Sargent, T. J. (1987), *Macroeconomic Theory*, 2nd edn. New York: Academic Press.
Sattinger, M. (1984), 'Value of an Additional Firm in Monopolistic Competition'. *Review of Economic Studies*, 51: 321–32.
Schultz, C. (1989), 'The Impossibility of "Involuntary Unemployment" in an Overlapping Generations Model with Rational Expectations'. Discussion Paper 89–18, University of Copenhagen, October.
Schultze, C. L. (1981), 'Some Macro Foundations for Micro Theory'. *Brookings Papers on Economic Activity*, 2: 521–76.
—— (1986), *Other Times, Other Places: Macroeconomic Lessons from US and European History*. Washington, DC: Brookings Institution.
Sheshinski, E., and Weiss, Y. (1977), 'Inflation and Costs of Price Adjustment'. *Review of Economic Studies*, 44: 287–303.
—— (1983), 'Optimum Pricing Policy under Stochastic Inflation'. *Review of Economic Studies,* 50: 513–29.
Silvestre, J. (1988), 'Undominated Prices in the Three-Good Model'. *European Economic Review*, 32: 161–78.
Sneessens, H. R. (1987), 'Investment and the Inflation–Unemployment Tradeoff in a Macroeconomic Rationing Model with Monopolistic Competition'. *European Economic Review*, 31: 781–815.
Snower, D. J. (1983), 'Imperfect Competition, Underemployment, and Crowding-Out'. *Oxford Economic Papers*, 35: 245–70.
Spear, S. E. (1989), 'Learning Rational Expectations under Computability Constraint'. *Econometrica*, 57: 889–910.

Spence, M. (1976), 'Product Selection, Fixed Costs, and Monopolistic Competition'. *Review of Economic Studies*, 43: 217–35.

Stefanou, S. E. (1987), 'Technical Change, Uncertainty, and Investment'. *American Journal of Agricultural Economics*, 69: 158–65.

Stigler, G. J., and Kindahl, J. K. (1970), *The Behavior of Industrial Prices*. New York: National Bureau of Economic Research.

Stiglitz, J. E. (1979), 'Equilibrium in Product Markets with Imperfect Information'. *American Economic Review, Papers and Proceedings*, 69: 339–45.

—— (1989), 'Imperfect Information in the Product Market'. In R. Schmalensee and R. D. Willig (eds.), *Handbook of Industrial Organization*, i. Amsterdam: North-Holland.

Svensson, L. (1986), 'Sticky Goods Prices, Flexible Asset Prices, Monopolistic Competition and Monetary Policy'. *Review of Economic Studies*, 53: 385–405.

Sweezy, P. W. (1939), 'Demand under Condition of Oligopoly'. *Journal of Political Economy*, 47: 568–73.

Taha, H. (1982), *Operations Research*, 3rd edn. London: Collier Macmillan.

Taylor, J. B. (1979), 'Staggered Wage Setting in a Macro Model'. *American Economic Review, Papers and Proceedings*, 69: 108–13.

—— (1980), 'Aggregate Dynamics and Staggered Contracts'. *Journal of Political Economy*, 88: 1–23.

Tobin, J. (1969), 'A General Equilibrium Approach to Monetary Theory'. *Journal of Money, Credit, and Banking*, 1: 15–29.

—— (1972), 'The Wage–Price Mechanism: Overview of the Conference'. In O. Eckstein (ed.), *The Econometrics of Price Determination*. Washington, DC: Board of Governors of the Federal Reserve System, pp. 1–15.

—— and Brainard, W. (1977), 'Asset Markets and the Cost of Capital'. In R. Nelson et al. (eds.), *Economic Progress, Private Values and Public Policy: Essays in Honor of William Fellner*. Amsterdam: North-Holland, pp. 235–62.

Townsend, R. M. (1978), 'Market Anticipations, Rational Expectations, and Bayesian Analysis'. *International Economic Review*, 19: 481–94.

—— (1983), 'Forecasting the Forecasts of Others'. *Journal of Political Economy*, 91: 545–88.

Turnovsky, S. J., Shalit, H., and Schmitz, A. (1980), 'Consumer's Surplus, Price Instability, and Consumer Welfare'. *Econometrica*, 48: 135–52.

Ueda, K., and Yoshikawa, H. (1986), 'Financial Volatility and the *q* Theory of Investment'. *Economica,* 53: 11–27.

Vives, X. (1985), 'Duopoly Information Equilibrium: Cournot and Bertrand'. *Journal of Economic Theory*, 34: 71–94.

Waugh, F. V. (1944), 'Does the Consumer Benefit from Price Instability?' *Quarterly Journal of Economics*, 58: 602–14.

Weiss, L. (1982), 'Information Aggregation and Policy'. *Review of Economic Studies,* 44: 31–42.

Weitzman, M. L. (1982), 'Increasing Returns and the Foundations of Unemployment Theory'. *Economic Journal*, 92: 787–804.

—— (1984), *The Share Economy*. Cambridge, Mass.: Harvard University Press.

—— (1985), 'The Simple Macroeconomics of Profit Sharing'. *American Economic Review*, 75: 937–53.

Weizsacker, C. C. von (1984), 'The Costs of Substitution'. *Econometrica*, 52: 1085–116.

Williams, A. W. (1987), 'The Formation of Price Forecasts in Experimental Markets'. *Journal of Money, Credit, and Banking*, 19: 1–18.

Woglom, G. (1982), 'Underemployment Equilibrium with Rational Expectations'. *Quarterly Journal of Economics*, 97: 89–107.

Wolinsky, A. (1986), 'True Monopolistic Competition as a Result of Imperfect Information'. *Quarterly Journal of Economics*, 101: 493–511.

Yoshikawa, H. (1980), 'On the *q* Theory of Investment'. *American Economic Review*, 70: 739–43.

# INDEX

*Index compiled by Frank Pert*